The Military and the Market

AMERICAN BUSINESS, POLITICS, AND SOCIETY

Series editors: Andrew Wender Cohen, Shane Hamilton,
Kimberly Phillips-Fein, and Elizabeth Tandy Shermer

Books in the series American Business, Politics, and
Society explore the relationships over time between
politics, society, and the creation and performance
of markets, firms, and industries large and small.
The central theme of this series is that culture, law,
and public policy have been fundamental to the
evolution of American business from the colonial era
to the present. The series aims to explore, in particular,
developments that have enduring consequences.

A complete list of books in the series
is available from the publisher.

THE MILITARY AND
THE MARKET

EDITED BY
Jennifer Mittelstadt
and Mark R. Wilson

PENN

UNIVERSITY OF PENNSYLVANIA PRESS

PHILADELPHIA

Published by
University of Pennsylvania Press
Philadelphia, Pennsylvania 19104-4112
www.upenn.edu/pennpress

Printed in the United States of America on acid-free paper
10 9 8 7 6 5 4 3 2 1

Hardcover ISBN 9781512823233
Ebook ISBN 9781512823240

A catalog record for this book is available
from the Library of Congress

CONTENTS

The Military and the Market

Jennifer Mittelstadt and Mark R. Wilson

In 2020, the US Army piloted a new personnel management system for its more than four hundred thousand active-duty enlisted personnel. The Assignment Satisfaction Key-Enlisted Marketplace imagined its soldiers as individual actors in the "marketplace" of military occupational specialties, geographic posts, and commands. It asked soldiers to enter information about their "talents," "interests," and "preferences" into a database that the army said would sort and match them to their next billets not by using a traditional military method of command and control but via a marketplace. A leading architect and overseer of this system was the assistant secretary of the army for manpower and reserve affairs, Casey Wardynski. A retired army officer who had worked previously as an economics instructor at the US Military Academy, Wardynski was also a creator of the *America's Army* first-person shooter video game, released by the army in 2002 as a recruiting tool. From his positive experience in marketing military service through the lucrative world of online gaming, Wardynski developed a regard for the greater use of markets as a key to successful personnel reform. As he and his coauthors argued in a 2010 essay outlining the personnel policies he would implement a decade later, the military needed to ditch its command-oriented "feudal employment culture," which overemphasized "fairness," in favor of adopting "controlled market mechanisms." This change would generate "far more efficient and productive outcomes" like those seen in the private sector, where, Wardynski assumed, individual choice and maximized utility produced better results.

In 2020, as Wardynski and his team launched the new personnel system, they saw the need for adopting market mechanisms throughout the US military in order to provide the United States with a global strategic advantage. Wardynski wrote that one of the greatest strengths of the US military, in comparison to its peers abroad, was its willingness to solve problems with markets. Here Wardynski was likely thinking of growing US strategic rivalry with China, along with its ongoing contest with traditional competitors, such as Russia. "In terms of national security, I think it gives us a huge edge. I don't think other armies . . . are going to take this approach. That's not in their culture."[1]

Wardynski was hardly alone in his assessment of the need for close intermeshing of the US military and capitalist markets. By the early twenty-first century, it had become difficult to find any leaders in the military or the Department of Defense who do not believe the future success of the armed forces depends on its ability to engage private commercial markets and apply market-oriented solutions across the defense sector and the military. In their words and actions, military leaders and organizations suggest that in order to achieve greater efficiencies, innovation, and military effectiveness, the armed forces must do more to make use of markets and for-profit firms. By the time of the army's debut of the enlisted soldiers' marketplace personnel system, this sensibility had already penetrated deeply into military culture, informing well-known recent developments in military history ranging from the dramatic jump in the US government's employment of security and logistics contractors overseas, to the privatization of the Veterans Administration's health care, to the proliferation of "other transaction authority" contracts, designed to allow the military to purchase goods and services more easily in commercial markets.

Today's heavy reliance of the US military on the private sector is significant but not without precedent. The armed forces have always operated in close partnership with private entrepreneurs and firms, in wartime and peacetime, from the Revolutionary War to the present day. Although military-market relations have a long history, that history is far from simple or uniform. The US military has been and continues to be a complex, multifaceted institution. Over its history it has added branches, a veterans' administration, and an elaborate civilian defense and national security apparatus. And the military's relationships to markets have also evolved and diversified. Basic contracting relationships are only one facet of the US military's relationship to markets. Throughout its history, the military has relied on and affected a wide range of industries and institutions, far beyond the fields of weapons acquisition or contracted military services. The US military has run systems of free and unfree labor, taken over private sector firms, and both spurred and inhibited economic development in the private sector. It has created new markets, all around the world—markets for consumer products, for sex work, and for new technologies. It has operated as a regulator of industries and firms and an arbitrator of labor practices. It has rejected or embraced promarket ideologies and business management fads, adopting or refashioning them for its own purposes. And in recent decades it has gone so far as to redesign itself from the inside, so as to become more similar to a for-profit corporation and more committed to the idea that most efficiencies and innovations are to be found in commercial markets.

The Military and the Market brings to bear the scholarship of a diverse group of historians and political scientists, to enrich our understanding of the depth and complexity of such military-market relations. In the chapters collected in this volume, scholars offer innovative histories of markets and war, in the US and across the globe, from the nineteenth century through the present day. Many of the chapters focus on specific markets, in which buyers and sellers of goods or services—such as housing, or electronics, or sex—transact business. These microlevel case studies highlight specific military actors, such as particular services or departments, as well as individual civilian industries or entrepreneurs. At the same time, the volume as a whole traces changing relationships between the military and "the market" writ large, by exploring connections between two of the most important forces of the modern era: national armed forces and capitalism. Military actors past and present have not merely purchased from (and shaped) specific markets for pragmatic reasons but have also participated, knowingly or unknowingly, in political struggles over how much deference should be given to a broader "market"-oriented economic system based on private property, decentralized decisions, and the pursuit of profit. As the contents of this volume suggest, perhaps what is most remarkable about the long-run history of the military and the market is not the many tensions between them, but their record of accommodation and collaboration.

Military-market relationships have long been the object of scrutiny all around the world. A robust and often skeptical public discussion of the subject was evident in eighteenth-century Europe as capitalism ascended, when there was widespread public cynicism about for-profit military contractors, even in the most efficient of the fiscal-military states.[2] Deep concerns about illegitimate profit taking by military suppliers were also expressed by the public and policymakers in the early United States; during the Civil War, these concerns fueled street protests, abundant attacks on profiteering in popular culture, and, in a few cases, the trials of private contractors in military courts.[3] During the first half of the twentieth century, in the era of the world wars, profiteering during wartime, and in the arms industry more generally, was denounced by politicians, military authorities, members of the armed services, veterans' groups, and civilians. In Russia, for example, outrage over wartime profiteering contributed to revolution; elsewhere, it gave rise to new, elaborate regimes of taxation and price and profit control.[4] Throughout the Cold War, and especially during the US war in Vietnam, a variety of critics condemned the "military-industrial complex," which President Dwight D. Eisenhower had named in his farewell address of 1961. Some of these critics, including those affiliated with the New Left, went beyond traditional complaints about profiteering, by suggesting that competitive markets no longer existed in the US defense sector, because it had become a planned system, directed by the Pentagon, distributing jobs and profits to contractors who took no meaningful risks.[5] In more recent years, a diverse group of scholars, journalists, and activists, including libertarians and progressives, have continued to decry a wide range of alleged evils in military-market relationships, from individual cases of excessive profit taking to the wholesale corruption of US political economy and foreign policy.[6]

Analysis of the military's relationship to markets has also been offered by those within the armed forces and defense community. The military itself, at the Army Industrial College founded in the 1920s and in other institutions, began formal study of how to run a future war economy. After World War II, when the United States stood as the largest industrial and military power in the world, a wide range of policymakers and scholars undertook sophisticated treatments of military-market relationships. Most of these focused narrowly on procurements of big weapon systems, which were subjected to more formal economic analysis, both within the Pentagon, led by Defense Secretary Robert S. McNamara, and by scholars and analysts at think tanks and universities.[7] In more recent years, this line of investigation has continued, both inside the Defense Department in its efforts to learn from acquisition history, and also in Congress and the nonprofit sector, where experts have documented a seemingly endless effort to achieve helpful "defense acquisition reform."[8]

For many years, both outsider and insider studies of military-market relations shared certain assumptions about how to define the "military" and the "market." They have tended to view the military as an undifferentiated monolith, and mostly in a narrow strategic and operational capacity as a purchaser and deployer of weapons and materiel, and have viewed the market as those firms that supply those products. In recent years, some scholars have also included in this purchase and deployment model providers of military services, such as logistics, maintenance of weapons and materiel, and security provision.[9] But few have looked beyond the military's traditional acquisition and deployment of weapons from big prime contractors to other forms of military-economic activity. Nor have they fully appreciated the diversity of defense policy regimes, branches, and leadership and the variety of their encounters with markets.

Traditional approaches also often shared assumptions about a timeless functionalist relationship between the military and the market. Sometimes scholars, analysts, and critics have assumed that the military is naturally independent from capitalism, as it uses command, coercion, and bureaucracy, and seems to enjoy a monopoly or monopsony. Or, conversely, some have assumed the military is nothing more than the tool of capitalist interests, who use the military to advance private profits. By offering simplistic, ahistorical understandings of power and interests, traditional accounts of the subject have inhibited fuller and more precise understandings of the military, the markets, and the interactions between them.

In recent years, historians of business, labor, and the military have begun moving beyond these traditional studies of the military and the market. Their work defines both the military and the market capaciously. They have understood the military to constitute all the specific branches, the civilian department of defense, and other national security apparatuses. They have pulled into the view military education and veterans programs, selective service, and peacetime training and operations, and have taken seriously the military's influence in the wider polity, society, and culture through the process of militarization in such areas as policing, entertainment, and humanitarian efforts. In doing so they have also historicized and analyzed ideas and values forged in the military—hierarchy, order, domination, effectiveness, lethality, and more.[10]

Recent scholarship has meanwhile illuminated the diversity and complexity of markets, as sites of exchange, investment, production, and consumption. In our own field of US history, a new generation of scholars has gathered loosely under the banner of "the history of capitalism." Their work encompasses business, economic, and labor history and has offered new accounts, sensitive to the operations of power, race, gender, and culture, of specific industries and markets, including markets for labor, information, technology, finance, and real estate. These scholars have also done a great deal to trace the development of promarket discourses and ideologies, including those broadcast by business leaders, economists, and business schools.[11]

Little of this newer historical scholarship on markets and capitalism has focused on the military, just as little of the recent innovative work on military history is directly concerned with markets. But if new scholarship on the military and markets has not always been in direct conversation, the works share these understandings of "the military" and "the market" in ways that are broader than previous traditional scholarship and are deeply historically situated. This opens up new opportunities for enlarging our understanding of military-market relations over the long run.[12]

These more complicated understandings of military and market have often come from scholars who have asked new questions about the military's relationship to broader aspects of society—to gender roles and structures, to empire and global entanglements, to race and inequality. This work draws on important long-term shifts in historical inquiry and methods that considers social, cultural, and labor history as integral to military history and political and economic history and that employs insights from scholarship that is more global and transnational, that employs feminist and critical race analysis, and that seeks to place the military-market relationship within broader structures of social, state, and global power.[13]

The *Military and the Market* moves forward along the path blazed by these new works, opening up new questions about how war and the military have affected an enormous swath of economic life in the United States and abroad, and how ideas, practices, and people outside the military have, in turn, shaped the American military and way of war. Its chapters follow the US military and markets from the nineteenth century through the twenty-first, tracing stories within the United States and outward to the military's entanglements across the world. This volume brings to light the importance of long histories of struggles among a wide range of actors over the balance of public versus private military production and service provision. It shows military institutions and leaders negotiating and managing buyers and sellers in consumer markets from clothing to sex work, and laborers and corporations in less recognized areas of production like base and housing construction. It sets military and market relationships into the broader context of macroeconomic and welfare state policies. The volume brings these works together, placing them in conversation with each other and with the extant literature on the military and the market in order to generate fresh insights and new questions about the US history of war and economy.

Together, the chapters in this book make several important contributions.

First, they demonstrate that the United States has long relied on a hybrid, public-private political economy, which has been decisively transformed by a shift toward privatization over the past fifty years. The transformation was not simple or linear; it involved debate and accords among a wide range of actors in the military, Congress, and the private sector. This history is the subject of the book's first section, which begins with our own essay, offering a broad, long-run perspective on the rise and fall of the US military's in-house, public capacities. In the book's second chapter, A. Junn Murphy presents a rich new history of the US government's surprising turn, during the early Cold War, to a more nationalized scheme of military housing. The final chapter in this section is focused on more recent years, during which, as Daniel Wirls shows, the traditional "military-industrial complex" has become a broader entity, more focused on services, involving a wider range of government agencies, and more privatized.

Second, this volume emphasizes the ways in which military and market institutions and relationships have been structured by the intersections of race, gender, and class. This has been particularly important in the realm of consumption, which must be understood as taking place across a broad terrain of services and goods, not limited narrowly to contracting for weapons and materiel. This is made clear by the two chapters in the second part of the volume, both of which examine important aspects of military, markets, and consumption from fresh perspectives. Sarah Weicksel's chapter, on informal entrepreneurship and consumption within the ranks of the Union armies during the Civil War, shows that soldiers' engagement with markets for consumer goods was shaped by surprising connections between battlefront and home front, family economies, and women and men. The next chapter, by Kara Vuic, presents an original essay on the US military's complicated, long-run relationship with prostitution. Vuic shows that the US military has not only created markets for sex, domestically and around the world, but has also attempted to manage those sex markets, formally and informally, with decidedly mixed results.

As Vuic's contribution suggests, a third point emphasized by this volume is that the US military's economic activities, past and present, must be viewed from a global perspective recognizing disproportionate US power, which has reshaped domestic and foreign markets in important and sometimes surprising directions. This point is highlighted in the two chapters in the third part of the volume, both of which trace the US military's shaping of local and global markets during the Cold War. Gretchen Heefner's chapter reminds us that the US military's efforts to project power during the Cold War required a massive new construction project aimed at building air bases and other military installations all across the globe, from Greenland to North Africa and beyond. As Heefner shows, this work brought the US Army Corps of Engineers and other military organizations into close partnerships with large US-based construction firms, who in turn became important shapers of local markets for materials and labor, in a variety of locales around the world. The military's global reach is also emphasized in the chapter contributed by Patrick Chung, which uses the life story and global journeys of one prominent Korean industrial engineer to suggest the ways in which the US military inspired and regulated technological innovation, both inside and outside the boundaries of the United States.

Finally, this volume suggests the need to examine military and market relationships within the wider context of the nation's macroeconomy and socioeconomic policy. For decades, the military has not only been shaped by broad economic forces but has also served as an important element of macroeconomic policy and a key contributor to larger patterns of technological change and social welfare systems. This is demonstrated by the two chapters in the final section of the book, starting with Tim Barker's essay on military Keynesianism during the Cold War era. Barker offers a fresh perspective on this often discussed but poorly understood subject, by focusing on developments during the era of the Nixon administration, at the end of the US war in Vietnam. As Barker suggests, bringing the Pentagon and defense budgeting more squarely into histories of economic policy complicates and enriches our understanding of the broad shift from Keynesianism to neoliberalism at the end of the twentieth century. The volume's final chapter, by Jessica Adler, is also concerned with macroeconomic problems and economic policy in the later twentieth century. Adler's contribution focuses on the economic outcomes of military service for African American veterans after the Vietnam War, as they struggled to find satisfactory employment in racially discriminatory civilian labor markets. Adler's chapter explores how African American veterans responded to this injustice with political action in Congress and the Veterans Administration, demanding that military service should be linked to reforms in the realm of race and employment law and social welfare policy. Like many of the other chapters in the volume, the contributions by Adler and Barker demonstrate that military and market relationships must be

understood in relation to broad political movements and the ongoing transformation of the state.

Taken together, the chapters in this volume go beyond contributing to particular subjects and subfields and also point to implications for today's elected
officials, defense policymakers, and military members and leaders. The historical perspectives offered in this volume show that the dominant arrangements and sensibilities in our current moment with regard to military-market
relations—including a heavy reliance on contractors for weapons, equipment, and services, and a widespread admiration of the superior efficiencies
and innovations provided by markets—are in fact not timeless "best practices." Rather, they are the product of historically specific developments in the
realms of political ideologies and management practices, both outside and
inside the military and the broader public sector. A greater awareness of this
fact may allow those active today in defense policy and practice to consider a
broader, more imaginative range of solutions to new challenges as these arise
in the coming years.

    Policymakers and military leaders will also benefit from recognizing that
military markets include a great deal more than those that involve major prime
contractors and subcontractors and the largest, most expensive weapon systems. The branches of the US military, the defense department, the VA, and
the wider national security apparatus are involved deeply in markets they do
not always sufficiently consider or even acknowledge, such as those that provide sex, nonmilitary-provided consumer goods, or the often invisible labor
(much of it subcontracted) offered by support personnel, like cleaners, truck
drivers, or food workers. While apparent to any member of the military or
defense community on the ground, these traditionally underconsidered markets deserve more attention from policymakers and military leaders because
they can have powerful effects on military morale, strategy, and operations,
as well as international relations.

    Military members, leaders, and policymakers can also benefit from the
recognition of the close relationship between the military, the market, and
civilian governance in the realm of economic and social policy. Civilian systems of health, education, and social welfare, and structures of discrimination
in gender and race, directly impact military effectiveness in recruitment, training, and operations. Reduced economic returns of military service for nonwhite personnel, for example, harms recruitment and personnel sustainability

in the long term. The continued, albeit officially prohibited, reliance of military personnel on gendered sex work produces tensions in the US military's local relationships with other nations and in its internal personnel policies intended to reduce sexual harassment and violence. Similarly, the military's heavy use of contractors (and their subcontractors) for basic services tends to create new challenges for military leaders in management and labor relations, as well as in US foreign relations, defined broadly from the highest levels of diplomacy to routine ground-level interactions. In these areas, as in many others, military members and leaders, elected officials, and policymakers stand to gain from a more historically informed, critical understanding of military-market relations.

This volume offers a new, interdisciplinary perspective on an important and still narrowly understood subject. Intersections of the military and the market have shaped US history and world history for many decades, and will continue to do so in the years to come. Once we do more to recognize the complexity and dynamism of military-market relations, which have been consistently underappreciated by scholars and policymakers, we can gain a richer understanding of the past and a clear-eyed perspective on a wider range of alternatives available in our day and into the future.

CHAPTER 1

The Politics of US Military
Privatizations, 1945–2000

Jennifer Mittelstadt and Mark R. Wilson

In the late summer of 1953, at the end of the Korean War, US Navy Secretary Robert B. Anderson issued his end-of-fiscal-year report. Anderson oversaw an organization with an annual budget of about $12 billion and that employed more than one million uniformed navy personnel and marines, along with nearly half a million civilians. "A random selection of the activities of the navy, in addition to the operation of its fleets and forces," Anderson reported, "shows a scope and diversity touching on nearly every phase of human endeavor." Far from being focused entirely on combat power, the navy also employed "some 2,500 people and $12 million each year to catalog supplies numbering some 1.3 million items, roughly ten times the number carried by the world's largest retail organization. . . . Its lawyers handle more than 100,000 legal cases and legal opinions a year. . . . It runs a correspondence school with more than 150,000 navy and Marine students. . . . It is a rent-collecting landlord for more than 24,000 families. . . . It supervises more than 200 reserve industrial plants, including copper smelters, aircraft-engine facilities, and ammunition plants. . . . It cares for almost 18,000 patients a day in 29 hospitals. It owns four oil fields."[1]

But even as he boasted of the navy's immense, multidimensional operations, Secretary Anderson also hinted at pressures to limit those very same in-house capabilities. "One of the past year's developments of greatest interest to the businessman," Anderson reported, "was the trend toward getting the navy out of enterprises competing with private business. Early in 1953 the navy gave up the manufacture of clothing, and just before the end of the year it sharply curtailed the manufacture of paint." More significant in dollar terms was the navy's recent move in the direction of privatizing more of the production of warships, including aircraft carriers, submarines, and destroyers. "Since 1950," Anderson explained, "approximately 90 percent of the navy's new construction has been assigned to private shipyards."[2] As Anderson's report suggested, the shift from public to private enterprise aimed to please political conservatives, including many business leaders and sympathetic elected officials. Those critics were in the midst of a forceful campaign to restructure the American military establishment in ways that would cut its vast in-house operations, from property to production to services, in favor of contracting out or sale to the private sector.

This routine report by a top Defense Department official composed during the early Cold War captured the US military and the market at the outset of a profound transformation. While the US military had for most of its history relied on both the profit-seeking private sector and the public sector for provisioning, weapons, research, and operational support, by the mid-twentieth century, the balance had shifted toward the public side. Not just during World War II, but in the years that followed, the military was the largest public entity in the nation. In the mid-1950s, the Department of Defense employed directly more than four million people, close to 80 percent of all the people working for the federal government. At the same time, another three million Americans worked for military contractors. Across the country, there was about $150 billion worth of defense-related investment, in properties such as factories and bases. This was more than the combined assets of the one hundred largest American corporations.[3] But the military Leviathan of the early Cold War era would not last. In the second half of the twentieth century, many of its elements would be sold off and contracted out to the private sector. By the time Secretary Anderson penned his report, the military's real estate holdings, production capacities, and service provision, from equipment maintenance to food production, all faced scrutiny from an increasingly vocal private sector that questioned the large public military holdings. And as Anderson's assessment suggested, during the Cold War, all branches of the armed forces faced new pressures to transfer their public investments and services to private firms and other nongovernmental entities, large and small. Over time, these pressures caused a variety of important privatizations across the US defense sector, in a complex, punctuated process of transformation, extending across half a century.

This chapter tells the story of the decline of a "big government"–style, multicompetent US military in the twentieth century. The chapter describes resistance to the capacious public military that had been erected in preceding decades and tells the story of its dismantling and transfer to the private sector. This transformation was not a natural function of demobilization after World War II, or of natural cycles of alternation between public and private governance, or even purely pragmatic decisions based on sober assessments of costs and efficiencies. Rather, the transfer of public to private was the result of several specific new developments in the relationship between the American military and the market in the postwar period. We document a political movement to vivify private enterprise and reduce the ambit of federal government activity, particularly the military's in-house ownership, production, and management. The modern movement against "government competition" with the private sector began in earnest in the 1930s, during the New Deal; it continued into the 1950s, and beyond, taking ever-sharper aim at the military, as it constituted the biggest, most expensive component of the American state. As this political agenda gained legislative and executive power, it was accompanied by, and encouraged, the growing intellectual and cultural power of promarket ideologies, which took root in the US military itself, and in the Department of Defense, from the 1960s forward. Although some military leaders were dubious about the alleged benefits of privatization, others enthusiastically championed them or, perhaps more commonly, remained ambivalent as they implemented outsourcing reforms pushed by Congress and the Pentagon that seemed to offer the services some pragmatic benefits, along with costs. Together, political, cultural, and intellectual movements contributed to a successful campaign to transfer public military functions to the private sector, to a degree unprecedented in US history.

This important transformation has seldom been given sufficient attention by scholars and students of the history of the US military and defense acquisition.[4] To be sure, several parts of the story are well documented. For example, we have good accounts of the creation of the all-volunteer force (AVF) in the early 1970s, and the neoliberal economic thinking behind it. And both scholars and casual observers of twenty-first-century warfare and contracting are aware of the recent jump in the use of "private military companies" (i.e., mercenaries), such as Blackwater.[5] However, on the whole, the scholarship to date has not documented the breadth and depth of the long-run privatization of the US military since World War II, nor explained the ideological and political forces behind that transformation.[6]

The US military's transformation in the direction of privatization needs to be understood as part and parcel of a broader pattern of change in US and global political economy, many decades in the making. This chapter contributes to a growing scholarly conversation about the origins and development of neoliberalism, which is commonly defined as an ideology emphasizing the benefits of private property, entrepreneurial energy, free markets, deregulation, and free trade, while denigrating the competence of the public sector.[7] To date, scholarly conversations about neoliberalism have said too little about the military. In our discussion of the US military in this chapter, we address two important broader questions about neoliberalism: one about periodization, and one about the nature of the state.

When exactly did neoliberalism emerge as a powerful force in politics and policymaking? Some accounts, while acknowledging that neoliberalism's intellectual roots may run deep, emphasize a rather sudden rise of its political potency, in the 1970s and 1980s.[8] But many historians are offering a more complex story of periodization, which points to earlier struggles and manifestations.[9] Our chapter adds to this body of work by emphasizing a messier chronology of the rise of neoliberalism, and also suggesting that the US military's transformations must be counted among its most important components. We relate a story of a long-run process of ideologically driven privatizations, which started long before the 1970s and was not uniform or linear, but uneven and punctuated. In particular, we describe two distinct waves of privatization in the military sphere. The first of these, in the field of weapons production, real estate, and some basic services, began to take place during the early Cold War and continued through the 1970s. After a perhaps unexpected lull during the Reagan years, a second shift toward outsourcing commenced in the early 1990s, this one focused on the fields of social welfare provision, logistics, and the many additional services performed by the military. In other words, we offer a complex account of periodization, which is not compatible with simple, compact narratives of neoliberalism's ascent. This complicated history may be unwieldy, but it is more accurate; we see it as complementary to some of the best recent work on non-military subjects, which is similarly questioning narratives of a quick 1970s-80s neoliberal ascendance.

At the same time, our account departs slightly from some of the most sophisticated recent works on neoliberalism, in the area of our understanding of the recent transformations of the modern state. Some scholars have properly pointed out that neoliberalism in practice is not anti-statist, but rather requires positive state action, in favor of certain policies and interests, such as the creation of institutions of global trade, and the insulation of private interests from state intervention and democratic politics.[10] We endorse this important point; our account of the US military's recent history suggests the many ways in which privatization was achieved via new public policies, sometimes accompanied by the creation of new public authorities and entities. And yet, our understanding of the US military's transformation makes us skeptical of suggestions that neoliberal states are not much different from their more regulatory-minded, mixed-economy style counterparts, in terms of raw public power and predilection for interventionism. Our account of the military's transformations suggests a perhaps more conventional view of the later twentieth-century US state, in which state capacities were indeed hollowed out, altering the fundamental balance between public and private authority, and empowering an outsized corporate sector.

As this chapter shows, the post-1945 push to privatize the military met with frustrations and setbacks, but nonetheless was largely successful. The US military of the mid-twenty-first century is significantly smaller, and far more reliant on contractor support, than it was two generations ago. Like other, better-documented aspects of neoliberal reform, the transformation of the US military was sometimes presented by its advocates as an inevitable consequence of rational economic calculation, but in fact it more closely resembled a political campaign. Acknowledging this history is an essential starting point for anyone who seeks to understand the US military, both its recent past and its possible futures.

The First Wave of Privatization

The enormous American military of the mid-twentieth century, with its substantial in-house real estate, commercial services, and industrial assets, had been built up over two centuries in which the United States military pursued a mixed-economy, public-private approach to defense acquisition and operations. This approach was far from revolutionary: it was also practiced by the military establishments of early modern Britain and France,[11] as well in civilian governance in the early United States.[12] From the Civil War onward through the World Wars, a diverse alliance of actors drove the growth of an increasingly public sector military, combining numerous interests and impulses, including concerns about meeting technical, long-term military production needs; military professionalism; regional boosterism, and populist and progressive advocacy of public sector transparency and suspicions of big business and war profiteering.[13] Together these actors and impulses established a public development path that gathered support from local interests and Congressional representatives, and from ambitious military officers keen to expand their professional ambit.[14] Public military capacities were buoyed by the proven military effectiveness of the government-owned facilities in arms production and in the test of combat during World War I and II.[15] And to no small degree, new and continuing investments in the military's in-house capacities were also promoted by wariness—among the American public, legislators, and military authorities—of corruption and profiteering that often seemed to taint the military's purchases of goods and services from for-profit firms.

The growth of the public military did not take place without struggles over the proper scope of public versus private military functions. These debates dated back to the earliest years of the Republic and continued into the nineteenth century, with conflict occurring most often between specific interests and their allies in Congress and the military, such as private ship builders, laundry service providers, or the producers of firearms.[16] During the twentieth century, the stakes of such contests grew enormously, however, as the capacity and funding of the military grew to unprecedented proportions. By the middle of the century, a growing movement of anti-statist business leaders and political allies targeted the military, which, whether measured in terms of number of dollars or number of properties and programs, loomed—in their eyes—as the single most wasteful, anti-capitalist component of the American state. Those anti-statist critics began pressing Congress and the executive to issue directives privatizing substantial parts of the big military, in an effort that had increasing success, over the course of the second half of the twentieth century. Meanwhile, many Department of Defense officials, along with some officers in the military services, themselves began to embrace methods of business management that stressed the advantages of outsourcing. These sensibilities—and not simply technological or geopolitical shifts—help to explain the transformation of the US military, during the latter part of the twentieth century, into a leaner, less multi-functional entity, for better and for worse.

The modern anti-statist assault on the military's public property and functions began in earnest during the era of the New Deal, when new organizations such as the American Liberty League, as well as older business associations such as the National Association of Manufacturers (NAM) and the Chamber of Commerce, began to target the military's commercial and industrial activities. In 1932, just before the election of Franklin D. Roosevelt and the Democratic landslide, the House of Representatives formed a special committee charged with investigating "government competition with private enterprise." In its report issued in 1933, this body, acknowledging that it was formed in response to lobbying efforts by the NAM and the Chamber, examined a wide range of state operations, from prison enterprises to the Government Printing Office. But its central concern was the military. Poring over the federal government's budgets and programs of the 1930s, the committee cited the military's ownership of property, its productive capacities in weapons and materiel, and its undertaking of "commercial services," services defined as not "inherently governmental," which might be performed by the private sector. All of these features of the public military state, they argued, created "unfair competition" with the private sector.[17]

The political campaign for reining in the big military strengthened in the late 1940s and early 1950s, with the rise of domestic anticommunism and Republican gains in Congress.[18] The most important mechanisms for its articulation were the Hoover Commissions of 1947 and 1953, led by former president Herbert Hoover, a fierce critic of the New Deal order. The Hoover Commissions aimed officially at "reorganization of the Executive" branch of government, touting, organizational reform and efficiency. But one of their practical aims centered on the Defense Department, and at eliminating the military's commercial and industrial operations. The Hoover Commissions demanded that the Defense Department sell off many of its "commercial-industrial facilities" so as to reduce "government competition . . . with private enterprises." They targeted an enormous array of military state activities: "shipbuilding and ship repair yards, peacetime transportation in aircraft and seagoing vessels, commissary stores and post exchanges, bakeries, coffee roasting plants, meat cutting plants, laundries, dry cleaning plants, tailor shops, clothing factories, dental manufactories, watch repair shops, and many others."[19]

The Hoover Commission Report captured the postwar "free enterprise" mood of the Republican Party, and fiscally conservative, anticommunist and free-enterprise Republicans in Congress and in allied political groups rallied to the Hoover Commissions's findings.[20] Attentive to these calls from conservatives, the administration of President Dwight D. Eisenhower initiated what would become the foundational federal rule concerning contracting government activities to the private sector. In 1955 Eisenhower ordered his Bureau of the Budget to issue a new memorandum, 55-4, following directly from the Second Hoover Commission's complaints against government commercial activities. "It is the general policy of the administration," the budget chief Rowland R. Hughes wrote, "that the Federal Government will not start or carry on any commercial activity to provide a service or product for its own use if such product or service can be procured from private enterprise through ordinary business channels."[21] It was clear that the focus of this reform would be the big military. "Since most of the commercial activity is carried out by the Department of Defense," the Bureau of the Budget told Eisenhower and the cabinet, "most of the Congressional criticism has been directed to that Department."[22]

Although the new Eisenhower administration rules affected the big military, in the short run, their overall impact was modest. By October 1956, according to the Bureau of the Budget, the Defense Department had closed 355 of its own commercial enterprises.[23] However, the military of the 1950s resisted the wholesale contracting out of these activities. Although dozens of military industrial or commercial operations were outsourced, the scale of many of those establishments was small. During the first half of 1955, for example, the military services closed four coffee roasting facilities, a ropewalk, two paint manufacturing facilities, a bakery, a dry cleaning plant, and five cobbler shops, at installations all across the country. These fourteen facilities together employed about 300 people—hardly an impressive fraction of the big Cold War military, which at the time had about four million uniformed and civilian employees.[24]

Military privatization and government outsourcing increased in the 1960s, however, as President Lyndon B. Johnson pursued privatization in order to placate pro-business critics of his Great Society programs. Johnson reinvigorated the Eisenhower-era Bureau of the Budget memorandum favoring the private sector, and directed the Department of Defense in 1964 to evaluate its activities and to encourage additional private contracting. At the time, 43 percent of the DOD's $8 billion in annual spending on major services such as repair, housekeeping, and warehousing went to private contractors, with the remainder handled in-house.[25] In 1966, Johnson's administration clarified and formalized the policy of the Eisenhower years by issuing what is now understood on Capitol Hill as "the first permanent directive dealing with the issue of governmental reliance on the private sector."[26] The rules were encapsulated in Bureau of the Budget Circular A-76, which, as President Johnson stated when he promulgated this order, was intended "to maintain the Government's policy of reliance upon private enterprise."[27]

As the White House declared a fundamental public policy designed to limit in-house economic activities by the government, the Department of

Defense was already in the midst of a thoroughgoing effort to achieve greater efficiencies by slashing costs—including the high fixed costs of in-house capacities. This reform push was led in the 1960s by Defense Secretary Robert S. McNamara, a former Harvard Business School professor and top Ford Motor Co. executive.[28] More often than not, McNamara and his team of young "whiz kid" analysts favored privatization. Immediately after taking office in 1961, McNamara's team immediately launched "Project 71," a systematic assessment of the nation's military installations and military-industrial base. In this effort, McNamara and his aides understood themselves to be guided by the Eisenhower administration's directives, "which established the general administration policy to get the government out of competition with private industry." As they decided which military installations to retain and which to sell off, the McNamara team pursued a policy "based directly on the principle that free competitive enterprise must be fostered by the government"; the military itself should not own industrial plant unless it could be "clearly demonstrated" that the private sector could not do the job, or if "execution of the military mission makes government ownership of the facility a necessity."[29]

Under McNamara's leadership, the Pentagon shed hundreds of millions of dollars' worth of military-owned real estate, bases, and manufacturing plants, including some of the nation's oldest military-industrial facilities, such as the Brooklyn Navy Yard and the Springfield Armory, which had existed for over a century and a half.[30] The impact of the McNamara-era reforms was particularly strong in the field of naval shipbuilding. By the late 1960s, to the delight of industrial associations and lobbying groups such as the Shipbuilders Council of America, the navy entirely ceased building new warships in its own yards. This effort to close shipyards and other military-industrial facilities continued into the early 1970s, as Secretary of Defense Melvin Laird and his top deputy, David Packard, presided over additional rounds of closures and sell-offs, similar to those overseen by McNamara a few years before.[31]

McNamara's reforms, part of the broader Cold War push to privatize more military activities, were received in the military services with some suspicion and resistance. The military officer corps was a large and diverse group, charged with complex operational and administrative tasks. Many of these military leaders in the services were open to pragmatic reforms, but they regarded McNamara's team as excessively devoted to formal quantitative analysis, and disrespectful of military experience. They were also aware that private business lobbies tended to exaggerate the benefits of contracting out, while unfairly denigrating in-house establishments. As the navy awaited McNamara's decisions on shipyard closings in the mid-1960s, Commander J.J. Meyer, Jr., a submarine captain, published a long essay in a journal for naval professionals, defending the superior knowhow of the navy's own shipyards, especially for complex repair and overhaul work, while questioning the private yards' ability to meet national security needs. The essay appears to have resonated with Meyer's fellow officers, active and retired, two of whom submitted long letters praising his arguments and augmenting them with further examples of the hidden costs of relying on the private sector.[32] This conversation in the mid-1960s suggests that at that time, many military leaders in the services regarded the growing movement for privatization as something imposed by Congress and civilian leaders in the Department of Defense, who were unduly influenced by private lobbies, and whose focus on short-run efficiencies did not fully comprehend the real balance of the costs and benefits of outsourcing.

Military leaders' ambivalence about the growing use of contractors was also evident in their discussion of construction efforts in Vietnam. From 1966 to 1968, soon after President Johnson escalated the US war in Vietnam, the military turned to a consortium of big commercial construction companies, known as RMK-BRJ, to carry out a billion-dollar building program in South Vietnam, which included eight large air bases, six ports, 8,000 hospital beds, cantonments for 500,000 troops, and thousands of miles of new roads. From the point of view of top military officers, the decision to rely so heavily on contractors for this massive effort was not because of any perceived superiority of the private sector, but because of specific institutional constraints on the military's ability to mobilize its own forces. For largely political reasons, President Johnson had decided not to activate reserve units for service in Vietnam. Because the reserve units contained much of the military's standing in-house construction capacities, Johnson's decision had, as one army general observed in 1967, "dictated that contractor effort be relie[d] on to an extent unique in the annals of warfare." This jump in outsourcing big overseas military construction projects was not due to any lack of confidence among army and navy engineers in their own ability to handle the needed work, but by a pragmatic need to get work done fast under a specific set of rules established by civilian leaders. Indeed, in mid-1967, the navy's top engineer, Rear Admiral Alexander C. Husband, stated that if he were able to do it over again, he would have chosen to rely less on the private construction companies, despite their ability to quickly mobilize a large work force abroad, in part because of concerns about their ability to operate in a dangerous environment. Admiral Husband and his colleagues maintained this ambivalence about contractors despite a broader political environment in which the contractors were favored. As the defense journal reporter who interviewed Husband suggested, had the military opted in 1966 to do most of the construction on its own, "the charge of Government competition with private industry would surely have been levied."[33]

In the 1970s, the back-and-forth push to privatization on the one hand, and ambivalent reception in the military, on the other, continued. The historic establishment of a new AVF stoked a new call for privatization of the military from a new cadre of free enterprisers: academic economists. Renowned free market advocate Milton Friedman headed the Gates Commission, the group appointed in 1969 by President Richard Nixon to create the blueprint for the postconscription military, the AVF.[34] Viewing conscription as a "tax" levied by the government on its draftees, they argued instead for a recruited force that joined of free choice, having weighed their options in the labor market versus military service and determined for themselves to enlist. Free marketers advised a wholly cash-based system of increased pay in order to compensate for the elimination they proposed of all military-owned and military-provided services like housing, health care, and the many recreation and support programs officers and career personnel used. Using a rationale that mimicked the argument for education vouchers or a negative taxation program, the economists argued that rather than offering soldiers housing or medical care, the military should provide more cash income and let soldiers choose individually whatever "support" they wanted to "buy."[35]

The armed services successfully resisted the Friedman proposals to covert to an all-cash-incentive military, reasoning that it contradicted military values of public service and also substituted private sector support for direct military aid to personnel—aid that they perceived as central to the military value of "taking care of its own." Army leaders like General William Westmoreland and General Harold "Hal" Moore, Jr., instead proposed expanding military-provided benefits and social welfare services to help guarantee recruitment, retention, and loyalty to the new AVF.[36] The military had already begun to take on new services to serve military families, such as the 1950s-era Civilian Health and Medical Program of the Uniformed Services, which provided regular health coverage to military families and servicewide social work services, and Army Community Services, created in the 1960s.[37] Now, in the 1970s as the military abandoned conscription, military leaders argued successfully for a significant expansion of in-house social welfare capacities. Congress acceded and kicked off a twenty-year period of growth in military social welfare, housing, and support programs.

Though the military resisted the privatization of the new social welfare benefits, free market economists found success in continuing the trend toward privatizing other parts of the military. They were buoyed in the 1970s by the increasing influence of corporations in Washington—including the appointment by President Nixon of Roy Ash, president of military contractor Litton Industries, to lead the new Office of Management and Budget (OMB). Under Ash's leadership, the OMB promoted more contracting out of federal activities, especially in the military. In 1974, the OMB ordered civilian and military agencies to begin using quotas for privatization and outsourcing, thus ensuring timely transfers to the private sector. In 1976, the armed forces were ordered to locate "at least five functions presently performed in-house" that could qualify for immediate "transfer to the private sector."[38] Such directives continued into the administration of President Jimmy Carter, under whom the Government Accountability Office (GAO) criticized what it regarded as an unsatisfactorily small number of services contracts at the Defense Department. Reiterating the government policy—"to rely on the private enterprise system"— the GAO pressed Defense to outsource more of its "military base support services," such as trash collection, cleaning, food service, and utilities.[39]

The corporate and free market economics political pressures, in combination with defense budget cuts, produced significant transfers to the private sector. From 1973 to 1980, the army, for example, outsourced many more services and supports to private firms. First went dining facilities at several posts, including Fort Myer in Virginia and Fort Benjamin Harrison in Indiana. By the end of the 1970s, the army had moved decisively toward much more outsourcing of many other services, including mortuary and memorial affairs, laundry and dry cleaning, medical care, and policing.[40] The army's signature business management and research institutions, the Human Resources Research Office and the Resources Analysis Corporation, founded just two decades before, were spun off to the private sector.[41] As the army scoured its activities to determine more elements for contracting, even many of those very studies were contracted out to private firms. In 1977, the army's deputy chief of staff for personnel spent $402,000 on manpower contract studies telling him to contract out his services.[42] Meanwhile, a similar trend toward contracting was happening at air force installations. At Vance Air Force Base in Oklahoma, an important pilot training facility, the air force engaged Northrop Worldwide Aircraft Services, a division of the Northrop Corporation, a top manufacturer of supersonic fighter aircraft, to take over the gamut of support services at the base. By the late 1970s and early 1980s, the contract was worth about $30 million a year; Northrop had twelve hundred employees at Vance, which was understood to be a model for future outsourcing of support services at other installations across the country.[43]

As they surveyed these trends of the 1970s, many advocates for the private sector expected that President Ronald Reagan, elected in 1980, would hand them a decisive victory through the massive transfer of government services to private enterprise, especially in the military. In 1982 Reagan raised hopes when he created the President's Private Sector Survey on Cost Control, known as the Grace Commission, which aimed to reduce the "reliance on federal systems and employees to perform functions which could be performed more efficiently and at less cost by the private sector."[44] Like their predecessors on the Hoover commissions a generation before, Grace Commission members insisted that four hundred thousand defense positions were "commercial activities," not "inherently governmental," and demanded they be transferred to the private sector.[45] Proponents of defense outsourcing would not end up being fully satisfied by the Reagan administration, however, as the 1980s witnessed an overall slowdown in privatization and, even more conspicuously, significant new growth in in-house military construction and services, largely in the realm of social welfare provision begun in the 1970s.

The Reagan administration mounted only a tepid response to the concerns of the Grace Commission. It wrote stricter rules for the A-76 process, which encouraged more outsourcing, but Reagan's secretary of defense, Caspar Weinberger, limited its impact.[46] Weinberger conceded to an increased number of A-76 competitions, in which existing public entities had to bid against private contractors for the work they had been doing. Between 1979 and 1984, the DOD held 1,054 A-76 competitions for Defense Department base operations support, involving 35,500 federal jobs, and private sector firms won nearly half of these.[47] Nevertheless, the burst of new A-76 competitions failed to radically downsize the military's own service operations. Job cuts at public facilities were regarded with dismay by many members of Congress, which enacted new laws in the 1980s requiring the military to retain in-house capacity for "core" functions and capping at 40 percent the fraction of depot maintenance work that the military could have done by contractors.[48] More broadly, Secretary Weinberger, despite his personal faith in the benefits of free enterprise, did not approve of a massive defense outsourcing effort, as it ran counter to his Reagan-sponsored defense buildup. Instead, the Defense Department increased civilian hires by 130,000, a nearly 15 percent rise, and increased the numbers of active duty personnel and reserves.[49]

As the military of the 1980s expanded its public workforce, it also radically expanded its new, AVF-based in-house social welfare state for military personnel and their families.[50] Though the programs had started to grow in the late 1970s under Carter, Reagan in particular championed the AVF and vowed to support the troops like no president before. Fostering recruitment, retention, and the readiness of new volunteers, generous social welfare services grew to a historic size. The family housing construction budget skyrocketed, and numerous costly services were created in universal military health care and childcare. In addition, the military services created dozens of additional new programs, from family counseling to legal and financial services, to violence prevention services. In 1985, army leaders touted more than twenty substantial welfare-related activities performed inhouse by the army itself.[51]

The expansion of the military's own social welfare activities in the 1970s and 1980s suggests the complexity of the chronology of military-market relations and the broader history of neoliberalism. By the final years of the Cold War, the US military, under pressure from a variety of efficiency-minded reformers, lobbyists, and ideologues, had already seen three decades of substantial privatizations, especially in the areas of industrial production, real estate, and facilities management. However, as late as the 1980s, many social welfare and administrative functions, as well as the bulk of logistical activities, were handled by the military's own organizations and personnel. This incoherence in military-market relations was perhaps an inevitable consequence of the military's wide-ranging activities across so many economic sectors, each of which had unique characteristics and complicated histories. However, as the Cold War came to an end, there would be a new round of transformations in military-market relations, this one more consistently aimed at outsourcing.

The Second Wave of Privatization

The Reagan-era expansion of the public military functions and the limits on privatization disappointed free market advocates, but this setback proved temporary. In the 1990s, the decades-old goals of anti–New Dealers and Hoover Commission supporters were realized in a second and massive wave of privatization. This new boost to privatization occurred during the drawdown of the immediate post–Cold War era, a new period of austerity for the military. While during previous postwar retrenchment periods of American history, the military establishment and Congress had typically preserved or expanded some public capacities, even as it cut or privatized others, in the 1990s, a more powerfully unidirectional move toward outsourcing took place. In this phase, both elected officials and business leaders from outside the military continued to pressure the military toward privatization. But they were also increasingly joined by top officials inside the military establishment, who, by the time of the post–Cold War drawdown, responded to budgetary and political pressures by turning to outsourcing.

The military's growing interest in adopting private sector philosophies and solutions, driven in part by Congressionally-imposed limits on numbers of uniformed personnel, was embodied in its shift toward the use of contractors for major logistical support services overseas. As noted above, during the US war in Vietnam, the Defense Department had engaged large commercial construction companies to build infrastructure abroad, even as some military leaders suggested that the military's own engineering organizations were capable of handling more of the work. A generation later, the Pentagon embraced the outsourcing of construction and logistics functions more deliberately, and with more enthusiasm. The Logistics Civil Augmentation Program (LOGCAP), created in 1985, came to life in earnest during the tenure of Defense Secretary Dick Cheney, who commissioned private firms to study the possibilities of expanded logistical roles for contractors. One of the companies called on to study the question was Halliburton, the oil services giant that included Brown & Root, a construction company that had built many military installations, domestically and abroad, across much of the twentieth century. Halliburton advised Cheney (who would be named CEO of Halliburton a few years later) to make more use of contractors. The first major LOGCAP contract was issued in 1992, to Halliburton's Brown & Root subsidiary. More comprehensive than previous contracting arrangements in the field of military logistics and service provision, the LOGCAP agreements called on the contractor to perform a wide range of tasks in a given overseas region, from facilities construction to the provision of basic services, such as food and showers. Used first in the Balkans and Africa, the LOGCAP contracts, which paid tens of billions of dollars to Brown & Root (later, KBR) and other private firms, would become much more important in the years to come, during the post-9/11 operations in Afghanistan and Iraq.[52]

Privatization trends within the military accelerated in other ways during the same period of the drawdown. A prime example was the hard-hit Army Materiel Command. The Materiel Command was forced to radically "restructure and downsize" between 1987 and 1991, as it faced a reduction in forces across the board of fifty-two hundred jobs, including a 30 percent reduction at headquarters, and the closure of many of its installations through the Base Realignment and Closure Commission process.[53] According to the organization's own official history, "By 1995 . . . AMC was reduced to a size operating with less than half of the strength it possessed during the 1980s."[54]

As military leaders downsized their own functions to meet budget cuts, they made more use of corporate management methods and philosophies. Logisticians took courses in business management and tested contractor-provided supports in everything from food service to payroll to preplanning for overseas mobilizations.[55] In the late 1980s, Secretary of Defense Frank Carlucci required the Defense Department, the military services, and their contractors to implement total quality management (TQM), which had become popular in the US business community in recent years. TQM, which had been developed by Japanese companies (and their American advisors) in the 1950s and 1960s, proposed to create a process of continuous improvement of goods or services through a focus on "customer satisfaction," as well as more input from ordinary employees about ways to achieve efficiencies in day-to-day operations. By the early 1990s, the army had initiated new courses in TQM, "throughout the Army's training and educational systems." All army components that supported soldiers through infrastructure or services or programs would manage their cuts through corporate-style management planning and practices.[56]

By the 1990s, the military establishment was increasingly suffused with corporate methods and logics. Whereas in the past, uniformed military officers had often defended in-house industrial and commercial operations, during the 1990s, more of them joined the privatization bandwagon. Vice chief of staff of the army General Dennis Reimer in 1992 ordered commanders to "critically examine which services we should provide, which we should divest, and which ones should be contracted." Reimer told them, "You will be given more discretion to employ business practices from the private sector."[57] Especially in the army, where cuts were deepest, many officers turned to corporate America and business schools, whose methods such as strategic planning, determining core competencies, and outsourcing they hoped would help them manage the institutional impact of the drawdown. The army joined the Conference Board (an industry-funded think tank), created a Captains of Industry Conference, and sent some of its best officers to earn MBAs from schools such as Syracuse University and the Massachusetts Institute of Technology.[58] Influenced by this education, which was helping business

leaders downsize American industry in a new era of globalization and dein-
dustrialization, military officers increasingly embraced the outsourcing of
services.[59] One of the army's in-house historians researching the effect of
1990s defense reforms reported that senior army officials held "deep misgivings" about the brisk change and the force of the mandate to outsource in the
Clinton years.[60] But if they did, the sentiments did not become public. Typical
venues for questioning and discussion of army policy—the research papers at
the military war colleges, articles in *Army* magazine, testimony before Congress—contained relatively little discussion of the dramatic policy change.
When officers did write about outsourcing in these venues, they assumed
its worthiness as strategy—"essential to achieving the DOD mission," as one
medical logistics officer put it—and offered their thoughts on the best ways to
implement it in their respective commands and communities.[61]

The presidency of Bill Clinton, during which corporate practices gained
even more influence over governance, accelerated the military's transfer of
its activities to for-profit entities. Such reform was an important element of
the Clinton administration's National Performance Review, a descendant
of previous executive-branch-led efforts to cut government by using more
businesslike management, including the Hoover commissions and the Grace
Commission.[62] Though the National Performance Review of Clinton and
Vice President Al Gore was less stridently conservative than those boards,
it nevertheless shared their assumptions about the poor performance of
government agencies and the superiority of the private sector.[63]

The Clinton administration's enthusiasm for outsourcing was helpful to
defense contractors, many of which were struggling to survive in the midst
of the defense budget cuts that came with the end of the Cold War. In the
early 1990s, defense industry associations, including Business Executives for
National Security, founded in 1982, became more aggressive in their calls
for the government to use private companies for more research, consulting,
and depot maintenance work.[64] This new push by the White House and lobbyists was noticed in the military services, which were charged with finding
more opportunities to contract out. As General James Link, the deputy commander of the Army Materiel Command, observed in 2000, recent years had
seen a marked uptick in outsourcing. "It's a significant change. Now why is
that?" General Link explained that, with the end of the Cold War, "we have
a few companies scrambling for defense work with very few defense dollars.
So they're interested in where they can take over what has heretofore been
government work and have the dollars to go with that."[65]

The Clinton-era reforms had especially impressive results. During the 1990s, expenditures on contracted military support services grew steadily, increasing from about 30 percent of all military contracting in the late 1980s to nearly 45 percent by 1999, when they matched or exceeded total military spending on products (weapons and materiel), traditionally the lion's share of military contracting. The money value of these contracts was so large that for the first time, corporate providers of consulting, housing, and health care made the list of top military contractors in dollar value of contracts.[66] This meant that the last major addition to the Cold War–era big military—in the fields of in-house welfare and social services—was being substantially privatized. More broadly, the last years of the twentieth century saw a marked decline in the scale and scope of the big military, as outsourcing became de rigueur. Many military officers and uniformed personnel, whether they worked inside the Pentagon or far outside it, recognized the shifted terrain. As one army officer wrote in a 1997 research paper, "Privatization and outsourcing are buzzwords that are all the rage these days inside the beltway. DOD is looking at any and all work currently being accomplished by military and civil servants that can be transferred to the private sector."[67]

By the new millennium, the United States government's military had stopped performing many of its activities and services and was divested of much of its production power and property. The military had off-loaded huge swaths of its real estate, capital, and production capabilities. It had also passed into the private sector many of its non-war-fighting services and activities. In sharp contrast to the big, multicompetent military of the earlier Cold War era, the new American military was becoming something closer to a collection of privately contracted goods and services, in support of a small set of warfighters. Reforms instituted from the 1950s through the 1990s, while never fully satisfactory to the most thoroughgoing critics of "government competition," had, by the turn of the millennium, produced very substantial results. The United States military of the early twenty-first century, more than its predecessors in any period, would attempt to ride on the back of the private sector.

Conclusion

On September 10, 2001, Defense Secretary Donald Rumsfeld delivered a speech at the Pentagon during the opening ceremony for its Acquisition and Logistics Excellence Week. In his address to military and civilian DOD employees, Rumsfeld described the Pentagon itself as a formidable "adversary," which stood as "one of the world's last bastions of central planning." According to the defense secretary, the military was still far too big and multifunctional. "Why is DOD one of the last organizations around that still cuts its own checks?" asked Rumsfeld. "When an entire industry exists to run warehouses efficiently, why do we own and operate so many of our own? At bases around the world, why do we pick up our own garbage and mop our own floors, rather than contracting services out, as many businesses do?" Announcing a "war on bureaucracy" and a "campaign to shift Pentagon resources from the tail to the tooth," Rumsfeld promised to cut costs by privatizing even more defense functions, including housing, utilities, and health care.[68]

Just one day after Rumsfeld's speech, attacks on the World Trade Center and the Pentagon killed nearly three thousand people; over the following months, the George W. Bush administration launched major new military operations in Afghanistan and Iraq. In waging these wars, which were among the most expensive in dollar terms in history, the United States relied to an unprecedented extent on outsourcing. The most widely discussed aspect of this more privatized way of war was the rise of security contractors—providers of private soldiers—such as Blackwater. But most contractors supporting the wars of the 2000s, in the United States and abroad, were in logistics, health services, housing, food services, and other noncombat functions. As Rumsfeld's speech showed, the George W. Bush administration was committed to privatizing more of these functions. But Rumsfeld's 2001 address failed to suggest the extent to which they had already been outsourced, even before Bush took office. It is those earlier reforms, as much as or more than Rumsfeld's preferences, that explain the unprecedented, dramatic change in the ratio of contractors to uniformed personnel in theatre, which for most of American history had been approximately one to four, to a new norm of one to one, or even higher, by the 2000s.[69]

A few years after the start of the wars in Afghanistan and Iraq, there was something of a pause in the long-term privatizing trend, as Congress and the Obama administration raised questions about the wisdom of additional outsourcing. In 2008, a Democratic Party–controlled Congress halted A-76 competitions, which had been used by the George W. Bush administration to transfer more governance work to private entities. This policy shift was inspired by increasing concerns about mismanagement in the contractor-heavy war and reconstruction effort in Iraq, as well as a 2007 exposé of scandalously poor care for soldiers at the Walter Reed Army Medical Center. Journalists and legislators initially blamed military bureaucracy for many of the problems at the facility; however, following the lead of Senator Barbara Mikulski (D-MD), they soon

attributed some of the failures to IAP Worldwide Services, the contractor chosen after the Bush administration had pushed the army, several years earlier, to
outsource more work at Walter Reed.[70] By the 2010s, some top DOD officials
had become wary of what they came to regard as excessive outsourcing, including total system performance responsibility (TSPR) arrangements, adopted
widely by the air force in the 1990s, under which contractors assumed near-
total responsibility for the long-run logistics support and maintenance of several major weapon systems, including aircraft and missiles.[71]

The lull in the pace of outsourcing, together with the complaints registered
by Rumsfeld in his 2001 speech, may be interpreted as evidence that despite all
the sound and fury of would-be privatizers, the big, multicompetent military
has remained unassailable. Alternatively, it is possible to argue that for technological and political reasons, the postwar national security state, like other
parts of the American state, has become an overwhelmingly associational or
hybrid institution, in which the concept of privatization has little meaning,
because public and private have long been fully entangled and inseparable.
Some of these accounts are sanguine about the current state of this public-
private balance, suggesting that it allows considerable innovation and agility.[72]

This chapter suggests the limitations of both of these views by showing that
over the long run of American history, there have in fact been far-reaching
changes in the balance of public and private responsibility and power, not
least when it comes to the provision of military goods and services. The history of the deconstruction of the big military state suggests that in this recent
area, the turn to private providers was often neither especially pragmatic nor
popular. Rather, the late-twentieth-century shift to a more privatized military
was largely a political project, pushed by business leaders, economists, policymakers, and elected officials whose preferences for private sector solutions
were informed both by rigid ideological positions in favor of private enterprise and by self-interested searches for greater profits through takeovers of
government resources and functions. Much of this shift occurred without
any mandate from the general public and against the wishes of many military
leaders, members of Congress, workers' organizations, and many military
personnel. It is a change that deserves more acknowledgment and reckoning,
as a new generation of policymakers, military leaders, and voters works to
reimagine national and global security.

CHAPTER 2

The World's Biggest Landlord: How the Cold War Military Built Its Arsenal of Houses

A. Junn Murphy

Representing a group of housing developers and landlords, Texas lawyer Roland Boyd delivered an extensive photo-illustrated presentation to Congress in 1959. Boyd showed the House Armed Services Committee slide after slide of housing tracts in Virginia, Alabama, Florida, Texas, and California, commenting on the attractiveness of their homes, the lush landscaping, and the fertility of their inhabitants. He boasted to the representatives that if they ever drove through one of his client's neighborhoods, they would find themselves thinking, "Well, I never saw so many kids and so many dogs in such a short distance in my life."[1] Boyd declared that the builders he spoke on behalf of were "a cross-section of America"; more specifically, they embodied "free enterprise."[2] Expounding on the fundamental incompatibility of government and private enterprise, he explained to the assembled legislators that the prospect of profit was not only "the basis of our capitalistic system" but "the foundation of our greatness" and a natural and righteous basis for private industry.[3] At first glance, Boyd's performance appears to be a familiar rehearsal of standard midcentury probusiness, free market rhetoric.[4] Odd, then, that the reason he and his clients were there in the halls of Congress was to convince the US government to take ownership of their eighty-two thousand apartments, duplexes, and detached homes in suburban housing developments across the country.[5]

The houses Boyd showcased were by all appearances normal midcentury American homes, built and owned by private developers. But Boyd's houses were actually of a peculiar and specific kind: they had been built on military bases for the express purpose of housing military personnel and their families.[6] In 1949, in the midst of a national housing shortage, Congress authorized a plan to incentivize and subsidize private developers to construct, own, and manage large amounts of military family housing called Wherry housing, after Senator Kenneth S. Wherry (R-NE), who sponsored the legislation. Following three years of rapid construction and a contracting scandal, Congress altered the program so that future construction would be privately built but government owned. This second iteration became known as the Capehart plan after another senator, Homer E. Capehart (R-IN). Perceiving the Capehart program as competition, the private owners of the Wherry housing appealed to Congress for relief, resulting in the strange scene of landlords lobbying for their own (compensated) expropriation by the federal government. Together, the Wherry and Capehart programs generated the bulk of the Cold War military's family housing and made the military a landlord to hundreds of thousands of families, a role it had only haphazardly filled before World War II.

This essay makes two main interventions. First, it centers housing as one of the defining features of the Cold War military by examining Defense Department property data, which show a decisive growth in the absolute and relative importance of residential housing in the US military's overall program in the 1950s. The Wherry and Capehart family housing programs represent one of the key transformations that the military underwent over the course of the Cold War, physically embodying its increasing capacities in the field of human services.[7] At the same time that the military was closing many of its industrial facilities in favor of contracting, in the field of housing it made a decisive move toward increased state ownership, ultimately nationalizing significant amounts of privately owned housing.[8] Between 1950 and 1964, the military and its private partners constructed approximately two hundred thousand units of family housing—close to half of the total amount of civilian public housing units built across the country in that same period.[9] These figures point to a hidden military welfare state, one that reproduced racial and gender ideologies in ways that mirrored more familiar midcentury public provisions.[10] The cumulative result of the family housing program meant no less than the remaking of the military itself: into an owner and manager of hundreds of suburban housing tracts. Recognizing family housing's place in the defense establishment reveals that an essential part of America's Cold War strategy was the building up of the military's infrastructure for social reproduction.

By venturing into the field of housing, the military invested in the architecture of social reproduction for its members and their families. Developed by Marxist feminist scholars, social reproduction theory calls attention to the totality of social relationships required to reproduce a capitalist economy as a whole—especially forms of work not considered "productive" because they are domestic or otherwise outside the conventional capital-labor relation patterned on industrial wage work.[11] The concept of social reproduction sets into relief the importance of housing and family arrangements in the military's strategic-level manpower plans. In the aggregate, these policies encouraged heterosexual marriage, reproduction, and cohabitation in nuclear family units, complementing other military and federal policies that promulgated gender and sexual norms.[12] The expansion of military family housing was an intervention in social reproduction in that it set up infrastructure for sustaining its members, providing the venue for the unwaged support of individual service members in single-family homes occupied by nuclear families. Read through this feminist lens, the story of military family housing shows how markets are dependent on social relationships far beyond the direct participants in exchange, predicated on domestic and unwaged labor, and created and shaped by the state. This insight brings us to the second main intervention of the essay.

In addition to highlighting the importance of domestic relationships in defense policy, this chapter explains the circumstances that allowed a remarkable expansion of state capacity to be achieved through programs that were paradoxically marketed as (and have since largely been described as) privatization initiatives.[13] Anti–New Deal forces crafted the Wherry program in an attempt to rely on private enterprise to solve the military's housing problem, but it ironically resulted in a mass nationalization of private property into the military's new inventory of residential housing. The story of the military's turn to nationalizing housing challenges common conceptions of public-private partnerships that view them as mere tools of business interests seeking to extract public resources and undermine state power.[14] Congress, landlords, and defense officials disagreed about the economic prerogatives of the state and the proper relationship of the military to the market, but they shifted in their commitments as accusations of profiteering led to the abandonment of the Wherry model. In this way, the military's postwar turn to the market for housing ultimately resulted in a massive expansion in the scale and scope of state capacity, all in the name of defending the world from socialism.[15] Military family housing was both a poignant example and constitutive

component of the military Keynesianism and uneven welfare state that char-
acterized America's Cold War political economy.[16]

Family Housing as Strategy: Military
Infrastructure Investment by the Numbers

Military family housing was a Cold War phenomenon that developed in
response to both the new reality of a large standing army as well as broader
postwar shifts in family patterns. The military had long been in the business of
human sustainment and held an obligation to provide housing to personnel, but
the number of people it housed grew dramatically after World War II.[17] Even
in 1948, when postwar manpower levels were at their lowest point, the military consisted of 1.4 million active duty personnel, compared to just 250,000 in
1935.[18] At the same time, the consolidation of the postwar heterosexual nuclear
family entailed a shift in the military's social composition.[19] Thanks in part to
public policy that encouraged marriage and childbearing, millions of Americans married and produced children at much higher rates than preceding generations—and military personnel did the same.[20] In addition to the absolute
growth of manpower to six times the size of prewar levels, service members
more frequently had families in the postwar period: 80 to 85 percent of officers
and 20 percent of enlisted men were married by 1955.[21] Before World War II,
the relatively small stock of family housing the military controlled was available
only to commissioned officers and senior enlisted career noncommissioned
officers, leaving the vast majority of military personnel housed in what were
called barracks or bachelor quarters.[22] At the end of World War II, the army
had only 13,000 family housing units and some 25,000 more temporary apartments converted from wartime civilian housing and nonhousing buildings.[23]
With increased manpower levels taken into account, the military estimated that
it had a deficit of 235,000 family housing units in 1949.[24]

    As a result of this deficit, the majority of married service members secured
housing for themselves and their families through the private market: by
renting or buying housing within reach of their station, or by housing their
families elsewhere while they lived in barracks or bachelors' quarters. But in
the postwar period, a national housing shortage made relying on the private
market a difficult proposition. A long-term housing shortage had been growing since 1926, even as the establishment of the Federal Housing Administration (FHA) in 1934 boosted construction.[25] World War II moved millions of

Americans, especially rural, female, and African American workers, into new cities and jobs.[26] After the war, the housing shortage was exacerbated by the return of fifteen million veterans.

In the context of the general civilian housing shortage in the late 1940s, the housing that service members found on the private market was often both substandard and expensive. Cold War living conditions for military families were publicized in sensational new stories detailing beer trucks and chicken coops that had been converted into domiciles.[27] Prominent journalist and social reformer Agnes E. Meyer presented military housing as an urgent problem threatening the country's very social order, warning that housing conditions in military communities were creating a "morally rotten situation" by breaking up families and breeding vice and delinquency.[28] Even Secretary of Defense Louis A. Johnson called the housing conditions "disgraceful."[29] The housing problem drew attention not only for the indignity suffered by service members and their families, but also because it was the top factor that military personnel cited in explaining their decisions not to reenlist.[30]

All of these housing scarcity and quality problems were compounded for African American service members. Across the country, citizens, businesses, and government agencies collaborated to build and enforce all-white residential areas through redlining, racial covenants, restrictive zoning blocking low-income construction, and violence.[31] The GI Bill loans that fueled suburban development were denied to African Americans, with banks in the New York City area approving only one hundred out of sixty-seven thousand such mortgages to nonwhite veterans.[32] Together, these practices constituted America's hidden and racialized form of Keynesianism that systematically redistributed wealth to white people through credit programs that boosted white homeownership.[33] Truman's 1948 executive order to desegregate the military was carried out in stages, over several years, and involved the integration of small units and military-owned housing and facilities.[34] While desegregation was uneven and often resisted by those tasked with carrying it out, the military was quickly becoming one of the less segregated institutions in American society, introducing integrated on-base housing in areas that were otherwise strictly segregated.[35] Discrimination in local housing and facilities, however, remained major problems: until the passage of the Fair Housing Act of 1968, private real estate actors across the country could openly discriminate against African American military personnel who sought to live off base.[36]

By 1949, with housing conditions for all service members at a nadir, defense leaders agreed that lack of adequate housing posed a serious threat to

military retention.[37] The army proposed barring lower-ranking enlisted personnel from reenlisting if they had families.[38] But the army was also failing
to recruit the amount of personnel that Congress authorized, let alone the
amount that their war plans called for.[39] Excluding married men from enlisting would only aggravate the problem. Instead, Congress pivoted toward
internalizing social reproduction by approving a massive plan to finance the
construction of military family housing. With the plan passed in 1949, the US
military committed to providing or subsidizing housing for the spouses and
children of all of its career personnel, not just commissioned officers.[40] The
significance and scale of this investment is perhaps best expressed in data on
the material composition of the military's real estate inventory.

To be sure, the military had long managed a diverse portfolio of real
estate, including the aforementioned bachelors' quarters or barracks, ammunition manufacturing plants, shipyards, office space, pipelines, warehouses,
and maintenance shops. What was new about the postwar moment was the
military's enthusiastic advance into family housing—a new kind of real estate
that situated the military as the user and eventually owner of vast swathes
of suburban housing tracts. If the data that the Department of Defense
collected on its real property are broken down by type (Figure 2.1), one of
the most apparent trends is the long-term relative increase in housing and
"community property," reflecting the military's increasing commitments to
service members over the second half of the twentieth century.[41] The data
also show a relative decline in industrial capacity and supply facilities in the
wake of WWII, when the government owned the majority of manufacturing
plants for aircraft, ships, synthetic rubber, aluminum, and ordnance—nearly
a quarter of the value of all the factories in the country.[42] The military's family
housing inventory surged in the late 1950s and overtook its investments in all
other major categories of real property (including barracks, airfields, storage,
production, and maintenance facilities) by 1963. In terms of the proportional
makeup of its real estate inventory, by the early 1960s the military had developed into an institution invested first and foremost in housing.

Half of the Cold War military's stock of family housing was built under
the Wherry and Capehart programs during the short windows of 1950–1954
and 1956–1964.[43] Existing writing on the Wherry and Capehart programs
describes them as milestones in the larger arc of privatization of military
functions.[44] They were undoubtedly examples of public-private partnerships,
a pattern seen time and again in different forms in the long history of the
military.[45] The Wherry and Capehart programs in particular relied more on

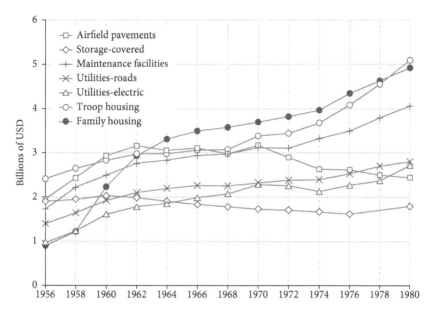

Figure. 2.1. Types of real property controlled by the Department of Defense, in billions of US dollars, 1956–1980. Source: *Real and Personal Property of the Department of Defense* (Washington, DC, 1956–1980).

private capital and enterprise than past housing projects had. Before and after these programs, domestic military family housing was provided through "appropriated funds" construction contracts financed up front by cash drawn from the Treasury, which had a high sticker price that made Congress reluctant to ever build very much at any given time.[46] However, while relying on the private sector was the original intent of the Wherry and Capehart programs, they ultimately facilitated the swift and decisive investment of the federal government in a massive arsenal of state-owned residential housing (Figure 2.2).

The Wherry program's design indeed reflected a broader trend toward private provision of military services, but this aim was undermined by conflict over the government's right to determine permissible and appropriate profit on taxpayer-funded ventures.[47] When Congress replaced the Wherry program with the Capehart program, it discarded a vision of privately owned military housing in favor of a new configuration of privately financed, state-owned housing. By deploying creative budgetary accounting, this hybrid configuration permitted the swift accumulation of a huge inventory of residential

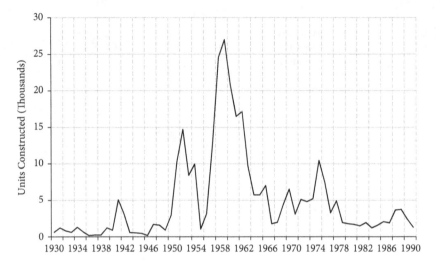

Figure. 2.2. The US military's family housing inventory as of 1991, by year built or acquired. Source: Congressional Budget Office, *Military Family Housing* (Washington, DC, 1993).

real estate that would not have been politically possible through the direct investment of federal funds budgeted by Congress. In other words, this public-private partnership—a form typically associated with privatization—in this case enabled an epochal state *expansion* of publicly-owned infrastructure for the social reproduction of the Cold War military.

The story of the military's provision of family housing in the postwar period represents an almost entirely unknown episode of large-scale nationalization of private property in the middle of the Cold War.[48] With good reason, the overarching narrative of the military's institutional transformation in the second half of the twentieth century is one of increasing privatization, culminating in the reliance on private security forces seen in America's twenty-first-century operations in Iraq and Afghanistan.[49] After World War II, conservative forces pushed for the privatization of many of the military's assets, especially production plants, using demobilization as an opportunity to fulfill anti–New Deal agendas.[50] However, there was an important and striking exception in the realm of family housing. In order to house service members, Congress and defense leaders chose increased state ownership and ultimately the nationalization of significant amounts of privately owned housing. These federal housing units—two hundred thousand in all—were maintained and used into the 1990s, when they were finally privatized through the 1996 Military Housing

Privatization Initiative.[51] How is it that, amidst an ongoing postwar campaign by conservative business leaders and their political allies to unmake the New Deal state and its productive capacity, the military simultaneously acquired a gigantic stock of residential housing?[52] Having established housing at the center of the Cold War military, the rest of this essay explains the contingent and contradictory series of events that led the military to build and acquire its arsenal of houses. This circuitous process began with Congress's attempt to jumpstart a new rental housing market by incentivizing private developers to embark on a construction boom.

The Wherry Program: A Public-Private Solution to the Postwar Housing Crisis

On March 5, 1949, Senator Wherry introduced a plan for building military family housing that boasted a distinctive mix of private and public contributions.[53] Part of the cohort of fervently anticommunist Republican senators that included Joseph McCarthy and Richard Nixon, Wherry is perhaps best known today for spearheading the "lavender scare" that purged lesbians and gay people from jobs in the federal government. Wherry personally did much to repeatedly push homosexuality onto the political stage, demanding an inquiry into homosexuals in federal employment in early 1950, leading a subcommittee investigation on the issue, and allegedly boasting privately that he was "the expert on homosexuality in the State Department."[54] Wherry's campaign against homosexuality in government was part of his larger political crusade against government institutions—one of the most conservative members of Congress, he was a fierce opponent of the New Deal and the Fair Deal, calling himself a "fundamentalist" against the "socialistic welfare state," including public housing.[55] These commitments were reflected in the new strategy of social reproduction he engineered for the Cold War military.

Wherry's military housing program proposed that private developers use FHA-insured mortgages to build, own, and maintain housing on military land in order to rent it to service members and their families.[56] Private real estate developers had failed to build housing near many of the remote locations of emerging Cold War bases, especially given the risks of catering to a pool of customers—military personnel—who might vanish at the drop of a hat (or, more aptly, bomb) on relocation orders. Under Wherry's plan, the FHA would guarantee the loans that builders took out from private banks as long as the loan covered no more than 90 percent of the total construction cost, in the expectation that builders would assume a "normal 'business risk'" with their equity investment of 10 percent.[57] The plan was modeled on an existing program of FHA insurance for private housing development, a core part of Cold War America's grand strategy for the domestic economy that relied on hidden but essential subsidies for widespread white homeowner- ship.[58] Along with the mortgage insurance, practically free land (leased from the military for nominal payments), and discounted utilities, the Wherry plan offered guaranteed demand by promising developers that the installations where they built housing were a "permanent part of the Military establish- ment." After an open bid process, the chosen developer would sign a fifty- to seventy-five-year ground lease and commit to build, rent, and maintain the homes for that period, at which point they would transfer the properties to the military. Rental rates charged to service members were to be determined through an agreement between the owner, the FHA, and the military and based on a calculation of mortgage servicing, operating costs, and a "rea- sonable profit" of five to seven percent.[59] Wherry housing would be privately owned and operated, but located on military land, filled with military ten- ants, and rented at rates set by the FHA. With these features, the Wherry plan was privatized compared to appropriated funds construction, but it was also a departure from the actual default way that housing had been delivered to the majority of married service members: through the private market.

The Wherry plan was passed in August 1949 and the military began accepting proposals shortly thereafter.[60] In terms of design, most Wherry plans were drawn from existing plans for civilian housing.[61] Charles Leavell of Morgan, Leavell and Ponder, one of the biggest Wherry builders, said plans for the program were "pulled right off the shelf: whatever was popular at the time, as long as they met the regulations."[62] The local military officials who received bids selected among proposals that ranged from single-family detached houses to six-story apartment buildings. Compared to private development projects, Wherry communities were often larger, amounting to hundreds of units at a given location. Fort Knox in Kentucky was one of the first and largest Wherry projects, consisting of one thousand apartments in two-story brick row houses that were "exact duplicates" of other government- subsidized housing projects that were being built for civilian use elsewhere in the country.[63]

With the commencement of Wherry construction, the military suddenly became a major player in the construction of American housing communities.

The military was an important force behind suburbanization across the country, a role amply documented in histories of the geographic distribution of defense spending, the Interstate highway system, and postwar mortgage assistance for veterans.[64] Beyond these relationships, however, the military was directly involved in shaping settlement patterns through its lesser-known status as a direct generator and user of housing.[65] Alongside civilian FHA mortgage insurance and the GI Bill—which established the financial architecture that made possible the settlement of the suburbs by white Americans in detached homes—the military also encouraged heterosexual nuclear families through the living spaces it provided its personnel.

The Wherry program's scale and ambition were impressive, but once underway, problems arose. Some installations were inundated with proposals, and many proposals overstated the quantity or quality of what they could deliver. As it cropped up around the country, Wherry housing elicited complaints about the units being cramped and shoddily built.[66] While many developers underestimated their costs in order to secure contracts, others developers completed their projects for less than they had proposed and pocketed the difference. This last practice was the most damning scandal to hit the Wherry program, and one that had troubled the FHA more broadly: that of windfall profits reaped by government-backed developers of rental properties.[67] The FHA was supposed to guarantee loans for 90 percent of the construction costs with the builder investing the last 10 percent. But many builders ended up completing construction with the loan funds alone, without staking any of their own capital to build the projects. Profits for the builders were already accounted for in the proposals chosen by the government and further limited profits were supposed to come from rent collection, not construction. Thus, some builders were collecting larger profits than Congress had intended or authorized.[68]

Forty-three days of Senate hearings on the FHA programs found a total of $75 million in so-called windfall profits on 437 projects of the 543 they investigated.[69] A widely publicized example concerned a two-thousand-unit apartment project built in Dayton, Ohio, for Wright-Patterson Airfield under the Wherry program. A company formed by four "investors" contributed only $2,000 in capital and received a $17.4 million loan insured by the FHA; the company stood to split the $908,000 left over from the mortgage among the four stockholders.[70] The windfall scandal culminated in the resignation and indictment of FHA head Clyde Powell and nearly a thousand other criminal investigations.[71] Somewhat dramatically, Republican senator of Indiana and investigation chair Homer Capehart called it "the biggest scandal in the history of the United States."[72]

In 1953, Congress passed an amendment to the Housing Act that required builders to return any money from FHA-guaranteed loans that was not used in construction.[73] After that, interest in building Wherry housing came to a virtual halt.[74] Scandal aside, the program had successfully built 83,742 units in 264 projects across the country.[75] However, a formidable shortage of family housing remained and continued to provoke the anxiety of top military leadership. In a testament to the fact that social services were a prime military concern, even Air Force General Curtis LeMay, commander of America's nuclear arsenal, worried in 1955 that the persistent lack of adequate military housing threatened "the survival of our civilization."[76] Coming away from the Wherry program, the Defense Department and Congress would double down on investment in housing through a variation on their public-private partnership that functionally revolutionized the government's involvement in family housing, turning the military into the world's biggest landlord.

The Capehart Proposal: Public Turn and Nationalization

In 1955, Senator Capehart came forward with a proposal to improve the military's family housing development program.[77] Proponents of Capehart's plan emphasized its similarity to the Wherry program, including its reliance on private developers and FHA guarantees, but with the major distinction of short-circuiting opportunities for windfall. Unlike Wherry projects, Capehart housing and the mortgage liabilities used to build it would be transferred to military ownership at a negotiated price as soon as construction was completed. By quickly transferring housing stock to the government, Capehart hoped to preclude windfalls by compensating builders only for their actual equity investment. However, by vesting ownership in and placing debt burdens on the federal government, the Capehart program actually marked a dramatic departure from the Wherry program. On first blush, it can be difficult to understand why Congress willingly committed to a mammoth investment in housing in the middle of a broader push to downsize federal property holdings. Democrats had taken control of the House and Senate in the 1954 midterm elections, but the program was sponsored by Capehart, a Republican. What lent the Capehart program its bipartisan appeal was its apparent costlessness, a product of creative accounting.[78] After the housing projects were transferred to the military, the military would pay off the mortgages with quarters allowances: the funds earmarked for individual service members who would have lived off base but were now military tenants in Capehart homes. The costs of this housing would show up in the budget not as military construction projects, but as personnel expenditures charged one year at a time for the duration of the mortgages. As conservative congressmembers like Virginia Senator Harry F. Byrd pointed out, the Capehart program concealed a massive long-term commitment of government funds for housing under the label of pay for service members.[79] A $2.5 billion investment in building 120,000 public houses in a span of five years would have had a politically unviable price tag, but the same exact purpose was achieved through the Capehart plan's budgetary sleight of hand.[80]

Wherry landlords were quick to recognize Capehart housing as competition to their own properties, which were typically smaller and less desirable.[81] The Capehart proposal made allowances for higher unit cost to increase the size and improve the quality of the three hundred thousand proposed units. Capehart had nearly double the per-unit cost ceiling: $13,500, and later $16,500, compared to Wherry's $9,000.[82] Some Wherry owners had already been disappointed by lower occupancy rates than they had expected and by demands for local taxes, and by 1956, six of these projects were in default.[83] Capehart would presumably exacerbate vacancy rates and Wherry owners' economic woes.

Wherry owners balked at the prospect of competing with the federal government as an owner and operator of military housing. Hearings on the Capehart proposal drew to Washington the Wherry Housing Association, which claimed to represent the owners of forty-thousand Wherry homes, or about half of all units constructed.[84] Dan R. Ponder, president of the Wherry Housing Association and owner of housing at Fort Bliss in El Paso, Texas, urged members in 1955 to write to Congress to "protect your own property and your rights" from "dangerous legislation" that promised to put Wherry housing out of business by providing unlimited and preferable public housing for the military.[85] Ponder explained that the Wherry owners were not against more military housing, but that those like him who had built housing "at the time when the Congress would not appropriate funds to provide it" were "entitled to some sort of preservation." Ignoring the subsidies that had kept his investments risk-free, Ponder treated the direct ownership of military housing as a threat to free market principles. "I respectfully submit that competition is the essence of American business," Ponder continued, "and we in the Wherry business are ready, willing and able to compete with private capital. . . . We cannot, however, compete with our own Government."[86] Ponder's rhetoric strongly echoed the arguments that the Chamber of Commerce and probusiness allies had long made about the unfair and destructive "invasion" of "government competition" into the free market.[87] Getting the government out of business became one of the central objectives of the presidential Hoover commissions (1947–1949 and 1953–1955), which together set an agenda for the privatization of the military's iconic shipyards, arsenals, and other manufacturing facilities over the subsequent years.[88] While the owners of military family housing propounded the same ideology, the fate of their industry would assume a very different trajectory.

Recognizing a dire need for more family housing, but faced with outrage from Wherry owners, Congress settled on a remarkable solution: nationalizing privately owned military housing. In addition to quieting Wherry landlords, Congress believed that nationalization would ultimately save costs. As one House report enthused, "the savings to be effected are so large that it would be an unreasonable man indeed who would deny the wisdom of embarking upon this program of purchase."[89] Proposals for the military to purchase the Wherry houses were first floated in 1955, and in the housing legislation passed that year, Congress authorized the military to begin acquiring them.[90] The military, however, was not particularly interested in buying: the army and navy denied that they were "in a position to budget" for the costs of acquisition.[91] They also would have likely preferred to receive upgraded Capehart units instead. In the 1956 Housing Act, Congress ultimately forced the military to acquire Wherry housing at all installations slated to receive Capehart housing.[92]

Wherry owners also initially resisted the notion of selling their units to the government that had backed their construction. In 1955, Ponder promised he would never relinquish his Wherry projects "unless they break me."[93] But it was not long before Wherry owners were petitioning for military buyouts.[94] By 1957, WHA counsel Roland Boyd reported his clients' unanimous resolution in favor of compulsory acquisition by the US government of all Wherry housing: "the only sensible answer is that the Government should acquire all Wherry within the continental United States."[95] Why would these landlords, who were so vocal about the virtues of entrepreneurs in free markets, advocate for their own expropriation by the federal government? The Wherry program was geared toward providing developers with modest rental income over a period of decades. Whether because of the real difficulties of operating under the military's constraints, or because of new investment opportunities, Wherry owners' free enterprise values did not stop them from seizing the opportunity for a one-time payout from selling their houses to the government.

In 1956, Congress laid out the procedure for acquiring Wherry housing at or below fair market value, as determined through independent appraisal considering original investment and depreciation.[96] The procedure required the military to make an offer, and if owners refused, the properties were put into condemnation proceedings. In practice, many units were acquired through eminent domain, following costly litigation.[97] The military services acquired most of the Wherry housing by 1959.[98] By June 1959, the military had spent or earmarked $66 million on equity payments, $55 million on repair, and $40 million on mortgage payments. Wherry developers and some in Congress called the whole program a mistake, but the members of the House Armed Services Subcommittee who heard Boyd's appeal disagreed, concluding, "We wanted houses and we got houses."[99]

In the meantime, the construction of Capehart housing had drawn military experts trained for warfare further into the business of designing the architectural setting for the reproduction of heterosexual norms. Designs for Capehart units were drawn up under the supervision of the Army Corps of Engineers. The design of military family housing catered to but also necessarily shaped expectations of what space and amenities families needed. Compared to Wherry houses, Capehart produced fewer apartment buildings and more detached housing, townhouses, and duplexes.[100] Military regulations specified design standards such as the number of bathrooms and square footage of storage for variously sized units.[101] Many Wherry housing units that had been acquired were deemed inadequate and were converted into larger dwellings; especially, "excess" one-bedroom units were combined into three- and four-bedroom units "to keep pace with the constantly increasing size of military families."[102]

More units were successfully built under Capehart than Wherry, but the newer program encountered its own problems, too. Local communities motivated in part by racial exclusion were able, with the help of their congressional representatives, to block the construction of Capehart projects in several cases.[103] In 1960, labor disputes between a prime contractor and subcontractors triggered a work stoppage scandal, with seven projects in progress grinding to a halt. The contractor at the center of the scandal claimed his financial problems were the result of "fancy demands" from officers' wives about color schemes and upgraded materials.[104] The military and FHA attempted to take possession of the construction in progress, but the public scandal had irreparably damaged the program. The last Capehart projects were approved in 1962, and family housing construction thereafter was funded through direct appropriation.[105]

While brief, the Wherry and Capehart programs together managed to produce two hundred thousand housing units between 1949 and 1964, arguably making the US military the world's biggest landlord in as much time.[106] To fully understand the scale of this program, it's worth drawing some comparisons. The unique purpose of this housing stock strains the concept of "market value," but one can approximate a comparison by assessing the total mortgage valuations of those properties. By the time the Wherry program was winding down, the FHA had insured $633 million worth of mortgages for that program, a figure approximately eight times the sum that the Egyptian government paid foreign shareholders for the expropriation of the Suez Canal in 1956.[107] Under the even larger Capehart program, Congress authorized the FHA to insure roughly $2.5 billion in mortgages.[108] For comparison, the entire Federal National Mortgage Association borrowing authority for purchasing civilian mortgages was $1.6 billion in 1957.[109] While they were public-private partnerships, the military family housing programs of the 1950s entailed massive federal investments that quite literally reshaped the United States' economic and social landscape.

In the thirty years that followed the Capehart program, the military switched back to building less government-funded, government-owned housing with appropriated funds, before ultimately privatizing most of its family housing in 1996.[110] While the story ends with privatization, it is crucial to remember that for the entirety of the Cold War period, a large portion of the American military community was housed in public housing units that had been bought, sometimes forcefully, from private housing developers across the country.[111] A model of actually existing government services, the military's public housing program was possible because it had a cover of national security and private provision.[112] The military built a social service infrastructure of its own to attract and retain manpower, becoming the most robust part of the American welfare state at the same time as civilian counterpart programs were disinvested from, in the later Cold War period.[113] Full of contradictions, the military's public-private family housing experiments of the 1950s resulted in a state-owned and operated inventory of residential housing that ought to be remembered as America's "other public-housing program."[114]

CHAPTER 3

Updating the Military Industrial Complex: The Evolution of the National Security Contracting Complex from the Cold War to the Forever War

Daniel Wirls

The term "military-industrial complex" is a venerable entry in the lexicon of American politics and scholarship on national security. But what the phrase describes or implies has often been frustratingly imprecise or elusive. Even in the heyday of the Cold War, with corporate giants bending metal for the Pentagon in its titanic competition with the Soviet Union, it was not clear whether the military-industrial complex was simply a general description of a material fact or a causal force driving spending and policy. That the United States had a vast and expensive arms industry supporting and dependent on American taxpayers' expensive commitment to military supremacy was undeniable; what effect this had on the economy and politics was less clear and subject to considerable debate.

Changes wrought around the end of the Cold War and particularly by national security policies in the wake of September 11, 2001, including those that led to the "forever war" in Iraq, Afghanistan, and beyond, require that the concept of a military-industrial complex be updated, along with the name applied to it.[1] Such things as new forms of military privatization, the revolution in digital technology, the post-9/11 tsunami of veterans, and the creation of the Department of Homeland Security (DHS), mean that the word "industrial" no longer captures the breadth of the activity and that the word "military" does not fully embrace the set of policies and interests involved. Instead, with myriad private enterprises, large and small, contracting for weapons, services, information technology (IT), health care, and a host of other things across several bureaucracies responsible for parts of national security, a far more accurate designation for the military-industrial complex is the *national security contracting complex*. This chapter traces and analyzes this transformation, with an emphasis on the expansion of contracting activities within *and beyond* the Pentagon, with the inclusion of departments such as Homeland Security, Veterans Affairs (the VA), and even State—in addition to the ongoing military programs in the Department of Energy—all tied to a diverse host of private enterprises providing an array of goods and services to all these departments.

What Is, or Was, the Military-Industrial Complex?

Although the concept was anticipated in the work of sociologist C. Wright Mills, President Dwight D. Eisenhower's 1961 farewell speech as president provided the name and precise definition. Eisenhower's "military-industrial complex" was the relatively new American "conjunction of an immense military establishment and a large arms industry," with a "total influence—economic, political, even spiritual—[that] is felt in every city, every State house, every office of the Federal government."[2] While historians have traced elements of an emerging complex back to the early 1900s, most analysts see the complex as a product of the sustained increases in military expenditures following the onset of the Cold War.[3] "These high levels of military expenditure," writes Steven Rosen, "have given rise to powerful domestic groups within the major states who have vested interests in the continuance of military spending and international conflict."[4] The groups include the professional military, the military contractors, civilian bureaucratic governmental officials, and members of Congress whose districts benefit from military spending.

The concept is closely related to, and arguably the same thing as, the idea of an "iron triangle" in military policy.[5] Paralleling Eisenhower's formulation, the corners of the triangle are occupied by the military establishment, the private arms industry, and governmental institutions that control policy formation and budgets, particularly Congress. Just as military-industrial complexes might exist in other countries, iron triangles can exist in various policy arenas, and agriculture has been used as an example.[6] But it is the scale and character of the US national security enterprise that sets the American military-industrial complex and iron triangle apart from other triangles within the government or complexes in other countries. Whether portrayed as a complex or triangle, "[t]hese various segments of the complex occupy powerful positions within the internal political structures of the major states, and they exercise their influence in a coordinated and mutually-supportive way to achieve and maintain optimal levels of military expenditure and war preparation, and to direct national security policy. On defense-related matters, their influence exceeds that of any countervailing coalitions or interests that may exist."[7]

Scholars and journalists are fond of adding "military-industrial complex" to their titles, but what follows often sheds surprisingly little light on the phrase. It often serves as a floating signifier, invoking the broad and general topic of the political economy of military spending and production, particularly in the post–World War II United States, but allowing or even inviting readers to fill the term with meaning or ignore it altogether. Under this big conceptual umbrella authors discuss or probe almost anything related to the political economy of military spending and production. Frequently there is no attempt to define, locate, or operationalize, let alone test the term for any analytic utility. The conclusion of Jerome Slater and Terry Nardin in 1973 still applies to much of this terrain: "In most of the literature, the concept of a military-industrial complex functions as both a description and an explanation (or theory) of what is being described."[8] This frequently loose mix of description and theory can become tautological.[9]

Whether or not they cause or influence US defense policy, the array of interests with a stake in consistently high national security spending can change and has changed over time. Weapons have always been the core of the complex, along with other products and services. However much the nexus of vast resources and interests has been a fixed part of US national security policy for more than seventy years, the complex should not be treated as a given or as a fixed concept. Just as the nature of warfare has changed, so has the complex, and we need to take account of those changes. Especially in the wake of the unprecedented nature of the wars and military buildup that followed 9/11, it is time to assess the state of Eisenhower's "conjunction."[10] Some, such as journalist Nick Turse and social scientist Linda Weiss, have analyzed important elements of the evolution of the complex. Turse notes that authors began to use a variety of terms to get at dimensions of what seemed new in the military-industrial complex, such as the "security-industrial complex," the "homeland security complex," and the "cybersecurity industrial complex," alongside familiar and related adaptations like the "prison-industrial complex."[11] Linda Weiss traces the evolution of what she calls the "national security state" from the familiar Cold War understanding to a more diverse techno-security complex featuring more extensive blending of public power and private enterprise in the post–Cold War and post 9/11 era.[12] This chapter complements and builds on such work by bringing into focus changes in budgets and contracting both within the Pentagon and across several other national security departments that together have superseded the Cold War military-industrial complex and produced a more diverse and expansive national security contracting complex.

The End of the Cold War . . . and the End of the Military-Industrial Complex?

The first phase of this transformation began with the end of the Cold War, when the military-industrial complex was looking like it might be assigned to the ash heap of history along with the communist system it was designed to thwart. The demise of the Soviet empire and then the Soviet Union itself spurred significant reductions in US military spending. Following the fraught militarism and high levels of spending in the Reagan years, the end of the Cold War was perceived as bringing substantial and lasting changes to the military-industrial complex through what became known as the "peace dividend," which was the general understanding that military spending would drop considerably and be devoted to other priorities. Even the 1991 Gulf War and the replacement of the Soviet threat with the rogue states doctrine centered on the "major regional powers" such as Iraq, Iran, and North Korea would not stop the decline in spending.[13] There was a general lessening of national security concerns, even during the belligerent presidency of George H. W. Bush, and especially with the purposive and nearly exclusive focus on domestic issues under President Bill Clinton.

These reductions in defense spending, however, were relative to the mountaintop of the military buildup of President Ronald Reagan—the largest and most sustained in peacetime—that had eclipsed spending during the Korean and Vietnam wars.[14] Long-term cuts were both strategically logical but also easier to swallow because the Reagan era had recapitalized the conventional and nuclear arsenals: there was not much left to build.[15] Overall, the military budget dropped by 27 percent in real terms from the peak of the Reagan buildup in 1989 to the low point of the post–Cold War era in 1998 (measured in budget outlays). But by far the biggest cut in both absolute value and percentage terms was to the procurement portion of the Pentagon budget, which dropped more than 40 percent in nominal terms, far larger than the cuts to research and development (R&D), operations, and even personnel, which dropped by less than 15 percent.[16] The weapons contracts that defined and sustained the military-industrial complex were drying up, and it was not clear if and when that might change.

But it was in this period, and in part because of the end of the Cold War and budget cuts, that the national security contracting complex would take shape and become the more accurate term for the reality on the ground. Events such as the 1993 "Last Supper," a dinner meeting with major contractors hosted by Defense Secretary Les Aspin and his deputy William Perry, seemed to indicate the vulnerability if not impotence of contractors. Perry emphasized that the defense industry had excess capacity in the potential production of major weapons systems and the government would let the market handle the necessary restructuring of the military market. A massive consolidation of the US defense industry was already underway and would continue, with some companies getting out of the military market altogether. Mergers and acquisitions created a smaller number of giants, including Lockheed Martin, that went all in on the defense market and seemed poised to dominate the industry.[17] Like others who took this route, including Raytheon, Lockheed Martin made multiple acquisitions of other defense companies, including Ford Aerospace and Loral. By 1997 the five giants in the US aerospace industry (Lockheed Martin, Boeing, Raytheon, Litton, and Northrop Grumman) were made up of what had been fifty-one separate companies.[18] They were more vertically integrated within particular areas of military production and in some cases horizontally diversified across national security needs. Faced with what appeared to be long-term reductions in military procurement, some companies used diversification into services, including the growing area of IT, as one strategy. As well, Pentagon subsidies that facilitated so-called payoffs for layoffs during the consolidation—including bonuses to executives such as those involved in the Lockheed Martin merger—reminded many of the substantial influence that supposedly characterizes the military-industrial complex.[19] Perhaps the overall complex was smaller, but the remaining major contractors had as much or more influence in the process.

The cuts and consolidation among contractors of major weapons systems were accompanied by the initial implementation of policies that became known as "privatization."[20] Given that the complex was premised on the long-standing dominance of private industry in military arms production, what was new about the privatization that developed near the end of the Cold War? In a more general conservative wave of policy-making, privatization was part of the neoliberal push to outsource various governmental functions—mostly services—to the market of private capital and labor, not just in national security but of the government as a whole.[21] Previously, military privatization was more necessity than the result of a political philosophy aimed at broader and more enduring changes in policy and governance. For example, the Vietnam War included the use of thousands of contractors in that nation and region to support the US war effort.[22] The wave of neoliberalism sought to take privatization, as part of a conscious policy of market-driven efficiency, well beyond weapons production to include lots of service and support functions in both peacetime and wartime. Gathering strength during the latter part of the Reagan administration, this neoliberal turn in security policy became more formalized under George H. W. Bush, and it accelerated under Bill Clinton and the reinventing government effort led by his vice president, Al Gore.

In the realm of national security this produced several policies and trends. The most concrete policy change was the Logistics Civil Augmentation Program (LOGCAP). Conceived during the Reagan administration and implemented on several occasions from 1989 through the 1990s in places like Somalia and Bosnia, the army used LOGCAP to contract out logistical services in support of combat or conflict operations.[23] These early contracts went to companies such as Brown & Root and DynCorp. They proved to be harbingers of vastly more significant applications in and around Iraq and Afghanistan, allowing for fewer boots on the ground but also creating their own problems in cost, effectiveness, and accountability. Meanwhile, private security firms had blossomed in the wake of the Cold War, and the United States (and other countries) was starting to use and incorporate them into its planning and operations.

Finally, during these years a more general tide of changes integrated a wider array of contractors, especially in the realm of services and IT, into the implementation of national security policy, at the level of such things as personnel management and benefits, housing, health care, and command, control, and intelligence.[24] These vital and growing tasks were seen as benefitting from the infusion of private sector skills and innovation particularly in digital technologies—the most efficient and effective way to bring the Pentagon into the information age in an era of budgetary restrictions.

As part of these developments in and around the end of the Cold War, and as most carefully documented in the work of Linda Weiss, the national security state had to "retool its incentive system" for R&D and procurement to "reach outside the traditional pool of large contractors to attract the most innovative companies, by building commercial goals into its programs."[25] This worked through the creation of such things as public-private venture capital entities in which the Pentagon and other agencies were partners.[26] As well, regulations regarding patents and other policies were changed to directly encourage what Weiss labels "spin arounds," that is, innovations that are created more or less simultaneously for their military and commercial applications.[27]

In sum, it was the convergence of such things as the end of the Cold War, the onset of relative budgetary austerity, the security implications of the digital revolution, and a strong tilt toward a neoliberal Washington consensus that contributed to this phase in the evolution of the original military-industrial complex into an increasingly diverse and broader array of contracting across several departments involved in national security. The Cold War group of major weapons contractors might have been in some ways diminished, at least temporarily, but it was also in the process of transformation. Where this might have gone in the absence of the American response to the attacks of September 11, 2001, is hard to say. That response, however, added the wars, resources, and policies to complete the transformation.

The Expansion of the National Security State and Diversification of the Military Market

The movement toward a more diverse and wide-ranging national security contracting complex grew over the 1990s. The wars that followed 9/11 would accelerate those developments in several ways, including by removing the smaller budgets that had simultaneously encouraged much of the change but also prevented the full manifestation of the developments underway. The attacks of September 11 did not automatically change anything, of course. US decisions following the attacks produced the changes. The decisions to go to war, especially in Iraq, brought forth the political and economic forces and consequences that have attended major wars, especially from the twentieth century onward. The first such force is war as an accelerator of technology and engineering. In this case, the acceleration of the revolution in military affairs centered on digital technologies. The second is war as a ratchet of governmental spending and power. In this case, there were vast budget increases for the very expensive wars but also for a military buildup by the Pentagon separate from the wars, which all went along with expansions of presidential and bureaucratic power at home and abroad.[28] In sum, the new characteristics of the military market emerged from changes in demand and supply. While the US national security state demanded a full range of traditional hardware, tens of billions of dollars of contracts were being made each year for other things related to the wars and the general buildup of American martial power in the era of digital technologies. And emerging from the post–Cold War era, the market of suppliers—a vast and diverse array of private enterprises—grew and changed to meet that demand.

As national security contracting ramped up after 2001 within the Pentagon and across government agencies, the range and diversity of contracts expanded accordingly. During the wars in Iraq and Afghanistan, a great deal of media attention focused on contracts with private security firms like Blackwater and logistics firms like Halliburton, which became KBR. But that was only part of the story. Within both the Pentagon and other agencies, increasingly diverse needs were being contracted, creating opportunities for an extensive array of private enterprises. National security departments further expanded their contracting in IT, for tasks ranging from the prosaic, like bookkeeping, to the exotic, including cyberwarfare and artificial intelligence. That work went both to traditional arms-making giants such as Lockheed Martin and General Dynamics but also, as we shall see, to enterprises such as Booz Allen Hamilton and Leidos that specialize in such work.

The government also expanded its outsourcing of military and veterans' health care. Just as health care came to consume a larger portion of the US economy, so too it made up a greater part of the national security state, but the wars following 9/11 shifted this from a national trend to a flood of change within the national security state. One measure is the changes in the percentage of the Pentagon budget devoted to aggregated categories of contracting (Figure 3.1). In 1986, near the peak of the Reagan military buildup, the category of supplies and equipment dominated Pentagon contracts, with services and IT far behind, along with R&D and construction.[29] After the end of the Cold War, supplies and equipment dropped dramatically, while services and information technology increased substantially. By 2006, supplies and equipment had rebounded with the Bush buildup and the wars in Iraq and Afghanistan, but services and IT continued its significant growth relative to the other categories, from 18 percent to almost 31 percent of Pentagon contracting

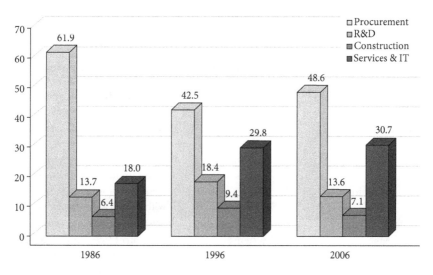

Figure 3.1. The growth of services and information technology in the defense budget, 1986–2006 (percentages of total defense acquisition budget). Source: Federal Procurement Data System.

over the twenty-year period.[30] Using a similar division of Pentagon contracting into services, products, and R&D, a Congressional Research Service study confirmed that this trend continued: services constituted 41 percent of defense contracting in 2017, compared to 51 percent for products and 8 percent for R&D.[31]

Another way to illustrate this change is to compare the top Pentagon contractors during the Cold War to those in recent years (Table 3.1). In 1986, the top twenty-five were dominated by manufacturers of major weapons systems and other tangible products, with IBM, GTE, and AT&T in the area of telecommunications (and this was still largely in the form of equipment). Thirty years later, in 2016, three major changes had emerged. First was the presence of five health care companies in the top twenty-five, including Humana and McKesson. Second was the appearance of such companies as SAIC, Booz Allen, and Leidos that specialize in IT largely if not exclusively in the nonmaterial realm of the digital and virtual.[32] Finally, and this is not evident in simply the list of corporate names, was the fact that most of the top major weapons systems contractors, the pillars of the Cold War military-industrial complex—including Lockheed Martin and General Dynamics—had by 2016 diversified into other areas, including IT and other services, as I will discuss below.

Table 3.1. Department of Defense Top Twenty-Five Contractors, 1986 and 2016.

1986	2016	2016 Diversification
General Dynamics	Lockheed Martin	Procurement (weapons systems) with significant services/IT
General Electric	Boeing	Procurement (weapons systems) with significant services/IT
McDonnell Douglas	Raytheon	Procurement (weapons systems) with significant services/IT
Rockwell	General Dynamics	Procurement (weapons systems) with significant services/IT
General Motors	Northrop Grumman	Procurement (weapons systems) with significant services/IT
Lockheed Corp	United Technologies	Procurement (weapons systems)
Raytheon	BAE Systems	Procurement (weapons systems) with significant services/IT
Boeing	L-3 Communications	Procurement (weapons systems) with significant services/IT
United Technologies	Huntington Ingalls	Procurement (weapons systems) with significant services/IT
Grumman	Humana	Health
Martin Marietta	Bechtel Group	Construction/engineering
Honeywell	UnitedHealth Group	Health
Westinghouse	McKesson	Health
Textron	Health Net	Health
Litton Industries	Bell Boeing Joint Project Office	Procurement (weapons systems)
Sperry	SAIC	Services/IT
LTV Corp	AmerisourceBergen	Health
Texas Instruments	Textron	Procurement (weapons systems)
IBM	Harris	Procurement (IT) plus IT services
Eaton Corp	General Atomic Technologies	Procurement (weapons systems)
TRW	Booz Allen Hamilton	Services/IT
AlliedSignal	General Electric	Procurement (weapon components) with services/IT
GTE	United Launch Alliance	Services
Royal Dutch Petroleum	Leidos Holding	Services/IT
AT&T	Oshkosh	Procurement (weapons systems)

Source: Federal Procurement Data System.

The Horizontal Expansion of National Security Contracting Across Government Departments

The policies and budgets that followed the attacks of September 11, 2001, vastly expanded the size and scope of spending and contracting not only by the Pentagon but also across several other departments, including a new one created specifically for the new security regime. Before 9/11 and the resulting military actions in Afghanistan, Iraq, and elsewhere, the Department of Energy was the only executive branch department other than the Pentagon with major military or security contracts. The Department of Energy was involved because it built and dismantled nuclear warheads. After 9/11, more agencies got deeply involved in national security spending and contracting. In addition to the Departments of Defense and Energy, the VA, the State Department, and DHS engaged in significant private contracting.

In terms of overall departmental spending, the combined budgets of DHS, the VA, State, and Energy kept pace as a percentage of the Pentagon budget from 2001 through the peak of the Pentagon's outlays in 2011, averaging 30 percent. When Pentagon spending dropped because of the end of major war operations in Afghanistan and budget constraints, the ratio rose to nearly 50 percent, averaging more than 49 percent from 2016 to 2018 (Figure 3.2). As a

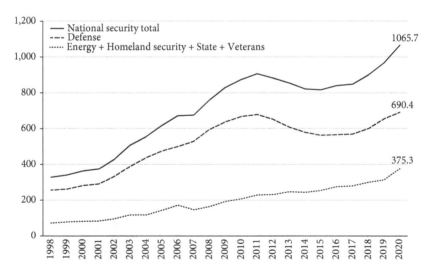

Figure 3.2. National security spending, 1998–2020 (outlays in billions of dollars). Source: Office of Management and Budget, Historical Tables, Table 4.1, Outlays by Agency: 1962–2026.

result of the government's expanded spending on national security, including the VA, and diversification of what the departments contract for, many corporations, both large and small, have had sizable contracts with more than one federal agency in recent years. American policies following 9/11 produced not simply another military buildup with an attendant resurgence of the military-industrial complex. The complex, which had been changing already, was transformed in important ways. Developments that predated the policies and spending that followed 9/11 accelerated, converged, and consolidated. Whether considered revolutionary or evolutionary, the changes have produced a national security contracting complex defined by several characteristics.

As the budgets of these other national security departments grew, so did their level of contracting with private companies. Government data show the changes from 1981 to 2018 in contracting by departments, other than the Pentagon, involved in national security (Figure 3.3). Outside the Defense Department, much of the jump in post-9/11 national security contracting came from the creation of DHS in late 2002 and early 2003.[33] Before DHS was created, some of that contracting was already being done by agencies brought together to form the new department, particularly the Coast Guard. But the scope and amount of DHS contracting increased dramatically—averaging nearly $14 billion a year from 2005 onward.[34] Other departments also expanded their contracting substantially after 9/11. In the 1990s, the State Department had an average of less than $700 million in contracts per year in national security–related matters. From 2009 onward, that average jumped

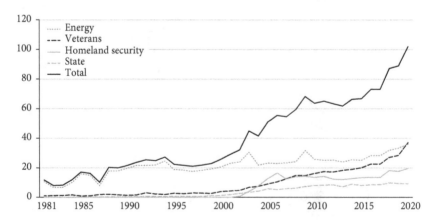

Figure 3.3. Contracting by national security departments excluding the Pentagon, 1981–2020 (in billions of dollars). Source: Federal Procurement Data System.

to \$8.4 billion a year. At a much smaller level, and not included here, the Departments of Justice, the Treasury, and even Commerce (in the realm of cybersecurity) have been spending more money on security contracting.[35]

But the VA experienced the most stunning increases in both overall budgets and contracting. Few Americans would guess that from 2001 to 2011, the VA's budget grew faster than the Defense Department's—271 percent compared to 240 percent—even including the Pentagon's extra spending for the wars, known as the Overseas Contingencies Operations supplementary budget.[36] Part of the VA's growth came in contracting. The VA had contracted out less than \$2.4 billion in work per year averaged across the 1990s. From 2009 onward, the VA contracted out nearly \$20 billion of work each year. Because the VA functions largely as a check-writing operation, rather than as a builder of things or manager of R&D, the percentage of its budget devoted to contracting does not match that of the DOD or the Department of Energy. But in absolute numbers it is now second in the entire government behind Defense, eclipsing Energy in 2020. The VA budget was large enough in 2020 to result in more than \$37 billion in total contracts, including to some of the same companies that are top Pentagon contractors, such as Lockheed Martin, Northrop Grumman, General Dynamics, and General Electric. This was not the case historically. The VA budget was much smaller in real terms and did not rely on contractors to the same extent. For example, in 1981 the VA contracting budget was \$990 million compared to the Pentagon's \$96 billion, or just over 1 percent its size. By 2020 VA contracting had grown more than 3,700 percent, making it nearly 9 percent the size of Pentagon contracting, and this following significant increases in defense spending under the Trump administration.

The Diversification of Contractors Within and Across Government Agencies

As noted earlier, during the 1990s, Lockheed Martin and General Dynamics in particular engaged in mergers and acquisitions to go all in on the defense market. Over time they responded to changes in the military market by diversifying beyond weapons research, development, and production. They became diversified "Walmarts of War," delivering a wide range of goods and services to various parts of the federal government.[37] And Lockheed Martin and General Dynamics were joined in 2020 by Raytheon Technologies, a merger that combined Raytheon with United Technologies. In size and scope no company comes near Lockheed Martin. Lockheed Martin diversified its Pentagon portfolio by developing capabilities in IT and other areas. In recent years, Lockheed Martin has been best known for the F-35 fighter program, the most expensive weapons program in history. But Lockheed is also the top contractor in other areas of Pentagon activity, such as missile defense—a hefty $2.6 billion in 2018—special operations at nearly $900 million, and the Defense Advanced Research Projects Agency at just over $240 million, not to mention seventh for defense logistics at just under $900 million. This diversity and depth made the company the Pentagon's perennial number one contractor, including every year from 2006 to 2015. The company also spread itself across more of the national security state beyond the Pentagon, and it has been a top Department of Energy contactor (for example, number two in 2006, number two in 2009, and number one in 2015). Lockheed Martin went from nineteenth for DHS in 2006 to second in 2009 and third in 2015, then dropped to twenty-first in 2017. Finally, not even in the top hundred for the VA as late as 2009, Lockheed Martin became its third largest contractor by 2015, but then disappeared in 2018.

Paralleling Lockheed Martin has been General Dynamics. General Dynamics' first reaction to the end of the Cold War was to shed divisions and downsize to its core weapons production portfolios in military vehicles and submarines, and this including getting rid of its relatively small data systems division. Starting in 1995 with the acquisition of Bath Iron Works (a major navy shipyard), General Dynamics grew and diversified by acquisitions in "combat-vehicle-related businesses, IT product and service companies and additional shipyards."[38] The company formed its information systems and technology group in 1998 from a series of acquisitions. During the next decade, General Dynamics acquired IT companies such as Digital Systems Resources and Anteon and, in 2011, acquired Vangent in the field of health care IT and business systems for government. This series culminated in the nearly $10 billion acquisition of CSRA, a major national security IT contractor, in 2018. General Dynamics, while typically ranked lower where it overlaps with Lockheed Martin, is spread across, and ranked highly in, as many or more major Department of Defense subcategories as listed in the government's contracting database. Among other things, General Dynamics provides "management support for projects such as the Defense Health Information Management System" and, as I found out when I received a call from a General Dynamics worker, does employment security checks for government agencies, including DHS. In 2015 the company was the Pentagon's fourth largest contractor, the fifth largest for the State Department, and four-teenth for DHS (it was fourth for DHS in 2009), and it has been in the top fifty for the VA in some years. In 2019 the company's IT division was awarded a $2 billion State Department contract for its global supply chain.

Beyond the Walmarts of War are other large companies that are more specialized but still find contracts across agencies. One prominent sector is composed of firms with an IT focus or IT combined with other skills such as engineering. In 2018 Leidos, formerly SAIC, was the government's ninth largest contractor, ranking fourteenth for the Pentagon, third for the VA, and first for DHS. Booz Allen Hamilton was the government's fourteenth largest contractor in 2018, ranking nineteenth for the Pentagon, seventh for VA, and thirty-second for DHS. Engineering giant Fluor Corporation was in the top fifteen for Defense, the Department of Energy, and DHS. Other examples include CACI and Jacobs Engineering. As well, more familiar names from the consumer sectors of IT are seeking national security contracts in this area. For example, the Pentagon's $10 billion Joint Enterprise Defense Infrastructure (JEDI) contract attracted the attention of Amazon, Google, Microsoft, Oracle, and IBM when it was put out for bids in 2018. Google dropped out of the competition after its employees protested that such a contract would violate its corporate values. Such concerns did not inhibit the others, which engaged in a headline-generating battle for the contract. After delays and lawsuits, Microsoft finally emerged the winner in September 2020, only to see the Pentagon cancel the JEDI contract altogether.[39]

The MITRE Corporation is a different example of a multiple-agency player. MITRE, which has more than eight thousand employees, is a not-for-profit corporation that runs federally funded research and development centers (FFRDCs), much like the RAND Corporation.[40] Formed in 1958, MITRE was a steady Pentagon contractor through the Cold War, at work on high tech projects in areas such as ballistic missile early warning systems. As of 2019 MITRE was running seven FFRDCs for seven different departments of the US government, including three of the core national security departments (Defense, Homeland Security, Veterans), with another national security–related FFRDC, the National Cybersecurity FFRDC, under the Department of Commerce. In 2015 MITRE was forty-sixth among DOD contractors, pulling in $755 million. But MITRE was also twentieth for the VA ($105 million) and eighteenth for DHS ($103 million), as well as sixty-seventh for State ($19.3 million), these together accounting for two-thirds of MITRE's total revenue of just under $1.5 billion.

In contrast to MITRE's steady participation and evolution in national security contracting, the McKesson Corporation became a major player only in this century. Much as Lockheed Martin rules as the king of Pentagon contracting, the McKesson Corporation has dominated VA contracting in recent years, but also ranks in the top twenty for the Pentagon. In 2018 McKesson was the US government's sixth largest contractor, and 95 percent of McKesson's governmental business was with the VA and the DOD.[41] With more than $200 billion in annual revenue in 2018, sixth on that year's Fortune 500, McKesson is the giant of pharmaceutical distribution and far from dependent on the national security state.[42] Nevertheless, McKesson took in almost $6 billion from the VA and almost $2.7 billion from the Pentagon. Depending on the year in question, McKesson has been joined by other health care companies that contract with the VA and the Pentagon, such as Centene, as well as other Pentagon players such as General Electric.

From Backwater to Behemoth:
The Veterans Administration

As the growth in contracting by McKesson and the other health care companies suggests, the VA is worth a closer look: the mammoth growth in the VA focuses our attention on the astounding level of health and welfare spending now done by the national security state as a whole. As noted earlier, the VA budget grew even faster than the Pentagon's during the decade after 9/11. Due primarily to the drawdown of the forever war, Pentagon spending (including war supplemental appropriations) decreased in real terms each year from 2012 through 2017 from the peak of $706 billion to $598 billion in 2017. By contrast, the VA budget continued to increase rapidly in nominal and real terms from $127 billion to $177 billion (a 39 percent increase). In 2000, Pentagon spending was 6.7 times the VA's; in 2017 it was 3.4 times as large. That year, the VA budget by itself would have been the third largest military budget in the world. And the growth continued under President Trump: in fiscal year 2019 the VA reached $200 billion and it hit $219 billion in 2020.[43]

Parsing the growth of VA spending is complicated. The wars and the needs they produced, as thousands of Iraq and Afghanistan warriors became veterans, account for much of the growth. From 2001 to 2014, the total population of veterans actually dropped by more than 17 percent from just over 26 million to 21.6 million. But the number of VA-enrolled veterans increased by almost 78 percent, growing from 5.1 million to 9.1 million. In addition to hundreds of thousands of new veterans enrolling in other benefits such as education, life insurance, and compensation benefits, the number of VA medical patients increased by nearly 2.4 million during the same period.[44] The mammoth growth of VA spending had been both overshadowed and facilitated by the scandals regarding the treatment of our veterans: difficult access to care, poor care, fraudulent record keeping.[45] Much as with waste, fraud, and abuse in Pentagon programs, the same Congress that got to scold and deprecate the VA leadership (and the president) over those scandals added huge new budget appropriations in part to address the alleged shortcomings in care but also to enhance other veterans programs, such as education benefits. In other words, as the demand for veterans' care changed in quantity and quality (that is, both the number of veterans and the relative expense of the medical or disability problems they confronted), the supply of programs and funding increased in ways that were sometimes as politically driven as they were necessitated by the consequences of the wars. The politics of "support the troops" that protected much of military spending from scrutiny, let alone opposition, applied even more to the VA.

It is worth making a final point about the VA's role in the contracting complex. After the passage of the Budget Control Act of 2011, Congress each year would negotiate subsequent agreements to modify or evade the caps on discretionary spending set by the 2011 act.[46] The act put separate caps on defense and "domestic" discretionary spending, which together make up about one third of the entire federal budget. These agreements, for the most part, were compromises between Republicans and Democrats in which Republicans got more money for defense and Democrats got more funds for domestic programs. In 2018, $85 billion or 46 percent of the VA's almost $197 billion budget was classified as discretionary spending.[47] That means that a good deal of the significant increases in VA spending, ironically, have counted as "domestic" in this partisan battle over guns and butter.

The United States is the quintessential "welfare-warfare state." This term captures the post–World War II national commitment to large-scale domestic welfare programs paired with a simultaneous commitment to being a global military power prepared to deter or fight World War III. Nothing better represents the fusion of the two than the programs and spending of the Department of Veterans Affairs. For most of its history the VA was relatively unremarkable in its scope and spending. It was at times a significant departmental budget, but not subject to the seemingly ineluctable growth of welfare entitlements such as Social Security or Medicare. All that changed after the United States committed itself to the open-ended wars after 9/11.

In years gone by when VA spending was relatively limited, Congress quietly supported the distribution of VA hospitals and clinics to as many localities as possible. That distributive politics continues. It is still quiet and mostly uncontroversial, disturbed only temporarily by scandals about access or quality of care. But now the vast scale of VA spending, projected to continue into the indefinite future, injects hundreds of billions of dollars into the economy every year. This has attracted hundreds of contractors, including, as we have seen, some of the long-standing behemoths of the Cold War military-industrial complex. More than ever, the subgovernment of Congress, the VA, and the associated contractors and interests form a happy triangle of interests, now with control over one of the largest single pots of money in either the warfare or the welfare state.

Conclusion

Some observers have argued that the general decline in overall military spending and weapons procurement, at least during the presidency of Barack Obama, meant the United States no longer had to worry about the influence of a military-industrial complex. The mammoth commitment of resources to the so-called forever wars and general US military superiority after 9/11 notwithstanding, there are always analysts and pundits who claim the United States is not spending enough, or not spending enough on the right things. Some would no doubt make the same argument even with the substantial real increases during the Trump presidency. Regardless, such observers see the complex as an increasingly diminished force. In 2017, and citing such things as the persistently small percentage of the economy represented by military spending, defense analyst Loren Thompson claimed the "idea of a military-industrial complex shaping federal priorities has become more myth than reality, the artifact of an era now long gone."[48] Charles Dunlap cited a variety of factors in the post-9/11 era that were in his view "*emasculating* America's military-industrial complex" (emphasis added).[49] And former Deputy Secretary of Defense William J. Lynn III proclaimed "The End of the Military-Industrial Complex," the title of his 2014 article in *Foreign Affairs*.[50] In fact, these contrarian arguments fail to see that some of their evidence for the demise of the military-industrial complex is in fact substantiation of the new, more diversified national security contracting complex. For example, Lynn points out that "more than one third of what the Pentagon spends on procurement and services goes to nontraditional companies such as Apple and Dell," as if that should not count.[51] Dunlap quotes then-Secretary of Defense Robert Gates's lament "that health care expenses, topping $50 billion a year around 2010, are 'eating the Defense Department alive.'"[52] "Most of the defense budget is not spent on weapons," writes Thompson, "it is spent on items like military pay and benefits, training, maintenance and the like." Because the amount for military equipment is "barely 1% of GDP . . . how much of a problem can the 'military-industrial complex' be"? Healthcare is 17%, but nobody refers to the 'healthcare-industrial complex.'"[53]

Actually, many have referred to a healthcare-industrial complex, and have for decades.[54] Whatever might be the size and influence of other complexes, we need to get away from the idea that what we thought of as the military-industrial complex is only about the procurement of major weapons systems and platforms, in the same way that military planners have recognized that contemporary security policy is about a "competition continuum" rather than "the obsolete peace/war binary."[55] Martial force is no longer only about traditional weaponry, but is also about things such as cyberwarfare and even social media. And all this has come together in an era defined by the unprecedented horizontal global reach and presence of US martial power beyond its borders, in the new levels of activity and capability in such things as the National Security Agency and the Special Operations Command, combined with unprecedented vertical integration within the country, represented by DHS and the involvement of state and local law enforcement in national security.

Yes, the sine qua non of Eisenhower's military-industrial complex was the new "permanent armaments industry of vast proportions," but the national security state has always included other things, including real estate and services. If the core of the phenomenon is "an informal coalition of groups with vested interests in high levels of defense spending," then what matters is less what the "vested interests" are than their existence and extent.[56] And those interests by some measures have grown and diversified since the end of the Cold War that fueled Eisenhower's concerns. Seen from one angle, some see these changes as a chance to redefine the national security contracting complex in a new and positive way. With so-called "hybrid warfare" spanning the competition continuum from traditional use of force to cyberwarfare to social-media manipulation, closer "collaboration among the commercial, nonprofit and military sectors is a matter of survival."[57] From another perspective, the dangers of such overlapping and reinforcing interests might be as great as they ever were, and possibly more varied.

Consequently, a narrow focus on weapons procurement misses the bigger picture. Since 9/11, a diverse array of firms has had a significant stake in federal national security spending across several government agencies. Those funds now flow from a large portion of the federal government into many sectors of the US economy. The national security contracting complex is probably more diverse and geographically distributed than at any time since World War II. "The reason why the MIC might be privileged," according to economist Ben Fine, "is that . . . it may attain what might be thought of as a 'critical mass', a weight of linkages and agencies that render it uniquely significant in the economy."[58] Like the military-industrial complex of old, the national security contracting complex might not dominate the economy, but it is the most multilayered, pervasive, and powerfully interrelated set of linkages between the state—its resources and decisionmakers—and the private sector, which in turn could further insulate it from rigorous oversight and reform. This chapter, which did not attempt to characterize the political influence of the new complex, has sought to clarify the changed and changing contours of what constitutes the national security contracting complex. As was the case during the heyday of work on the military-industrial complex during the Cold War, locating and measuring the political influence of today's complex remains a formidable analytic puzzle.[59] While by no means a complete portrait, this analysis has shown that Eisenhower's complex has become more varied and pervasive, which suggests, perhaps, the same for its influence on national security policy and spending.

CHAPTER 4

"Make Up a Box to Send Me": Consumer Culture and Camp Life in the American Civil War

Sarah Jones Weicksel

In 1864, Union soldier James Fitzsimmons wrote a note to his comrade, William Willoughby (then at home in Connecticut), urgently requesting a box of goods be sent to Virginia. He was so anxious to receive his order, likely for new clothing, that a fellow soldier added a note to Willoughby at the bottom of Fitzsimmons's letter: "for gods sake send the Box don't delay for he will have a fit if you do. Send the Box. Send the Box. . . . SEND THE BOX."[1]

The sense of urgency with which Fitzsimmons wrote was not unusual. The nature of army life created a ready market of soldiers eager to acquire a broad array of consumer goods ranging from writing supplies and cooking utensils to shoes and clothing. Soldiers obtained such items in a variety of ways—the quartermaster, civilian sutlers who contracted to sell in military camps, and family and friends at home. In addition, some soldiers, aided by connections to the home front, ran their own informal businesses, seizing the opportunity presented by their comrades' desires to acquire goods. It was through one such entrepreneurial soldier—William Willoughby—that Fitzsimmons had placed his order.

Historians' understanding of the relationship between US Civil War–era business and the military is a story of mobilization and contracts for war materiel and weapons. In this context, the needs of scale and war coincided with the scale of business and the growth and development of a capitalist industrial economy. Yet the archaeological record and soldiers' writings attest to the vital place of consumer goods in wartime and the remarkable variety of merchandise to which soldiers had access, ranging from patent medicines to paper collars to hair dye.[2] Shifting our vantage point away from war materiel to instead consider the marketing, pricing, and supply chains that sustained consumer practices reveals a more varied economic landscape in which government contracting, government licensing of small and medium-sized retailers, philanthropic organizations, and soldier-retailers coexisted and competed with one another. While the Civil War is generally understood to be a watershed moment in the history of large-scale manufacturing and regulation, the existence of soldier-retailers like William Willoughby suggest that the persistence of small-scale, unregulated, and family-supported consumption was essential to war and to the US economy. What did it mean for soldiers themselves to become actors in the military marketplace?

A US Army camp might seem an unlikely place to study consumption, but Civil War soldiers came from communities that were part of a growing consumer market and brought with them to camp a desire to partake in that world of goods. In the decades preceding the war, advances in production, advertising and marketing, and retail display and practices, and the accompanying changes in consumer tastes, created a bustling marketplace of consumer goods.[3] By 1861, Joanna Cohen argues, "although they continued to grapple with the inequities of the marketplace, northerners imagined a citizen's opportunity to shop for new goods as a symbol of America's success in creating a civilized democratic republic."[4] When war broke out, northern volunteers took that mindset with them to the warfront.

As Union volunteers marched south, manufacturers, retailers, and advertisers were hard at work marketing goods to a new consumer: the citizen soldier. Not yet an army regular, this potential customer was not accustomed to life in the field, presumably making him—and his family—more readily accepting of advertisements' promise of improving the soldier's life. Countless goods sold before the war were newly marketed using language of war, secession, and soldiering.[5] Merchandise advertised to soldiers and their families ranged from the utilitarian (weapons, envelopes, and watches) to the entertaining (board games and books) to the macabre (artificial legs and coffins) to the dangerous (body armor and many patent medicines). All in all, there was no shortage of goods to be had; the problem was how to access them.

The means by which soldiers accessed goods beyond those supplied by the quartermaster or through distribution by soldiers' aid societies remain relatively obscure. Yet economic activity and market dynamics were important features of camp life. Civilians living near encampments were known to hock goods, but sutlers, those merchants commissioned to sell supplies and food to soldiers in camp, were the most common figures in camp. Historians' attention to sutlers has focused on their reputation as "sharks" and "swindlers," including regulations intended to govern them, the poor quality and high prices of their goods, abuses of the suttling system, and forms of credit.[6] Yet experiences with suttling also paved the way for other, unofficial routes of accessing consumer goods, including supply chains established by families and soldier-entrepreneurs.

This essay explores the consumer culture of US Army camp life during the American Civil War through the lens of William Willoughby's unsanctioned business—a business that relied on his wife Nancy Willoughby's sewing skills and her access to consumer goods in New Haven, Connecticut. I situate the Willoughbys' business venture and their marketing, pricing, and supply within the broader context of soldiers' consumer practices as they related to sutlers and other businesses located near camps. Military-market relationships surrounding consumption were defined not solely by firms, institutions, and contracts but also by personal and private family and gendered relationships. Although official regulations applied to sutlers, the military did not officially regulate businesses like that of the Willoughbys.

Women like Nancy Willoughby were central to the functioning of the wartime economy and to the consumer market within it. They performed vital work supplying the armies by working in munitions and textile manufactories and sewing clothing for federal, state, and local employers and benevolent organizations.[7] They managed businesses, fundraised, petitioned government officials, oversaw plantations, farmed, and supplied relatives with both necessities and niceties during wartime.[8] Yet, we still have much to learn about women's provisioning of the war—both North and South—through what LeeAnn Whites has called (in the case of Southern guerrillas) the "domestic supply line."[9] Historians have generally regarded the family economy, in which parents and children combined their work and individual earnings for the support of the household, to have been replaced by a new gendered capitalist economy defined by separate spheres during the Early Republic.[10] Yet, as evidenced by the Willoughbys' story, the family economy persisted within this larger, industrial capitalist transformation. At the same time, wartime experiences expanded women's engagement with entrepreneurial capitalism.

Assumptions about the austerity of military life and the clash between military hardship and civilian consumer abundance are often at the center of our understanding of the relationship between the military and the market. Yet the Willoughbys' story reveals continuities and connections between the military and civilian sides, as well as a powerful demand among soldiers for goods that were not standard issue. Despite their more limited access to the marketplace, soldiers were discriminating consumers who enjoyed small pleasures and were not always thrifty.[11] By focusing on the intersection of consumer desires and unsanctioned business ventures, I show how the military-consumer marketplace breaks down the artificial boundaries historians have constructed between home front and war front. Certainly, Union soldiers experienced grim conditions throughout the war; their material deprivations have been well documented.[12] Yet we must also remember that many remained avid consumers and entrepreneurs, even when they were distant from the home front.

Accessing Goods During Wartime

When war erupted in 1861, the US government was unprepared to supply the tens of thousands of men who volunteered—it simply did not have the organizational or manufacturing capacity to do so. According to regulations, a soldier's first-year clothing allowance included two caps, one hat, one fatigue forage cap, two covers, two coats, three trousers, three flannel shirts, three pair of drawers, four bootees and four pairs of stockings, a leather stock, one greatcoat, and one blanket, as well as a knapsack, a haversack, a canteen, and various uniform trimmings. In April 1861, however, the US government's supply chain was equipped to support only the Regular Army—a force of seventeen thousand men. By June 1861, quartermaster operations had increased twentyfold to outfit a rapidly expanding Union Army of more than five-hundred thousand.[13]

Supplying the Union Army was an imperfect process that evolved over the course of the war and involved public and private enterprise, including federal, state, community, and family-based efforts.[14] Benevolent institutions such as the United States Sanitary Commission were established alongside hundreds of local soldiers' aid societies in response to the government's ongoing struggle to adequately supply and care for soldiers.[15] Women supported departing relatives and outfitted local regiments. Boxes packed with surplus household goods, clothing, and hospital supplies, along with canned fruits, jams, cakes, and produce, were shipped south, either directly to companies or for general distribution.[16] The movement of goods across the nation during wartime was extensive. Military supplies, shipments from soldiers' aid societies, and boxes of clothing, food, writing materials, and luxuries packed the holds of ships, wagons, and railcars, bound for southern locations. Battlefield souvenirs and objects stolen from southern houses, soldiers' impractical possessions, and excess gear filled express boxes and the knapsacks of furloughed and discharged soldiers returning north.[17]

As the war pressed on and US soldiers moved to distant camps, they experienced more acutely the challenges posed by their increasing distance from consumer spaces, including longer shipping times. Movement into remote areas away from the coastline also meant more difficult modes of transportation—wagons instead of ships—and the increased risk of Confederate raids on supply trains. One man found his company outside of the "regular channel of supply" and himself unable to replace his shirt, shoes, or socks—all of which were in poor shape.[18] The unreliability of quartermasters persisted. Some soldiers' encounters with the quartermaster were contentious and infuriating, in part due to problems resulting from insufficient supply, poor coordination of supply lines, the theft of knapsacks from transport wagons, and the distribution of goods made from too much shoddy (recycled fabric). There was much clamor "about the soldier being cheated by quartermasters as by sutlers. He has had rotten cloth and shoddy and wooden soles to his shoes, and the cheating has been as great in the quartermaster's department as in any other department of the Government."[19] Union soldiers, not only Confederates, found themselves nearly barefoot, without overcoats, and in desperate need of a new pair of pants.

Governmental failures to provide soldiers adequate access to new clothing meant that not only individual men but the government, too, needed help keeping men supplied. While the US government increased its efficiency in supplying clothing, the shortcomings of supply chains during the first years of the war created a space in which many soldiers engaged their families in a "domestic supply line." Once it was established, many continued to rely on that supply line for both physical and emotional support from home. Yet, writing home for new clothing or consumer goods also had challenges and drawbacks. Families might not have extra money to purchase goods, the postal service and express companies charged delivery fees, and soldiers on the move could miss the arrival of packages.[20] Furthermore, the length of shipping time limited the kind of perishables that could be sent—it was not uncommon for a soldier to open a box from home only to find its contents were "partially decayed" or that spoiled foodstuffs had ruined the entire box.[21]

Family shipments were one way to gain access to consumer goods, but the more readily available option was the army sutler, who served as both a grocer and a dry goods store. As Brian Luskey explains, "Enlisted men whose

Figure 4.1 Arthur Lumley, a sutler's tent near headquarters, August 1862. Source: Library of Congress Prints and Photographs Division, Washington, DC, LCCN 2004661305, https://lccn.loc.gov/2004661305.

supply of money was uncertain also came to understand that they were dependent on a market managed by army contractors and sutlers."[22] A camp follower, the sutler transported a wide variety of goods by wagon, setting up a semipermanent shop-like environment when an army encamped for lengths of time. In an 1862 sketch of the interior of a sutler's tent, long boards set atop barrels served as makeshift counters behind which dozens of articles for purchase are displayed on shelves, lending the air of a shopping experience to those who entered the tent or approached the window of a winter quarters log structure (Figure 4.1). Soldiers' options ranged from a new shirt and boots to liquor, patent medicines, oranges, pies, armor vests, and, as one soldier put it, "numberless other articles, useful and useless."[23]

Illnesses, problems in the army supply chain, supplementing rations, and the desire for a "treat," as one soldier put it, all led men to the sutler's tent. At the outbreak of war, people were still learning to navigate and assess the quality of the burgeoning array of available retail goods. Soldier Charles Brewster, once a store clerk, was "knowledgeable enough about the quality and price of products to know when he was being cheated" before making a purchase.[24] But many soldiers fell victim to deceptive marketing and found out the hard way—when pants tore out at the seams, when they were struck by bouts of diarrhea after eating pies fried in condemned lard, or as they witnessed a bullet easily perforate a purportedly bulletproof armor vest.[25] Although soldiers often enjoyed their sutler purchases, they also complained of the "exorbitant prices" and poor quality of foodstuffs. Many considered sutlers to be "vultures" who "preyed upon the misfortune of others in the market."[26]

Army regulations and congressional action ostensibly regulated sutlers' practices. Only one sutler was allowed per regiment and that sutler was forbidden from farming out or underletting "the business and privileges of their appointment." By March 1862, sutler activities prompted an act of Congress that detailed the conduct of sutlers' businesses, including a set schedule of goods and pricing.[27] In practice, however, sutlers were infrequently regulated. The US Sanitary Commission asserted that "proper control and supervision of the sutler is scarcely ever maintained in volunteer regiments" and "corrupt bargains" were frequently struck between sutlers and regimental officers.[28]

Sutlers were, nevertheless, tolerated, in part because providing for soldiers' small, ordinary needs and wants was considered necessary for the smooth functioning of an army. Access to goods, according to one US congressman, made a soldier "more comfortable, his service more agreeable, and renders him content in camp."[29] Furthermore, sutlers were preferable to allowing locals to sell goods to soldiers because they were subject to army regulations, however poorly enforced. As another US congressman explained, "When you throw open your camps to everybody who chooses to come there to peddle to the soldiers, you will find the most disastrous consequences following—that the officers will be utterly powerless to control."[30] Similarly, officers may have been willing to overlook schemes like the Willoughbys' in order to keep soldiers—and themselves—supplied in terms of both morale and small material needs without having to leave camp. Several of the Willoughbys' customers were, in fact, officers. While they operated their businesses outside of regulations, soldier-entrepreneurs were, in the end, still soldiers who were otherwise subject to army discipline, unlike civilian hucksters.

The failure of official military consumer markets—those supplied by the quartermaster and the contracted, licensed sutler—to meet soldiers' expectations meant that a soldier-marketer like Willoughby could fulfill soldiers' needs for reliable access to consumer goods and offer another site for bargaining in a consumer military market. It was a risk. Although army regulations did not explicitly address businesses like the Willoughbys', their business was unsanctioned by the government, making running it potentially punishable. Still, William's understanding of his and his comrades' dealings with the sutler informed his own business practices: he needed to make a profit, while also offering quality goods to maintain the trust—and repeat orders—of his fellow soldiers.

Willoughby gained first-hand experience with suttling while serving a several-month stint as the sutler's clerk, during which time he continued to run his own side business, presumably in competition with the sutler. In theory, all soldiers could avoid making sutler purchases by writing to their families at home to request goods. However, between the process of explaining what precisely they wanted, the question of whether those at home had accessible cash or credit, and the challenges posed by shipping, many soldiers likely considered it easier to simply make a purchase from the sutler. Others took advantage of acquiring goods through someone like Willoughby, who not only sold his goods at a lower price than the sutler, but also accepted the financial risk of lost shipments. Payment, after all, occurred when William provided the goods to his customer.

William's business scheme was particularly well articulated, and he frequently discussed business in his correspondence. Yet he was not alone in using to his benefit his connections at home and in the field. Confederate soldier William Allen, too, was an entrepreneur, relying on his mother to ship whiskey and apples, which he sold to his comrades for a large profit.[31] Soldiers' accounts of their debts and those owed to them—often found in the back pages of diaries—demonstrate the market dynamics at work in camp, including the common practice of purchasing goods and exchanging services with fellow soldiers.

Going into Business

A carriage maker by trade, William Willoughby was forty-three years old and unemployed when he enlisted in the 10th Connecticut Infantry Regiment, in 1861. A married father of an infant son, he and his family lived in a rented house in New Haven, and their personal estate was valued at only $100.[32] According to family history, "displacement through technological advance and a catastrophe involving a fire in his first shop at Darby, Connecticut, gave him an economic handicap which he never entirely overcame."[33] William was adamant that his motivation for enlisting had nothing to do with his job status, but he nevertheless sought out possible opportunities presented by army life to increase his monthly income. More generally, he hoped "to turn these scenes to some good account and return a better man than when I left home."[34]

Army enlistment brought with it the seeming surety of monthly pay. How-ever, delays in payroll and the deduction of gear, food, and sutler purchases meant a reduced payment. Willoughby's own experience was not uncommon. As a member of the drum corps, his monthly pay was twelve dollars, paid every two months. He elected to participate in the allotment system, which automatically deducted and sent home part of his pay. On one pay-day, William received only four dollars in cash for two months of service. He attributed this to the fact that he had been sick and "was obliged to purchase many little articles of convenience and necessity for three months." This, he told his wife Nancy, "has prevented me from sending you as much money as I otherwise should have done."[35] Throughout the war, Nancy was anxious about her ability to make rent and purchase necessities. Eventually, she began letting out rooms in their rented house to defray the costs. Anticipating the challenges of the winter, Nancy wrote to William, who replied, "I think if you manage prudently you will get over the winter without much suffering. And I have confidence that you will do so."[36] The Willoughbys' was not an unusual situation. As Peter Carmichael explains, during wartime, "fragile household economies were inseparable from a perilous soldier economy that kept enlisted men hanging on by a gossamer thread."[37]

Such financial instability, infrequent government pay, and pressing bills motivated soldiers, including William Willoughby, to engage in various schemes made possible by wartime circumstances. Laundering other sol-diers' clothing, preparing meals, selling goods, taking valuables from enemy houses, and trading in bounty certificates were among the ways in which sol-diers attempted to get ahead. For many soldiers, some—or much—of their twelve-dollar monthly pay was sent home, often leaving them short on cash. Yet soldiers possessed considerable potential consumer purchasing power in the form of recruitment bounties from state and local governments. These bounties—extra pay for enlisting—ranged from one hundred to several hun-dred dollars, divided up and paid in monthly installments.[38] The certificates could be signed over to another individual to redeem, making them a kind of currency at soldiers' disposal.

Early in the war, William began purchasing his comrades' enlistment bounty certificates at a discount and mailing them to his wife to redeem when they came due, pocketing the difference. In one instance, he purchased a hundred-dollar bounty for eighty dollars, providing him with a potential nominal profit of twenty dollars.[39] The scheme worked well for Willoughby— other soldiers wanted ready cash for their own expenses, likely in part to pay off the regiment's sutler. As Peter Carmichael explains, cash-hungry soldiers secured credit from sutlers and rank-and-file soldiers were "always vulnerable to a cycle of debt."[40] Indeed, Willoughby preferred to keep some cash on hand in camp, explaining, "Money is in great demand and brings a good bonus. . . . It brings $2 on every $10."[41] Willoughby traded cash for bounties through- out his enlistment, but after several months in the army, he was also ready to attempt selling goods to his fellow soldiers, often accepting bounty certificates as payment. The ability to negotiate such bounty certificates offered common soldiers access to more purchasing power than perhaps they had ever seen in their lives; William was prepared to take advantage of this.

In the early summer of 1862, William, having been encamped in New Bern, North Carolina, for several months, began his business venture. The idea began quite simply—he needed a few items and wanted some variation in his bland diet. Instead of a single shirt for himself, he asked his wife, Nancy, for four and gave her different measurements for the neck bands. Instead of a few tamarinds, he asked her to send him a keg. "See that the tamarinds are good ones," he directed. He also requested she hem and send "1 Doz Cheap White Cotton Pockett Hankerchiff with figured border."[42] William advised her to note the prices of all of the items, including "what they cost you, your labor included and also the freight you may hereafter pay." He further explained, "I shall probably sell some of them and shall want to know the cost."[43] William wanted to ensure he turned a profit.

This was the beginning of the Willoughbys' business, a joint venture dependent on the cooperation of both William and Nancy. Soldiers' ability to engage in consumer provisioning during wartime relied on gendered pri- vate relations and joint ventures between family members. While the rise of a capitalist middle class was enhancing gendered divisions of labor in the nineteenth century, in the case of wartime consumer provisioning, the family economy remained paramount, with women's domestic labor continuing to be an important source of household prosperity. Nancy and William both played relatively equally involved roles in their business—Nancy as pro- curer, wholesaler, and shipper, and William as marketer and retailer. Without

Nancy, William could not have participated in the informal market economy that existed within soldiers' camps; Nancy was the conduit for William to supply soldiers' demands for consumer goods. The couple's success in turning a profit depended on four central mechanisms: Nancy's ability to access and pay for materials and goods in New Haven, a ready market for William's merchandise, Nancy's sewing skills, and the reliability of shipping to the locations at which William was encamped.

Proximity to shipping was one of the determining factors as to whether soldiers could carry on such a business. Absent a widely available and reliable method of mailing and shipping, the Willoughbys' business could not have succeeded. Located in New Haven, along the Connecticut shoreline, Nancy had ready access to a shipping port. Likewise, William remained encamped with the 10th Connecticut for months at a time in coastal locations with active ports, including New Bern, North Carolina; South Carolina's Sea Islands; and St. Petersburg, Florida. William's letters detailing orders needed to reach Nancy, while merchandise needed to reach William in a timely manner and in good condition. Indeed, a reliable post was crucial to commercial transactions more generally and was a central part of wartime experience for both soldiers and civilians.[44] Yet, private express services were the critical denominator for people like the Willoughbys who depended on the ability to reliably ship packages economically, quickly, and safely across state lines during a sectional war.

When the war began, several express shipping companies existed. Founded by private entrepreneurs, these companies directly competed with the postal service to carry packages, letters, and money.[45] During the war, Adams Express garnered the bulk of soldiers' and their families' shipments, in part because it strategically located its offices near army encampments. Adams Express promised fast service. In 1861, the company announced the establishment of daily service between New York and the Washington, DC, area. Customers were advised that they "can send parcels daily by the express, with the certainty of having them delivered inside of twenty-four hours."[46] The company also advertised their services to soldiers in the field, assuring readers of a Union regimental newspaper that "you can safely send money, or any other valuable by this Company," whose office was conveniently located adjacent to camp.[47]

Considered more reliable and less expensive than the postal service when it came to shipping boxes, express services were widely used by US and Confederate soldiers, and the US army itself, to ship packages and send money. On one day in January 1862, for instance, an express agent delivered an envelope containing $100.17 to an individual, as well as "10 boxes weighing 1300 lbs" to the acting quartermaster at Camp Frazer, Kentucky.[48] References to the shipment, arrival, and loss of express packages pepper soldiers' wartime correspondence. To the Willoughbys' favor, the 10th Connecticut remained encamped for months at a time in various locations during 1862 and 1863, enabling William to receive and ship packages more reliably. His location—often a southern port controlled by the United States that had an established express office—was key to his success. Nevertheless, shipments did not always arrive on time or in perfect condition. In one instance, he reported, "My box arrived last friday night 36 Days after you paid the freight the vessell having been blown to sea in a storm. Most of the express matter was in a ruinous condition. Mine however was in excellent condition not a thing hurt."[49] The majority of packages sent from Nancy in New Haven to William in North Carolina, Florida, and Virginia seem to have arrived without great delay or damage. For the two and a half years that the Willoughbys ran their business, Adams Express and the postal service provided a key line of communication and a method of transporting consumer goods across several hundred miles.

What precisely those goods were was another matter altogether. Choosing inventory at a distance was difficult, but soldier-marketers like Willoughby developed market expertise in the field—by overhearing complaints and wishes from their messmates, recognizing their own desires, surveilling the sutler's offerings, and assessing the adequacy of quartermaster-supplied goods. Within the Willoughbys' partnership, William saw himself as the strategist and decisionmaker when it came to their stock, its quantity, and pricing. Yet he based his decisions on Nancy's access to and assessment of available goods.

William Willoughby drew on his own experiences as a soldier to determine what he could sell and how it should be priced. He once told Nancy that "the trials, denials and discomforts of a Soldiers life is not even imagined by the citizen he has not Idea of the life we live."[50] Indeed, he chastised Nancy for inaccurately anticipating his needs and what was worthwhile to ship, writing, "you do not use the best judgement in selecting articles to send." Vinegar, he assured her, was already in plentiful supply; potatoes and turnips were bulky and already furnished by the government. "Then as for crackers why the Commissary almost kills us with hardbread now!" Of dried apples, peaches, and prunes, he asked, "what can I do with them?"[51] Timing, too, was important to the Willoughbys' venture. Certain items were more desirable at particular times of the year. In late 1863, William saw an opportunity to profit from the new year and soldiers' desire to document their war, asking Nancy to "find the price for two dozen Diaries for 1864."[52]

As he began to take individual orders from comrades, William's ability to describe the desired goods and Nancy's attention to fulfilling those details were critical to both the profitability of the scheme and William's reputation in camp. Communication in general was key—costs, time, orders, and changes in those orders were all valuable information for running the business smoothly and for a profit. Yet that information was relayed by letter, and like many soldiers and families, the Willoughbys struggled with the unreliability of the postal service throughout the war. Accusations against the other for not writing regularly are interspersed throughout their correspondence. To facilitate description, William relied on both words and physical items. In describing the ream of paper Nancy should purchase for resale, he noted that he wanted the same-sized paper as his previous letter, but with "more distinctly ruled" lines. "As you will see," he continued, referencing the paper on which his letter was written, "this is not distinct."[53] In other instances, he sent shirts along with descriptions of the measurements, cut, and fabric for making new shirts. Occasionally he sent a swatch of fabric.

Home-sewn shirts were popular among soldiers. Technically, a soldier's outer garments—his coat and pants—were governed by army regulations in terms of color, cut, and style, but undergarments, including shirts and drawers, seem to have drawn little attention from officers. Furthermore, while the army provided strict uniform regulations, in practice, policies were often lax according to local circumstances. The advantage in having clothing sent from the home front or purchased from a local seamstress included the ability to make special requests in terms of materials, construction, decoration, and fit—options unavailable to those purchasing mass-produced clothing issued according to a still-developing sizing system.

William capitalized on soldiers' desire for better fitting, bespoke clothing. Initially, William requested shirts with generic measurements. As he began to sell clothing that was specifically sized to particular customers, William faced the challenge of communicating measurements without possessing the knowledge of a tailor. He described for Nancy how he came to them: "I get this measurement by laying the tape measure on the Shoulder joint, on top, the arm being Straight, Or in other words suppose the arm hanging down by the Side. I measure from the top of the Shoulder, at the point where it begins to turn downwards to the end of the sleeve. So you must make your calculations."[54]

Eventually, Nancy must have begun keeping a record of customers' names and measurements, as William referenced them in his requests: "One pair for Tom Fowler same as Whitneys with the Exception that the neck band be narrow like Boardmans and the sleeves a little longer say an inch or more."[55]

Fabric choice was also a key element in William's orders. Soldiers possessed limited access to the burgeoning array of available fabric, yet they still had the desire to wear it. William was careful to select fabric that would both withstand the demands of soldiering life and appeal to his customers, requesting shirts made from sturdy cloth "that will not fade by washing," as well as a variety of prints and fabrics, typically differently sized patterns and colors of woolen or cotton plaid. Yet, even the strongest of fabrics could not withstand the abuse of infrequent washing and manual labor, so William provided an additional service by having Nancy "enclose 2 or 3 Small pieces of the cloth Say 3 or 4 inches Square suitable for mending or patching the elbows" from the same cloth as that from which the shirts were made.[56] Such attention to detail enabled his customers to avoid a "patched up" appearance.

Shirts were the mainstay of the Willoughbys' business, but William quickly diversified and began keeping limited stock on hand, something that was possible only given the long periods of time he spent encamped. As a private, William would have had no access to transportation beyond the knapsack he carried. The goods he stocked tended to be useful items that made life in camp or on the march easier without adding bulk to a soldier's gear. One of his requested shipments included "three dozen Fabers lead pencils, I want 6 or 8 small sized Diaries one page for each day. And 1 Doz paper packages the paper to be good. also one Doz pencil Sharpeners like those you brought me at Hartford, four pocket knives to cost about 75 cts each, also half a Doz or a Doz if you can get them pairs of suspenders of good quality, also one Doz yards of Musketoe netting, colour blue You may get 1 Doz papers large size and 2 Doz papers Small Size of John Andersons honey dew best Tobacco for chewing."[57] In addition, William requested a variety of patent medicines, for his own use, specific buyers, and general sale. In one instance, he instructed Nancy to send two bottles of "Dr. Kennady's Discovery," a patent medicine, and to "write on the label of each bottle 'for Joe Tyler.'" In the same shipment, he wanted "some of Dr Nortons Exterminator or 'Dr Trues Pain Killer' a 1/2 Doz bottles of each or a Doz bottles of either, 4 bottles of 'Grays Hair Restorative,'" and one dozen "pairs knit wollen Gloves of some good collor and quality." He also wanted "one box of One Hundred cigars." An additional "One Doz Pairs cotten socks," he suspected, "would sell readily."[58]

Like many business partners, Nancy and William did not always see eye to eye. Once, Nancy questioned the business and her role within it, resisting making more shirts. William argued the point with her: "You give me a reason why you should not make any shirts. 'That it is very Expensive, or quite Expensive making them.'" He found that to be "no good reason." Instead, he suspected that the "real reason why you do not wish to make any more, is because it is taxing and laborious" when "added to your other daily duties." That Nancy may have been overwhelmed by her daily duties is not surprising—she not only ran a household, but also cared for a young son and managed boarders. Such was the challenge of participating in a family economy, as business matters ran up against household work. If Nancy was, indeed, overwhelmed, William suggested that she buy the material and have someone else make the shirts. He told her to consider their situation, and noted, "I think after you think over the matter and see that through your efforts at home and mine here you are from 6 to 10 Dollars a month better off and I none the worse off you will think better of it."[59] Nancy seems to have agreed that her labor was worth the additional money, as she continued sending shirts at his request.

In pricing his goods, William appears to have settled on prices that would net a profit yet seem like a discount compared to the sutler. When ordering handkerchiefs, for instance, he asked for "Something I can sell for 75 cents and make twenty five cents on them."[60] William's goods were akin to what a soldier might find in a sutler's store. But his prices were more reasonable. One Union soldier complained that "Army shirts—no better than those issued to us—cost six dollars at the sutler's."[61] Willoughby, on the other hand, was known to charge $4.50 for a cotton shirt and accepted the risks of shipping.[62] As a result, he was able to both compete with the 10th Connecticut's sutler and offer soldiers a better alternative to writing home.

Purchasing quality goods during wartime presented a challenge. William warned Nancy to "look out" for poor quality goods, but she, along with the federal government and many a soldier, occasionally purchased goods of inferior quality produced by manufacturers looking to profit from the war.[63] Yet, while government distribution of shoddy goods merely drew the ire of soldiers who had little recourse, for entrepreneurs like the Willoughbys, the mistake was much more personal and could threaten their business. To keep customers satisfied, William was occasionally forced to make right the problems arising from poorly sewn seams or poor-quality goods. Once, Nancy inadvertently purchased inferior soldiers' caps, the brims of which were made of improperly sealed paperboard. William explained the problem created by the caps in terms of both deception and loss. "I want to say a word about those last caps you sent The forepieces to them was made of paper covered over with a thin piece of leather and the first time worn in a dew they blistered right up and showed the deception." That "deception" was "too barefaced to smooth over easily" with his comrades.[64] In order to retain their trust, William took a loss. He refunded half of the soldiers' money who had already purchased the caps and offered the remaining merchandise for sale at a discounted price with the upfront admission that the caps' brims were poorly made.

While William negotiated with customers and managed pricing, Nancy navigated a challenging retail environment to maintain their supply chain. By 1860, women regularly performed retail shopping for themselves and their families in dedicated shopping districts. Yet, the marketplace and its mechanisms of credit remained largely male oriented.[65] The ebb and flow of access to cash and credit was one of the greatest challenges for a family business modeled on the family economy. The Willoughbys' business relied on Nancy's ability to purchase both raw materials and items for resale. And this depended on her ability to pay. Apparently drawing on his own previous experience in the marketplace, William instructed Nancy on how to succeed in retail transactions, directing her both in forms of payment and the prices she should expect. After placing a particularly large order with Nancy, William asked, "Well now how are you a going to buy them?" If payday was on time, he believed he could send her enough to cover the costs, but in his hurry to have her send the goods, he advised: "You had better take your Bank Book to Stephen D Pardee of Savings Bank and ask how you can best get $100.00 for Ninety Days." The bank was a dead end and Nancy instead borrowed $100.00 from her landlord, with interest. Paying interest on a 90-day loan was worthwhile to William, who had a ready market waiting. He believed he could bring a profit of nearly $90.00, a number certainly worth the $1.25 in interest. Better to take a loan than miss the opportunity for significant sales.[66]

The Willoughbys both purchased and sold on credit. It was a risk. Army payrolls could be delayed and the cash distributed on payday less than expected. Nevertheless, William knew the importance of timing the arrival of goods to coincide with payday to ensure that he could collect payment when soldiers had cash on hand. In extending credit, William was further reassured by the possibility of collecting bounty drafts as payment. One payday, he found that "a number of the boys who owed me had little or nothing coming to them [in cash] so . . . they turned over to me their next State bounty drafts at a discount." The Willoughbys' realization of money was not immediate, however—sometimes bounty drafts were not payable for a few, or even several, months. When that was the case, William advised Nancy: "You must get along the best way you can for money untill then."[67]

Mistakes about payment were also made. At one point, William accepted a coat and blanket as insurance against a soldier's debt who "boasted he would pay me when he 'Damned pleased.'" That a coat and blanket would be acceptable to William as a form of potential payment is unsurprising— textiles and clothing retained significant value on the secondhand and rag markets and soldiers regularly bartered with one another.[68] In this scenario, William shipped the coat and blanket to Nancy for safekeeping, but she misunderstood his instructions and gave the articles to another person. William was livid and attacked Nancy's business skills: "I supposed you had lived long enough [to] know it was not business like" to deliver the items without his instruction. He further berated her: "I should have supposed a child a Dozen years old would have known better. I feel really provoked about it." He advised her to never "be caught so again."[69] That William accused Nancy of being unbusinesslike in a scenario in which the transaction itself was irregular reveals the fluidity of wartime business practices within soldiers' camps. Cash, barter, bounties, promises, and accepting other material items as insurance were all within the realm of reasonable forms of payment.

Returning Home

Between the spring of 1862 and the end of William's three-year enlistment in the fall of 1864, the Willoughbys had established a regular business. When he left the army in October, the 10th Connecticut was then part of the Siege of Petersburg, where the US Army would engage in nine months of trench warfare against Confederate forces. Despite the shelling going on around him, William was intent on wrapping up his business affairs before his anticipated departure, collecting bounties and placing final orders for shirts.

Yet William's departure did not put an end to the Willoughbys' business: his friends and fellow soldiers continued to consider him a reliable source through which to acquire consumer goods. Immediately on returning home, William resumed business, taking up Nancy's mantle of interpreting orders placed by letter, corresponding with comrades, and making recommendations based on the goods available in local stores. One soldier wrote asking for several accoutrements, including "a Cap, you recollect the kind of Cap that we used to Wear so much when we first came out; with the top bearing over to the front, and the peak comeing down over the eyes; You may send one of those, size 7: and as good quality as you can find."[70] Here, the soldier relied on his and William's collective knowledge and memory to select an appropriate cap. Other soldiers commented on William's ability to provide good prices and quality compared to those available in camp. One man was pleased: "That Cap is a splendid article. just what I wanted. We can buy them here for $3 1/2 not half so good as the one you sent me."[71]

Certainly, the orders kept coming in, but the question of payment was complicated by William's absence. No longer in camp to pressure soldiers to settle accounts on payday or accept bounties, William relied on men's promises when they were unable to pay upfront. One customer recognized the situation. He was desperately in need of a new pair of shoes, writing, "I am almost barefoot, and do not like to draw Governments." But he acknowledged that he could not send the money "untill we get paid off again; so you can do as you like about sending to me."[72] Another soldier offered reassurances: "Willoughby if you haven't sent me the box I wish you would as soon as possable You need not stand in fear of not getting your pay for I will pay you the money as soon as I get it."[73]

Yet William and Nancy *did* fear not being paid. They were not shopkeepers who could let out lines of credit, but rather a couple with a young son and a rented house who were scraping by. They themselves took out lines of credit to purchase goods for resale. The Willoughbys' overall profit from their business was negligible in the broader marketplace, ranging in the hundreds of dollars over the course of the war. A dry goods store could profit thousands in the same period, making the Willoughbys' enterprise seem hardly like a business. Yet in the circumstances of war, it was precisely that.[74]

Although their profit might seem marginal, for the Willoughbys, it was critical, especially because William had been out of work before joining the army. That small profit was what made the difference in Nancy's ability to buy her winter coat and purchase coal. By letting out rooms in the house, she ensured that their rent would be met. Money was a persistent source of anxiety for the Willoughbys, and as Nancy followed through on transactions, cashed bounties, and accepted payments by mail, William cautioned her: "Be carefull you do not lose your money nor leave it where it may be stole if you have any in the house."[75] The Willoughbys' wartime business seems to have helped them get by, but it did not result in great financial success. On his return to Connecticut, William soon went to the Hartford Barracks to be paid. In the final line of his wartime diary, he wrote with irritation: "The Payroll was made out so as to wrong me out of 2 Dollars."[76]

Like many soldiers, William initially found his return to civilian life a difficult transition, writing, "I find the change from Camp life to one more homelike is great and is attended with difficulties, so much so I found I could not rest on a bed and found a relief to take the floor, to obtain sleep." Despite his ability to access and sell consumer goods in camp, camp life was incomparable to the comforts of civilian life. He was thrilled to "live a life of civilization to be able to get some thing to eat once more that may be considered food for man."[77] William's wartime experience with retailing consumer goods seems to have influenced the trajectory of his immediate postwar life. Unemployed at the start of the war, William did not have a job to which he might seek to return when his enlistment concluded. In 1865, he was working in retail, selling fruits and confectionary. He went on to work a series of jobs, including as a mechanic, a night watchman, and finally as a US mail carrier and a paper agent, until a few years before his death in 1887. Although he did not see great financial success, he eventually purchased a house for his family of four.[78]

Conclusion

The American Civil War created a ready market of soldiers with severely limited access to the broader, burgeoning consumer marketplace at a moment in which small comforts, like the ability to wear a plaid shirt, write a letter, smoke a cigar, or take patent medicine, were central to combatting both the exigencies and the dullness of camp life. By agreeing that sutlers were "absolutely indispensable to the comfort and convenience of soldiers while they are prosecuting this war," members of Congress confirmed that consumer goods were essential to soldiers at war.[79] The importance of consumer goods to soldiers' morale became an enduring theme in US military history. Immediately following the Civil War, the army abolished the position of the sutler.[80] This led to the development of canteens and exchanges, precursors to the modern Army & Air Force Exchange Service, which promises to "deliver quality goods and services at competitively low prices" online and through more than three thousand locations worldwide.[81]

Despite the growth of military consumer outlets, family businesses led by individual soldiers persisted. During wartime, entrepreneurial soldiers like Willoughby continued to find ways to make money by selling goods to fellow soldiers, and sometimes to civilians. Immediately following World War II, soldiers used cigarettes as a form of currency in Berlin's black markets.[82] During the Vietnam War, Meredith Lair argues, soldiers participated in a fringe economy, procuring supplies for units, funneling consumer goods to the black market, and rerolling marijuana in cigarettes for sale. As one soldier observed, "there was money to be made for anyone willing to take the risk."[83]

Even in the recent wars in Iraq and Afghanistan, family consumer supply lines continued. When Michael T. was deployed to Afghanistan with the United States Marine Corps in the early 2000s, his mother often made up boxes to send him. Such care packages were more than an emotional effort to provide comfort or a sense of home: those boxes supplemented the consumer and edible goods to which Michael and his messmates had access. Homemade caramel bars were an addition to many boxes.[84] Treats, sweets, and other foods also functioned as currency among American and international soldiers. One newspaper correspondent wrote of the popularity of peanut M&Ms, noting, "They're currency. Want to swap out your shift pulling guard duty? A packet might well buy you a favor."[85] Soldiers have found ways to negotiate variety and better standards of living into their daily lives. And, like many a Civil War soldier, they often remain eager for someone at home to "make up a box to send me."[86]

Across time and space, military consumer markets have defied the artificial boundaries historians have constructed between home front and war front and between big business and personal family economies. During the American Civil War, sutlers and other retail-related trades made huge profits during the war, as did other industries. Yet the persistence of extremely modest family businesses modeled on family economies reveals just how essential businesses like that run by the Willoughbys were both to individuals and to the military. Gendered private relations and family members' joint ventures facilitated soldiers' engagement in consumer provisioning during wartime. The work of women like Nancy Willoughby was vitally important to the functioning of this wartime consumer marketplace. Nancy, and civilians like her on the home front, possessed the ability to respond to soldiers at the war front who were anxious for someone to "Send the Box. Send the Box. . . . SEND THE BOX."[87]

CHAPTER 5

A Girl in Every Port? The US Military and Prostitution in the Twentieth Century

Kara Dixon Vuic

From July to December 1967, Captain Jesse H. Denton commanded an infantry company stationed in lower III Corps, South Vietnam. Based in a hamlet of about 340 villagers, Company E lived and worked among the people. When not engaged in hostile actions, the soldiers built bridges and provided rudimentary health care. Most of the villagers were farmers who continued to work in the rice paddies nearby, though a few enterprising folks supplemented their income by tending to the needs of the soldiers with whom they lived. Some worked in the mess hall where the American men took their meals, others washed laundry, and four or five of the village women sold sex. The women operated under a regulated system of prostitution created by Captain Denton for his men. It was a little-known practice, but not an uncommon one. Four other company commanders in the battalion regulated similar systems of prostitution, Denton explained, because he and his colleagues decided that "it was the most efficient way of satisfying one problem without creating another."

Denton regulated sex work to address very specific concerns, but they were ones that military officials in other locations and in other eras would have recognized. The soldiers under Denton's command lived alongside the Vietnamese villagers, slept in their huts, and often developed close ties to the families with whom they lived. Friendly relations could symbolize the best of the US military's attempt to win hearts and minds in Vietnam, but living in such close and constant proximity also created problems. The "young hardchargers" Denton commanded were "just as virile as anyone their age," he explained, and soon began "making overtures toward Vietnamese wives . . . and against females that had no sexual interest." In an effort to keep the peace in the village—essentially, to prevent the soldiers from raping local women— as well as to manage the sexual appetites of his young soldiers and to prevent venereal disease, Denton provided prostitutes.

Working with village officials, Denton recruited four or five "long-time res- ident local girls," ensured they were not communist sympathizers, and required them to submit to penicillin shots every Monday. The women then received identification cards with their photograph that licensed them to work as prosti- tutes and to charge "regulated, not absorbitant [sic]" prices. The soldiers under- stood that they were to "focus their sexual outlets" on these women and that if they did not, they "would be cut off, so to speak." Denton was pleased that the system stymied the "horrendous problem developing" and kept the sol- diers and women healthy. Only one man in the company contracted a vene- real disease, Denton boasted, and he had acquired it while on R&R in Hong Kong. Still, even with these measures of success, Denton hesitated to brag to his brigade commanders. Knowing that "good people crucified one of our finer Junior Officers" for more openly regulating prostitution, Denton and his fellow company commanders managed their situation as they saw fit, without draw- ing attention to it.[1]

Denton's management of sex in a warzone highlights problems and con- cerns that military commanders throughout American history have faced and illustrates the deep roots of sexual economies in military operations. Although direct military management of sex workers was never universal and wasn't well known, many military commanders have provided prostitutes for their servicemen (never for their servicewomen) throughout history. Likely, few of them considered the economic consequences of their actions or thought of sex work as one of many economic markets that they managed. They endorsed prostitution because, like Denton, they considered it the best solution for a multitude of interwoven problems related to health, gender, morale, and diplomacy. Not all commanders, of course, have openly endorsed, much less organized, prostitution. Indeed, most have condemned sexual economies publicly, though many among them offered indirect support for or adopted a "wink-wink" attitude toward a practice that seemed inevitable.

As this chapter demonstrates, whether the military provided, endorsed, or tolerated prostitution, it regulated the consumption and labor of sex, with far-reaching consequences for local and national economies. Officials who directly managed sex markets involved themselves in matters of supply and demand, labor, and consumption. Even those who forbade or attempted to prohibit military personnel from engaging in sexual economies indirectly created and shaped sexual markets that operated outside of, but remained dependent on, the military.

Although there have been plenty of continuities in the US military's approach to sexual economies, broadly speaking, that approach has changed over time, moving gradually from more to less hands-on management. In the first half of the twentieth century, the US military intervened in and regulated sexual markets to meet needs related to hygiene, gender, and foreign relations. As the military expanded its global footprint during the Cold War, officials less overtly regulated existing sexual economies, even as they indirectly supported booming and entrenched sex markets near military installations. By the century's end, militarized sex markets formed essential components of many local and national economies and linked the US military and prostitution worldwide.

At the turn of the twentieth century, most military officials understood sexual health and sexual labor as intertwined issues. Sexually transmitted diseases, especially syphilis and gonorrhea, frequently sidelined troops for a considerable amount of time and posed very real threats to military operations. Officials blamed women for the spread of disease—despite men's obvious complicity—and believed that regulated prostitution offered the best chance for preserving the sexual health of soldiers. Thus, at western outposts and in warzones around the globe, military officials managed the sexual labor of women outside of military control, mobilizing prostitutes for military purposes. Military officials forced sex workers to submit to medical exams and treatment, dictated the terms of sexual transactions, and sometimes confined women against their will, while also negotiating with brothel owners, leaders of vice districts, and local governments as they managed the business of sex.

Military and civilian leaders also understood sex as a matter of consumption, a critical component of martial masculinity and morale. Americans' understanding of male sexuality—and particularly male martial sexuality—changed dramatically over the course of the twentieth century. At various times, Americans thought the male sex drive was irrepressible, feared that the military's homosocial environment could lead men to engage in homosexual sex, and believed that virile men in difficult situations were entitled to blow off steam through sex. In all situations, sex formed a critical part of what it meant to be a man in the military, and military officials directly and indirectly provided opportunities for men to purchase sex. Indeed, a significant portion of military entertainment and leisure culture has involved participating in sexual economies—whether transactional sex, patronizing institutions linked to prostitution, purchasing sexually explicit materials, or even participating in military-sponsored, sexually charged entertainment.

These sexual economies have been inseparable from broader military economic practices and markets and thus highlight the inseparable histories of prostitution, the US military, and American foreign relations. Although the mere presence of militaries has historically been sufficient to create a market for sex, as scholar Cynthia Enloe notes, "militarized, masculinized sexual desire, by itself, isn't sufficient to sustain a full-fledged prostitution industry." She argues that prostitution depends on broader economic factors, including "rural poverty, male [and, I would add, female] entrepreneurship, urban commercialized demand, police protection, and overlapping governmental economic interest."[2] Managing sexual economies has entangled military officials in economies of varying scales, legal and illicit markets, black markets of goods and people, criminal and legal enterprises, and a range of actors from the individual to the national level. Military officials have negotiated and managed these larger structures and supports, and in doing so have made sexual economies a critical consequence of the US military's presence in war zones and occupations.

This chapter explores the complex webs that entangled the US military and sexual economies across the twentieth century. It is not an exhaustive history but, instead, uses examples to illustrate key moments when concerns about health, gender, and foreign relations framed the military's management of sexual economies. It draws on examples from across the armed forces, even as it suggests that militarized sexual economies have varied by location, unique service culture, individual policymakers, and local officials. As an institution, the US military has never fully reckoned with its history of managing sexual economies. The long history of this subject demands more attention, not only from students and scholars of military history and US empire but also from today's military leaders, who, like their predecessors, all have to manage the multifaceted problem of sex. Indeed, well into the twenty-first century, the US military is no closer to solving this problem than it was a century ago.

Markets on the Margins

Militaries throughout history have relied on sutlers, businesses, and industries to provide a range of services and goods for their troops. From the beginnings of the US military during the Revolutionary War, many of these providers have been women who cooked food, laundered clothing, and tended camps. Some of them provided sexual services.[3] In the late nineteenth and early twentieth centuries, as the US military more directly managed economies of all kinds, it also regulated sexual economies that provided civilian women sex workers for soldiers stationed in remote posts. Military officials regulated sexual markets and sexual labor in increasingly overt ways to control soldiers' sexual health and to regulate the sexual behaviors of lower-class men presumed to need control on the western frontier and at colonial outposts.

Isolated both by class and geography from most Americans, the military of the late nineteenth and early twentieth centuries generally tolerated prostitution. Most Americans did not endorse the selling of sex, and indeed, a diverse collection of Progressive reformers, religious folks, social scientists, and public health officials consternated about prostitution, the evils it wrought, and the women supposedly being sold into "white slavery." But they made certain allowances when it came to the military. Although prostitution "remained unacceptable within society at large," writes historian Anne M. Butler, "it was not only an expected, but perhaps an encouraged accoutrement at military sites."[4]

At the time, the army was a small force garrisoned in western forts. Officers typically came from the educated middle class, while most of the enlisted ranks came from the lower classes. Life on the frontier was tough, and military officers generally turned a blind eye when the rugged, brawny, rough-and-tumble men had a bit of fun, whether through liquor or women or both. Although they neither controlled nor regulated sexual economies, officers generally ignored servicemen cavorting with prostitutes as long as they did not cause a scene or draw public ire. At Fort Riley, Kansas, for example, soldiers enjoyed "relatively free rein to indulge in sexual activity, even with prostitutes" at the brothels in nearby Junction City. As historian Andrew Byers explains, military officials disciplined only those soldiers who brought prostitutes onto the fort or who created a public nuisance while engaging their services.[5]

But as military commanders soon discovered, transactional sex was never entirely private, especially when soldiers were stationed among or near foreign populations. In the Philippines and on the Mexican border, military leaders feared that soldiers' sexual appetites would cause diplomatic crises if not carefully managed, and many of them organized sexual economies as a critical buffer between servicemen and local "respectable" women.

Sex workers had operated legally in the Philippines under Spanish colonial rule, and the market for sex grew as American forces began arriving in the summer of 1898. Motivated by a sweeping range of factors from desperation to opportunism, Filipino women sold sex in brothels, in their homes, and on the streets. As demand nonetheless outpaced supply, sex workers migrated from Japan and China, and even as far away as Europe and the United States, drawn by the promise of a burgeoning market. American soldiers sought out sex for all the usual reasons, but many of them also saw Asian women in particular as especially exotic and erotic. Racial differences that might have discouraged some white men from having sex with women of color at home seemed less significant, even alluring, far from it.[6]

In an attempt to establish control over what seemed a combustible situation, in November 1898, Brigadier General Robert Patterson Hughes, the provost marshal general, instated regulatory practices. Army officials cooperated with civilian health and police departments, established a clinic where prostitutes could receive medical examinations, operated a hospital where they could be treated, and designated specific brothels for officers and for enlisted men. Sex workers had to pay for their own medical exams but received identification and health certificates that officially licensed their operations. Many women worked outside of any regulated system, often on a part-time basis. Although regulations failed to curb the venereal disease rate among soldiers, US military and government officials seemed pleased with the system. Then governor general of the Philippines and future US president William Howard Taft justified legalized sex work as a "police measure [and a] military necessity."[7]

Military officials adopted similar practices closer to home as well. In a response to raids into Texas by Mexican revolutionary leader Francisco "Pancho" Villa and his bands in 1916 and 1917, the army deployed ten thousand men to the border. Within weeks, brothels encircled the camps, and red-light districts in cities from San Antonio to El Paso overflowed with newly arrived sex workers. Caught between their general opposition to prostitution and their belief that soldiers needed sex, army officials imposed haphazard regulations that required prostitutes to submit to medical exams and assigned military police to maintain order in brothels and vice districts.[8] Despite these efforts, illicit sex markets continued to flourish, and many officials believed they served a useful purpose on any account. Men "made poor soldiers if they did not have women," many insisted, linking sex and soldiering in ways that their successors in later wars would have recognized.[9] Officers stationed in Mexico feared that soldiers who did not satiate their sexual desires would "go to Mexican villages and get mixed up with the women," creating a volatile situation that could "possibly bring on war." To alleviate the demand, officers established sexual markets inside army camps, where they provided prostitutes, set prices, and policed patrons.[10]

In an era when the military remained small and generally far from the eyes of most Americans, military and civilian leaders overtly regulated sexual economies. Although very few openly condoned prostitution as a respectable business, many accepted it as a necessary evil that could ward off disease and help manage military and civilian relations. As General John Pershing put it, the army's open management of the sex trade was "the best way to handle a difficult problem."[11] Militarized prostitution transitioned slowly from an illicit but tolerated vice to a regulated but hidden economy that operated on the geographical and social margins of society.

Regulated Wartime Sex Markets

The extensive mobilizations of World War I and World War II, along with changing gender norms, public health concerns, and medical advances, further entangled the military in sexual economies. Conscription moved the military literally and figuratively closer to all Americans, many of whom were pulled into the ranks themselves. As training camps sprung up across the nation and brought service personnel into towns and cities, the military's management of sexual economies reflected this increasing familiarity and proximity. While military and civilian officials attempted to cut off sexual economies entirely during World War I, deeming them illicit and harmful to doughboys and the nation, World War II officials accepted regulated sexual economies as necessary in certain situations. In all cases, wartime economic pressures determined and shaped sexual economies that operated under martial control.

By 1917, Progressive Era gender and social norms had gained a foothold among much of American society. Fewer Americans—including military and civilian policymakers—were willing to rationalize prostitution as necessary for effective soldiering or as an appropriate way to manage relations with the people around military camps and stations. Men and women who had been willing to turn a blind eye to the prostitution on and around military encampments proved far less willing to do so now that their sons might be drafted into service. In response, Progressive military and government officials not only ended the military's toleration and regulation of sexual markets, but also embraced continence, not virility, as the measure of a good man and a good soldier.[12]

The Selective Service Act of 1917 institutionalized measures that reformers hoped would lead to a "clean" military. Sections 12 and 13 authorized Secretary of War Newton D. Baker "to suppress and prevent the keeping or setting up of houses of ill fame, brothels, or bawdy houses" near "any military camp, station, fort, post, cantonment, training, or mobilization place."[13] Municipal and business officials all over the country clamored for military training camps to be located in their areas, and the act forced them to trade illicit sexual economies for the prospect of other, legitimate, ones.[14] Cities like Fort Worth, Texas, for example, with its famed Hell's Half Acre, quickly closed brothels so that the army would build Camp Bowie on the edge of town. Closing brothels did not end the sex trade, of course. Women simply plied their wares on streets and in cars, where they faced more focused and intense police attention that had previously been directed toward brothel owners.[15] Still, Progressive reformers had made their mark and ended the military's official regulation and toleration of prostitution.

The American Expeditionary Force (AEF) transported this new vision to France, where General Pershing declined offers from Premier Georges Clemenceau to provide the doughboys with access to state-run brothels designated specifically for their use.[16] Instead, Pershing deemed all brothels off-limits and enacted a number of measures to discourage and even punish participation in sexual economies. The AEF required doughboys to attend sexual hygiene lectures that warned of the dangers of prostitution, and any soldier who contracted a venereal disease was court-martialed and forfeited his pay.[17] Still, as Secretary Baker warned, soldiers' sexual desires could not be eliminated "by either proclamation or prayer," and military officials attempted to steer the men's attention away from sex.[18] Both in the United States and in France, they enlisted civilian agencies to provide entertainment and recreation that would, in theory, divert doughboys' wandering eyes away from prostitutes and toward more wholesome versions of American women.[19]

None of these efforts to repress prostitution had the effect for which officials had hoped. One estimate held that only 30 percent of doughboys in France refrained from sex. Even with the lowest rate of venereal disease among belligerent nations, the American military lost seven million days of active duty to men who, instead of working for the war effort, lay in hospitals undergoing treatment for syphilis or gonorrhea. More American doughboys suffered from venereal disease than any other illness save influenza.[20]

Moreover, many military officials concluded that the Progressives' effort to reframe martial masculinity as a model of continence was futile, even counterproductive. By 1941, most military officials had returned to the more conventional thought that men needed sex, or at least that they deserved it. In the words of senior navy medical officer Captain Joel T. Boone, who had been a surgeon during World War I, martial training "induces sexual aggression," a necessary quality of "good soldiers and sailors."[21]

When the United States mobilized for another world war in the early 1940s, then, officials deemed the repression of sexual economies largely pointless. Instead, they adopted a pragmatic approach that publicly disavowed but privately regulated sexual markets in an attempt to manage servicemen's sexual encounters and minimize the consequences of venereal disease. Within the United States, the May Act (1941) criminalized sex markets near military camps and authorized the Justice Department to shut them down. Although some military commanders and local officials failed to repress sex work with as much determination as federal authorities demanded, many others generally cooperated. No prohibition could entirely end prostitution, of course, and thousands of women who operated their own clandestine sexual markets were arrested and detained.[22]

On foreign shores, away from the eyes of the American public, the military distributed condoms to GIs, ordered men to take prophylaxis treatment postcoitus, embarked on an extensive education campaign that equated sexual health (not necessarily continence) with victory, and in September 1944 ceased withholding the pay of those who acquired a venereal disease after deciding that punishment dissuaded men from seeking treatment.[23] As long as men did not acquire a venereal disease or cause a public nuisance, military officials publicly denounced, then privately ignored prostitution. In several locations, officials determined that the best way to cultivate healthy, virile, heterosexual soldiers and sailors was to provide regulated systems of prostitution. Carefully managed sexual economies also seemed the simplest solution to fears that sexually frustrated men would resort to rape and that men who could not fulfill their desires through sex with women would have sex with men.[24] Whatever their rationale, military officials imposed the era's racial ideologies on sexual economies, both by endorsing prostitution primarily in non-Western locations and by enforcing racial segregation in all transactions.

When American military personnel invaded North Africa and Italy, they encountered and participated in well-established sexual economies that licensed women to work either in houses of prostitution or as freelancers.

Many women also operated clandestinely to avoid any regulation, but none of the women—licensed or not—received adequate sexual health care. Medical officers scrambled to develop a plan to combat the rising venereal disease rates among servicemen, but theater commanders rejected the leading medical officer's recommendation to place brothels off-limits. Instead, military medical officers conferred with local officials about how best to manage "the prostitution problem" and decided that regulation offered the best hope. In Oran, Algeria, military officials initially closed all brothels to US personnel, then selected "a number of the better type of European brothels" for the American forces. White soldiers could choose between seven brothels, while African American soldiers could choose between two, though they were restricted to thirty minutes. All patrons were required to take a prophylaxis treatment before leaving the brothels. Similar practices occurred throughout Algeria, Tunisia, and Italy as American forces pushed northward through the peninsula. Regulated prostitution did little to stop the spread of venereal disease, but brothels reportedly "did a flourishing business."[25]

Military officials intervened most openly and directly in the sexual economy of Liberia. Astounded by the high rates of venereal disease among the local population and guided by racist assumptions about sexual promiscuity and physical attraction between African American troops and Liberian women, American preventive medicine officers decided that it was "useless" to try to repress prostitution or reduce infection rates. Instead, white medical officers cooperated with the Liberian Health Department and the medical director of the Firestone Tire and Rubber Company plantations to regulate sex work. The Liberian government constructed two "so-called tolerated women's villages" near army camps, then permitted only women who passed medical exams to live and work there. African American troops were free to visit the villages, though publicly, officials hoped that "education and recreation facilities" would discourage sexual contact.[26]

Racial ideologies similarly shaped sexual economies in New Caledonia, a French colony in the Pacific, where American forces arrived in 1942. The French military managed the Pink House brothel for its troops, and white American soldiers began patronizing the house soon after their arrival. When local representatives complained about African American soldiers, however, US military authorities proposed the creation of a segregated brothel for the black troops, to be staffed by indigenous Kanak women. French authorities rejected the proposal on the grounds that the Kanak people and French missionaries would be offended by the prospect and suggested instead that

Figure 5.1. Far from American shores, the US Army tacitly endorsed sex work both by licensing sex workers and by indirectly regulating the women with whom soldiers interacted. Source: John Boyd Coates, Jr., ed., *Preventive Medicine in World War II, Volume V, Communicable Diseases Transmitted Through Contact or by Unknown Means* (Washington, DC: Office of the Surgeon General, Department of the Army, 1960), 301, Figure 59.

"Negresses" from the United States be imported as sex workers. An American colonel dismissed the idea, not because he objected to providing sexual markets for soldiers, but because he could not utilize government resources in the process, and because the American public would never approve.[27]

The situation differed entirely in continental Europe in the wake of the Allied invasion, where military officials prohibited commanders from condoning prostitution, either "directly or indirectly," and from having any role in licensing sex workers.[28] For the most part, commanders followed orders, though there were exceptions. The chief of the army's preventive medicine division discovered a month after the invasion in Cherbourg, for example, that "houses of prostitution [were] being run for, and indirectly by, US troops, with the familiar pattern of the designation of one brothel for Negro troops and the others for white, with military police stationed at the doors to keep order in the queues which formed."[29] As historian Mary Louise Roberts notes, General Charles Gerhardt of the 29th Infantry Division briefly established a brothel for his men in Brittany, explaining that he feared his sex-deprived men would turn to homosexual sex if he did not provide them with women, before the assistant provost marshal shut it down.[30] Even without officially endorsed sexual markets, GIs had little trouble creating their own exchanges with sex workers in brothels, independent prostitutes, and French women who had suffered through years of deprivation under German occupation and traded sex for badly needed food, supplies, and money.[31]

The length and global reach of World War II led many military officials to see sexual economies as inevitable elements of wartime operations, but they remained reluctant to publicly endorse them as legitimate or necessary. Far from the eyes of American families, in the Pacific and North African theaters, as well as wartime Hawai'i, military officials regulated the work of women who sold sex. In Western Europe, they generally proved reluctant to openly intervene in local sex markets, even as soldiers and sailors proved eager customers. With or without official approval, both the conditions and desperations of war and the needs and relative prosperity of American personnel created sex markets. As an official army history acknowledged, "the lack of food and, later, of fuel, gave the US soldier with a K ration an unbeatable bargaining position."[32]

Permanent Militarized Sex Markets

In the second half of the twentieth century, sexual economies and the US military grew in tandem, together becoming more or less permanent, entangled, global institutions. Freed in part by penicillin, military commanders focused less on the ways that sexual economies threatened the health and efficiency of their troops and more on how best to manage the intertwined problems of morale and foreign relations. As the military expanded its footprint globally during the Cold War, soldiers' sexual encounters regularly threatened the United States' often fragile relations with nations that hosted military installations or bore the brunt of the era's many proxy wars.[33] In the early post–World War II period, military officials banned "fraternization" with foreign women and emphasized a martial ideal of contained sexuality in line with the era's social and gender norms.[34] Increasingly, however, in conflict zones, occupations, and installations from Europe to Asia, commanders publicly declared sexual economies illicit, though military police patrolled bars and camp towns, and medical officers examined and treated sex workers. The continual movement of military personnel around the globe connected foreign and domestic markets and created new patterns of voluntary and involuntary labor migration. Even without direct regulation by military officials, sexual economies developed into integral parts of local and national economies, alongside and because of a deepening American military presence.

In postwar occupations of Japan and South Korea, military commanders officially rejected legalized sex markets, but disavowals did nothing to stop markets from booming. Immediately after the Japanese surrender in August 1945, male Japanese authorities feared that occupying troops would rape local women and so cooperated with private entrepreneurs to organize lower-class and foreign women as a "female floodwall" of sex workers to protect them. In January 1946, however, General Douglas MacArthur rejected that rationale, declaring that the abolition of licensed sex markets would free Japanese women from male chauvinism and bring democracy to Japan.[35] Again, prohibition "did not even begin to end the sale of sex," writes historian Sarah Kovner, but "merely deregulated the market in sexual services" as women continued to sell sex independently.[36]

The US military developed a similarly tenuous relationship with sex workers in South Korea. In the early days of the American presence at the end of World War II, US military officials initially regulated prostitution in an attempt to control venereal disease. Both the US and South Korean governments vacillated between official endorsement and tacit approval (though always public condemnation) of prostitution throughout the 1950s and 1960s, but camp towns of sex workers nonetheless grew at "explosive" rates, as historian Seungsook Moon has described it, "in a symbiotic relationship with US military bases."[37] The abolition of licensed sex work, in fact, bolstered the growth of private sex work, much as it had in Japan. Within nine months, the number of sex workers increased from two thousand to fifty thousand.[38] By 1956, the South Korean Ministry of Health and Social Affairs estimated that 262,000 prostitutes catered to US military personnel.[39] American officials continued to publicly denounce sex work, but they examined sex workers, distributed condoms, and advertised the rates of venereal disease at clubs near military installations.[40] Military officials also failed to enforce their prohibition of participation in the sexual economy. Although "houses of ill fame" were ostensibly off-limits to servicemen, historian Kellie Wilson-Buford

Figure 5.2. As the US military presence in Asia deepened following World War II, sex work proliferated in camp towns, despite military officials' public denouncements of the practice. Source: John Boyd Coates, Jr., ed., *Preventive Medicine in World War II, Volume V, Communicable Diseases Transmitted Through Contact or by Unknown Means* (Washington, DC: Office of the Surgeon General, Department of the Army, 1960), 330, Figure 70.

found that only three men faced charges for patronizing them in the 1950s, and they received lenient punishments. Many men faced charges for committing violence in or around brothels, but absent violence, servicemen generally faced no repercussions for purchasing sex.[41]

Sexual economies again developed in tandem with the US military presence during the Vietnam War. Although some commanders like Captain Denton openly provided prostitutes for their soldiers, most publicly disavowed but privately embraced sexual economies as a morale-boosting form of entertainment. Numerous accounts note that US medical personnel administered medical exams for women who sold sex in bars, clubs, and brothels near American bases, while military police monitored the spaces.[42] The army's Special Services R&R program sponsored one-week trips to Pacific countries, where GIs could put into practice the official and unofficial advice they had received on how to find disease-free prostitutes.[43] And, in early 1972 when morale sagged as the American forces steadily withdrew from South Vietnam, the army allowed GIs to bring Vietnamese women onto some bases after it deemed local towns off limits. The women merely needed a government identification card to gain entry, and as one official snidely remarked, the "girls are not coming on the bases to go to square dancing."[44]

By the end of the twentieth century, the US military and sexual economies were deeply entangled around the globe, hidden in plain sight. Although military officials feigned ignorance, many continued to understand servicemen's sexuality as part and parcel of military culture and addressed their institution's connection to prostitution only when it became international news, as in the late summer of 1995 when two American marines and a sailor kidnapped a twelve-year-old Okinawan girl and at least one of them raped her. The men's initial plan had been to find prostitutes, they later recounted, but the ringleader was broke and proposed finding a woman to rape instead. It seemed not to matter that he found a child.[45] A couple of months later at a breakfast meeting with reporters, a frustrated Admiral Richard C. Macke, commander of United States Pacific Command, described the rape as "absolutely stupid." He did not express anger that the men had raped a child. Instead, what he found "stupid" was the men's lack of economic sense. "For the price they paid to rent the car," he explained, "they could have had a girl."[46] Echoing the concerns of countless predecessors, Macke saw sexual economies as the solution to sexual violence.

Coming only a few years after the 1991 Tailhook scandal had focused public attention on the unseemly ways sexuality figured in military culture,

Macke's comments probably seemed even more inappropriate than they might have in years past. US government officials apologized and forced Macke to retire, but his comment exposed the callous and dismissive ways that many military commanders continued to see transactional sex and rape as two sides of the same coin. Had the men simply paid a woman to meet their sexual urges, Macke implied, they would not have raped the girl. Military officials insisted that the assault stimulated institutional contemplation, ordered a day of reflection for all military personnel on the island, and deemed red light districts catering to Americans off limits from midnight to six in the morning. The prohibition, though only a partial one, dampened business for the women who worked in districts that catered to American servicemen.[47] Although Japanese officials generally praised their longstanding relationship with the United States, the assault also sparked massive protests and threatened to undermine impending talks about the number of troops stationed on the island (twenty-nine thousand), the size of American bases, and the future of the military agreement between the two countries.[48]

Despite the wave of bad press, some US military officials continued to condone and even provide sexual markets for servicemen. In the late 1990s, for example, the army's Morale, Welfare and Recreation program organized R&R trips to Budapest for service members stationed in the Balkans. Soldiers stayed in hotels arranged for them by the army, and an MWR bus transported the soldier-tourists to sightseeing spots. One of the stops, probably not on many tourist maps, was a big house behind an iron gate called Captain Jack's. Military police and Criminal Investigation Division personnel insisted that it was not a hub of organized crime, and they monitored it while the soldiers visited. After showing their military identification, the GIs entered the first floor of the house, where they found pool tables, a bar, and a stage for female strippers. For a hundred dollars they could hire a prostitute. Soldiers could avail themselves of similar entertainment on another MWR-sponsored R&R trip to Macedonia.[49]

Although the military continued to endorse sex markets as a form of entertainment, by the late 1990s and early 2000s, the connections between sex work and human trafficking were becoming harder to ignore. International agencies, think tanks, journalists, and academics all documented that organized human trafficking networks supplied sex workers in areas near US military bases, that military contractors employed trafficked sex workers, and that networks of sex workers had migrated from US bases abroad to towns near installations in the United States.[50] In October 2005, public attention on these connections to human trafficking—importantly, not transactional sex itself—prompted President George W. Bush to order that the Uniform Code of Military Justice specifically designate the selling or purchasing of sex a crime. Military commanders had long had the authority to punish service members for patronizing sex workers, even if they seldom chose to do so, but some hoped that specifically criminalizing participation of any kind in sexual economies might finally signal the end of the military's tolerance of and complicity in prostitution.[51]

Market Power

Unfortunately, it seems that military commanders' hopes were unfounded. In recent years, journalists have documented astounding examples of ongoing military ties to sex work. In 2013, for example, a sexual assault prevention officer at Fort Hood, Texas, lured enlisted female soldiers into a prostitution ring, and in 2020 an exposé revealed an expansive system of human trafficking among navy personnel stationed in Bahrain.[52] These especially grievous examples have drawn pubic ire and sparked public outcry, but far less acknowledged or considered are the more common, everyday instances in which service members support organized sex work and human trafficking by patronizing restaurants, bars, clubs, massage parlors, and any number of businesses in camp towns, entertainment districts, and strip malls that surround military installations worldwide. The military's continued problems with prostitution are not simply the result of poor choices made by individuals but the consequences of a long history of the military's management of sexual economies. Military leaders cannot hope to confront contemporary matters of sex without considering the relationship between the US military and local economies, or the connections between sex, gender, and morale. Relatedly, military officials cannot consider the military's impacts on local economies or communities without a discussion of sex.

Militarized sexual economies reflect and, in turn, perpetuate much larger economies of power and violence. Militarized sex work depends on the physical presence of US military personnel and is therefore inextricably linked to the continued operation of military installations. That relationship exacerbates imbalanced power relationships between the US military and local authorities, as well as military personnel and the local people whose livelihoods depend on sexual economies. It severely limits local people's ability to resist labor and living conditions they oppose, prevents sex workers from finding other means of employment, and prohibits localities from developing more stable, independent economies. Moreover, this relationship gives power to criminal forces that often dictate the terms of sex work and thereby perpetuates a cycle of poverty and abuse among sex workers.[53]

The military's long relationship with sexual economies may also have contemporary legacies in institutional cultures that utilize sex as a form of entertainment, diversion, or morale and that continue to value male sexual prowess. If military culture prioritizes sexual prowess as a virtue and commercializes sexual transactions in a way that gives power to the soldier with the money and the gun, how might this relationship affect servicemen's perceptions of local people who live and work near bases, as well as their perceptions of the women with whom they serve?[54] And, although military leaders of the twentieth century failed to consider servicewomen's sexual desires as they managed sexual economies, what role might servicewomen and female sexuality have played in military cultures of the twentieth, and now the twenty-first, century?

As the military continues to struggle with an intractable problem of sexual assault and harassment, the history of militarized sexual economies may allow us to rethink the function of sexual economies in service cultures. Any connections between the history of the military's management of sexual economies and contemporary matters are enormously complex, to be sure. Disentangling these webs will not be easy, but the task is essential to better military-civilian relationships, foreign policy, and military culture.

CHAPTER 6

Building the Bases of Empire:
The US Army Corps of Engineers and Military
Construction During the Early Cold War

Gretchen Heefner

In the middle of 1952, Senators Russell B. Long (D-LA) and Wayne Morse (D-OR) took a trip around the world. From August 5 to September 15, the men covered nearly thirty thousand miles as they followed an arc from Limestone, Maine, up across the North Atlantic, through Greenland and Iceland, and then down into the United Kingdom before dropping into continental Europe. After skipping across Spain, France, and Germany, the senators moved into Northern Africa and continued east across the Saudi Arabian Peninsula. Tourists these men were not. Rather the two members of the Senate Armed Services Committee were on a fact-finding mission. Over the previous two years the US military had pushed out into the world, reoccupying and expanding wartime bases or, as was the case in Greenland and Libya, building bases anew. Long and Morse wanted to see precisely how US taxpayer dollars were being deployed: some $500 million in French Morocco, nearly half that amount in Greenland; the list went on.[1]

The price tags were astronomical, to be sure, and the senators were determined to investigate rumors of waste and excess. Was the military squandering American money? Just a few months before, their colleague, Senator Lyndon B. Johnson (D-TX), had conducted a sensational set of hearings on base construction that revealed stories of "large-scale loafing [and] drunkenness."[2] Allegedly men were sent to far-flung locations to sit idle. Johnson declared that the air bases under construction in French Morocco were a "fiasco." Bad decisions, mismanagement, and ineffective planning had led to cost overruns, construction failures, and embarrassing delays. Seeking a scapegoat, Johnson criticized not the air force but Lt. Gen. Lewis A. Pick, chief of the US Army Corps of Engineers.

Many Americans would have been surprised to discover that the Corps of Engineers was involved at all. The organization was best known for overseeing massive civil works projects at home: dams, roads, flood control, and navigation measures.[3] What were they doing abroad? International military construction was, in fact, a relatively new role for the Corps. Before World War II, the group was primarily recognized for its domestic projects. War transformed the Corps into a military construction agency. In 1941, Congress explicitly mandated that the agency take over all military construction. By June, the engineers were spending nearly $20 million each day on domestic wartime work.[4] By 1943, men of the US Army Corps of Engineers could be found all over the world fixing roads, building air bases and bridges, preparing water and communication systems, and, when it came to it, fighting the enemy.

Few people anticipated that the US military—and thus the Corps's role—would expand after the war. Most Americans hoped the country would pull back from its military obligations. That did not happen. By the late 1940s and early 1950s concerns about the emerging Cold War led to a massive remobilization as the United States committed itself to containing the Soviet Union anywhere and everywhere. The Korean War accelerated and amplified these concerns. From 14 permanent overseas bases in the 1930s to 582 in 1949, the number of US military installations abroad grew to more than 1,000 by 1956. The Corps was involved in building nearly all of them. The army engineers surveyed sites, drew blueprints, purchased land, found local workers, shuttled materials around the world, considered obstacles, and rearranged space. They also had to entice and work with US-based construction firms and contractors. All the while they encountered new environments, regulations, and people.

While there is a growing literature on the local consequences of this empire of US military bases, the construction and maintenance of these facilities has been long overlooked.[5] This chapter puts the Corps of Engineers at the center of the story of how the United States military created an infrastructure of global power during the early Cold War.[6] Of course, the Corps of Engineers rarely acted alone. Corps personnel served as middleman for a host of private and public organizations that came together to build bases. I argue here that base construction during the early Cold War created new patterns of public-private partnership and chains of economic interactions among the Corps, its prime construction contractors, subcontractors, and workers. Corps officials experimented with different types of contracts to entice US-based firms to enter these far-flung locales. In trying to decide between cost-plus-fixed-fee contracts or open-bidding arrangements, Corps personnel had to weigh speed, cost, and resources. While the military's modern reliance on private military companies was decades in the future, in the early 1950s the Corps of Engineers—working under intense pressure and often in unfamiliar locations—experimented with how to deploy the nation's private resources for national security ends.[7] These examples also highlight the ways that the US military—the only organization capable of deploying such vast resources to disparate places—provided private entities with early access to some of the world's hardest-to-reach locations.

Corps representatives did far more than encourage US firms to enter into foreign construction contracts and diverse environments. They also established expertise in managing complicated cross-cultural projects. Throughout the 1950s (and beyond) the Corps crafted best practices for construction in extreme environments and for managing diverse labor markets. Corps officers fostered relationships with foreign governments and officials. Indeed, the Corps's ability to acquire and share coveted information about host countries and markets was central to its role as middleman. While these roles were a product of the early Cold War flurry of military construction, they continued to inform international construction practices throughout the Cold War. In the 1980s, for example, the Corps's Middle Eastern District continued to broker contracts between US and international firms in Saudi Arabia, Egypt, and Israel.

Most Favored Contractors: Knowledge, Access, and Experience

In late December 1950, Lt. Gen. Pick was asked to consider the "top of the world." Would it be possible, the air force wanted to know, for the Corps to build an air base in northeastern Greenland?[8] Pick readily accepted the challenge, though privately he was not sure it could be done.[9] Building an air base in the Arctic Circle was going to be a challenge under any circumstances. Making matters more difficult that winter was the fact that Pick and the Corps had already agreed to build a number of additional air force facilities, including in Iceland, Morocco, and Libya. Adding Greenland to the list would both stretch

Corps capacities and test the limits of how much the Americans knew about building in some of the world's most extreme environments. The Korean War only added urgency to these plans; suddenly the air force wanted all of these bases operational within a matter of months. The goal was to contain the Soviet Union with a ring of bases encircling the Communist Bloc. Air force bombers stationed at these facilities could quickly make round-trip runs to their targets behind the Iron Curtain without refueling, thus deterring aggression.[10]

Such was the situation when Pick began planning for a base in Greenland. Within days of his first meeting with the air force, Pick got on the phone to marshal the vast resources of the US military establishment. He needed to accumulate all information about building an air base—enough to house four thousand men—in the Arctic Circle. He enlisted the Engineering Intelligence Division and the Army Map Service to take photos and survey the Thule area.[11] The Corps asked for copies of any and all reports and information on Greenland and cold climate construction more generally. In particular they sought reconnaissance collected during World War II. The engineers consulted explorers and experts in university and military labs and centers, asking for details and studies on building on permafrost, the operation of equipment in extreme cold, and the types of clothing one should wear. The list of questions was long: How do you ship materials to northeast Greenland? Would lubricants work in the constant cold? How could you dig down into permafrost? What sorts of foundations were needed? Did machinery even work when the temperature sank to forty below? Could morale be maintained in a place that was dark much of the year?

In establishing basic information on how to build Thule Air Base, Pick drew on a small but growing body of research being done on military operations in the climatic extremes. In the 1940s each branch of the armed services had initiated its own program for operating in the polar north, all working under the assumption that the next world war might be fought there.[12] Importantly the engineers would add significantly to this body of knowledge. Through construction programs in places like Greenland and Alaska, the Corps of Engineers conducted its own studies and drafted best practices manuals and reports that were later passed along to industry partners.

The key point is that this type of work in remote and often hostile environments required the capacity of a powerful state apparatus. No other group would have the ability or the will to undertake such an illogical and costly project. Individual agencies or companies did not have the resources. Though the implications were not immediately obvious, over the coming years important private sector industries such as aviation and oil extraction benefited enormously from the legwork done by the Corps and the US military.

In addition to relying on the expertise of the US government, Pick knew he was going to need private partners to get the job done. Unlike conditions during World War II, when entire engineering units were deployed together, the Corps no longer had thousands of enlisted men and hundreds of engineers on hand. Thus, at the top of Pick's phone list that January were the heads of US companies, such as Peter Kiewit and S. J. Groves, presidents of their eponymous construction firms. Within hours of their first in-person meeting all agreed—with more than a few reservations—to take part in what was now being called Project Blue Jay. The men agreed to quickly assemble a new joint venture, North Atlantic Constructors, made up of Peter Kiewit Sons' Co., S. J. Groves & Sons, as well as Condon-Cunningham and the Al Johnson Construction Company of Minnesota. The prime contractor was responsible for hiring and managing labor, procurement of supplies and materials, as well as building out the facility. As the Corps explored questions about terrain and materials, North Atlantic Constructors had to consider the problems of recruitment and acquisition. How and where could they locate the workforce to spend months in Greenland? How much would the men be paid? What were the tax implications of working overseas? How many months of construction were possible in a place where winter sends the mercury down to −40°F and offers twenty-four hours of darkness? What would workers wear? What if someone wanted to return home?

While North Atlantic Constructors considered the question of human capital, the firms Metcalf & Eddy and Alfred Hopkins & Associates, were brought on for engineering and design.[13] They worked with Corps officers to evaluate terrain and soil, survey sites, and plot the best locations for runways, roads, and mess halls. Corps of Engineers personnel oversaw and managed the project, including getting all of the materials and men from the United States to Greenland (using navy ships and air force planes).[14]

That contract negotiations for a multimillion-dollar government program (eventually more than $200 million) took place with preselected companies behind closed doors was not particularly surprising in 1951, though it was increasingly frowned on. It was precisely such behind-closed-doors practices that Congress had in mind in 1947 when it passed the Armed Services Procurement Act (Public Law 413). The act intended to streamline and manage acquisition across the military establishment for both "economy and national security."[15] For much of the nation's history, Corps of Engineers contracts were made on a competitive basis: engineers advertised a project, accepted sealed bids, and chose the private contractor based on price. This provided the opportunity for any and all firms to enter into government work. During World War II, the practice was seen as cumbersome and inefficient. Facilities in the United States had to be constructed quickly and in unexpected places. Cost-plus-fixed-fee (CPFF) contracts thus became the norm. Military agents (usually Corps of Engineers officers) would identify firms that would be a good fit for particular project and then enter into private negotiations for the work. The government guaranteed to pay the costs of the project while also providing for a set—or fixed—profit for the contractor.[16] While often faster and more streamlined than competitive bid contracts, CPFF had the negative effect of shifting risk to the US government and taxpayers. Contractors had little incentive to watch costs or project overruns.[17]

The 1947 act was a half-hearted effort to return procurement to the more competitive, prewar market-based system. In theory, competitive bidding was to be standard practice, though in reality the 1947 act was riven with so many exceptions that it was almost meaningless.[18] In fiscal year 1950, for example, nearly 73 percent of Department of Defense contracts were negotiated; the next year that number topped 80 percent.[19] While these numbers are for all procurement, not just construction, construction contracts for each service are represented in these numbers, not through the Corps's own accounting. Reviewing the numbers, the House Committee on Armed Services warned that the "habit of negotiation versus competitive advertised bidding is an easy one to acquire." The services had gotten so adept at it, the committee lamented, that they had basically given up on the "traditional American policy of free and open competitive bidding."[20]

Congressional worry did not trouble Pick in the winter of 1950–1951. Within a few weeks his teams were charged with building not only a massive air base in Greenland but also facilities around the world. To complete such complicated projects quickly the Corps was going to need trusted experts on the ground. Precisely as Pick was negotiating the CPFF contract with North Atlantic Constructors, his teams were engaged in similar negotiations with US-based firms for work in Morocco (Atlas Constructors), Libya (Crow-Steers-Shepherd), Saudi Arabia (Fluor Corporation). Pick and the engineers did not have time for the preferred bidding and vetting process.[21] The air force wanted functioning bases within months and so there was no time to advertise and accept bids, nor did the Corps have the specifications and plans available to distribute for potential bidders. Moreover, companies needed incentives to accept such potentially expensive jobs where the risks were nearly impossible to calculate. In January, when Pick met with the prime contractors for Thule Air Base, no one from the Corps had yet been to Greenland. The Corps admitted to that "lack of knowledge concerning the area of the job site [and] lack of information of the conditions existing at the proposed site" were important considerations when locating prime contractors.[22] Pick needed to work with companies that already had some experience in climatic extremes and had the connections and resources capable of undertaking a last-minute project of such size.

Peter Kiewit Sons' Co. was a good example of how this military-private relationship emerged. Founded in the late 1800s in Omaha, Nebraska, Kiewit got its first big break in 1939. That year the company was selected (through competitive bidding) to construct an army barracks at Fort Lewis, Washington. Their military work expanded from there. During World War II, they constructed nearly $500 million worth of facilities in the Great Plains, the Rocky Mountains, and eventually in Alaska.[23] The work transformed the company. In 1951, given the company's experience with military work *and* cold-weather construction, Pick knew it was the best possible fit for Greenland. In January 1951, North Atlantic Constructors and the Corps signed a CPFF agreement for the construction of Thule Air Base. Initially priced at $145 million, the final cost was well over $200 million. The initial contractor's fee, a set percentage of the total cost, rose accordingly.[24]

There were clearly sound reasons for the choice of CPFF contracts, but as internal Corps and Congressional reports later pointed out, there were many unintended consequences. Expense was just one. Nearly all overseas air base construction programs were significantly over budget. The bases in Morocco, for example, were $150 million over estimate by 1953.[25] Pick identified concurrency as the main problem. The air force insisted that planning, hiring, sourcing, and construction all happen at the same time rather than sequentially as normal construction protocols would suggest. Moreover, the air force frequently changed its plans and sometimes relocated facilities. Costs escalated as new materials were sent, men sat idle, or plans changed. For the Morocco base program, the prime contractors shipped equipment and supplies—including 500 generator plants, 200 earthmovers, 50 cranes and steam shovels, and 125 tractors—all before even knowing precisely where and what they were going to build. In CPFF contracts, the government bore the costs of such changes and delays. At the same time CPFF contracts created a heavy administrative burden for the Corps, whose representatives had to audit and oversee nearly all aspects of the job once started.[26] In 1953 the Corps actually revised its contract with Atlas Constructors in Morocco in order to curb excessive costs.[27] The use of CPFF contracts would come under increasing scrutiny in years to come. In fact, in the late 1970s when the Corps took on management of an air base program in Israel, initial plans for CPFF contracts were rejected in favor of competitive bidding procedures.[28]

The construction companies and contractors involved in these far-flung projects were quick to point out the risks they assumed. In the case of Project Blue Jay, Peter Kiewit and S. J. Groves insisted that it was work they did not want. Manpower, materials, and their energies would be tied up for months. The profit margin was slim. Their reputations would be grievously damaged if something went wrong. No one had ever tried to build a massive air base in the Arctic and they were certain that something could go terribly wrong. In June 1951, during another round of project negotiations, Groves exclaimed to Corps representatives, "We didn't want the job."[29]

So then why do it? The simple answer was that such work opened a path to additional contracts. Significantly, these companies acquired recession-resistant orders that provided for work even when commercial projects were hard to find. The companies acquired difficult-to-access information and experience that could be leveraged in the wider world—not just for military contracts but for private ones as well. In Greenland, for example, initial construction of Thule was just the first step in a multidecade process of building, maintaining, and expanding the military presence there. North American Constructors was guaranteed work for decades. Moreover, the individual firms gained valuable expertise and unparalleled experience in cold climates and terrain. They had access to the most up-to-date government research on these regions, which could be incorporated into their own plans and deployed around the world on other projects. Private corporate partners, then, acquired expertise from US government programs that they could channel into world-wide projects as a particularly American export. As scholars have shown, by the 1970s, US expertise was a highly lucrative global commodity.[30] Less under-stood is how much that expertise depended on US government largesse and on how early this set of relationships began to form.

Thus the benefits of military construction work went far beyond dol-lar signs. In 1958, for example, Kiewit was awarded a $5 million army con-tract to build Alaska's first nuclear reactor. In 1959, Kiewit crews and North Atlantic Constructors constructed two radar stations on the Greenland ice cap (a $13 million Defense Department contract). And so on. The projects in Greenland demonstrate the ways that military construction created new sorts of business relations and incentives. While postwar global military construction contracts might not offer tremendous financial reward, they did offer a *guaranteed* financial reward, as well as knowledge and experience in a rapidly expanding global setting in which the military would be operating for decades to come.

Building Bases: Men, Materials, and Local Conditions

In early 1951, the ads started appearing in newspapers across the Upper Midwest: "Construction Engineers, Construction Superintendents" needed for "work outside the Continental Limits of the United States in a Very Cold Climate." In the largest type of all: "TOP SALARIES."[31] Another ad explained that if a man between twenty-seven and fifty could answer three questions with a "yes," a job was his: "Can you take cold weather?" Are you "Ready for a long trip?" And, "Do you want quick or big money?"[32] Tens of thousands of men replied in the affirmative. Harold "Oakie" Priebe, a construction supervisor, admitted that when he applied all he knew of the job was that it had a high "wage scale and that it would be cold." He figured the job would be in Canada. Others guessed Korea.[33]

These were hardly the only military construction jobs being advertised in early 1951.[34] Work was scheduled to begin on five air bases in French Morocco that April.[35] Still more work was to be done in Libya, Saudi Arabia, Alaska, Iceland, and elsewhere. Not all of these projects required the same type and concentration of workers, of course, but in all cases Corps representatives and contractors had to carefully consider both the cost and the politics of labor at home and abroad. To be sure the general idea was to keep labor costs as low as possible, but the politics of recruitment and hiring often made that difficult to achieve. Take the question of skilled labor and craftsmen. For most overseas military projects skilled craftsmen were hired in the United States for two reasons: many of the places where the United States was building bases lacked skilled labor, and domestic political and labor leaders demanded that Americans be hired for such jobs, particularly because these jobs paid so well.[36] But wherever possible the US government hoped to hire local low-skilled workers to fill out the bulk of the construction crews, both to keep costs down and to appease host-country political and economic concerns. Countries accepting a US military base generally wanted the spillover benefits of having local people employed. In many places—such as Iceland and Libya—US engineers and contractors provided training and expertise for local laborers who until then had lacked such opportunities. In these ways local communities could materially benefit from the deployment of US forces.

Corps representatives had to manage these competing demands and expectations. Making matters even more difficult, no two places were the same. Totally different labor regimes were needed for projects in Greenland, Morocco, and Iceland. Everything and everyone had to be shipped to Greenland, more than five thousand men in all. In Morocco construction agents had to manage a patchwork of workers ranging from imported skilled labor from the United States to local French and Moroccan wage workers.[37] Stark divisions between local Arabs and French colonial personnel added difficulty to the task. So, too, in Libya, where the district engineer, Lt. Col. Paul D. Troxler, and his engineers had to manage a mix of local Arabs, Italians, refugees, and immigrants who came to Tripoli precisely to seek employment from the US military. The inflationary tendencies of US wages also weighed heavily on Corps officers and local governments.[38] Troxler spent a fair amount of time dealing with this in Libya, as did Corps representatives in Iceland. US military construction paid more than two times what local Icelandic projects paid. At the same time, officials in Reykjavik expressed concerns about how the importation of foreign labor could harm Iceland's culture. The minister for foreign affairs acknowledged the desire to avoid "endangering" "Icelandic nationality and national culture . . . by a long sojourn of a great number of foreigners."[39]

Even once the idiosyncrasies of hiring and wage scales were taken care of, managing local labor practices proved challenging. In Saudi Arabia, Troxler noted that construction work slowed nearly to a stop during the month of Ramadan. At other times heat and misunderstandings could be deadly. A Corps report noted that many local Saudi workers had taken to finding shade under machinery to avoid the sweltering sun, only to be crushed when the vehicles were used again. Local dress, too, led to new sets of problems as skirt-like wraps and tied turbans could get caught in machinery. Contractors had to cover gears and belts to avoid injury.[40]

The process of hiring workers at home was fraught as well. In early 1951, it seemed that dozens of overseas military construction programs were trying to draw from the same spring labor market, already busy with domestic construction programs. The question of how, then, to recruit top-notch labor for overseas construction had a relatively simple immediate answer with somewhat unintended long-term consequences: high wages. North Atlantic Constructors understood right away that to get the best people signed on for work in an undisclosed location, they had to offer top salaries and do so quickly. The urgency of the Thule program—combined with the logistical and financial power of the US government—meant that they were able to do so. In contrast, the Moroccan base program lagged. Atlas Constructors did not start recruitment until the spring of 1951, too late to tap into the best of seasonal labor markets. Many of men interested in overseas work had already taken jobs with other outfits, including for Project Blue Jay. Nowhere in the documentary record is there any indication that the Corps itself was concerned with the ways its own contracts could work against one another.

Harold Priebe, a construction supervisor, was one of the men hired that winter. He first heard about the Greenland project when half of his work crew in California stopped showing up in early 1951. They had left the dam project and gone to Bakersfield to follow up on rumors of high pay. Workers for Blue Jay were being promised nearly $2,000 a month (roughly $18,000 today). In Minnesota, where much of the recruitment and training for Blue Jay was centralized, carpenters made $2.12 per hour; on Blue Jay they would make $3.70. That topped even the pay scale for Alaska, which was around $3.14, or pay for work in North Africa, which averaged out to $2.45.[41] Negotiations between North Atlantic Constructors and the Corps of Engineers outlined seventy-hour workweeks (with overtime rates paid for work beyond 40 hours) without recognition of holidays or weekends. After all, one engineer mused, was it even possible "to identify a Saturday and a Sunday and holidays . . . in the North Pole?"[42] Most labor contracts were for the four months of the Arctic construction season. Priebe, like his coworkers, followed the money.

There was nothing unusual about construction workers following seasonal projects. Priebe in many ways is emblematic of the pool of labor available for projects at home and abroad. In the 1930s he fled Oklahoma and the dustbowl (thus his nickname) and, as he said, "hoboed" to California seeking work. He became a water boy on a Kaiser project and moved up from there, following the next major dam or construction project anywhere the work took him. By the late 1930s and through World War II, military construction was the most lucrative market and that is where Priebe found himself. While there was some contraction after the war, by the early 1950s base construction was picking up. Priebe followed the job ads for Blue Jay to Rosemont, Minnesota, where he was trained and fingerprinted, then to Westover Air Force Base in Massachusetts before taking a string of flights to Thule.[43] He returned every year for nearly a decade, earning the moniker "Thule old-timer" in the base newsletter.[44]

North Atlantic Constructors justified the high wages because of the distance and the short duration, hardship, and urgency of the work. Moreover, the Corps of Engineers and North Atlantic Constructors wanted to hire only the most competent people. The stakes were high: in 1950 nearly 30 percent of men sent overseas to work on base construction were sent home. (Congressional hearings identified "drunkenness," "lack of experience or skill," and outright "homesickness" for the high return rate).[45] The costs to the US government were considerable. North Atlantic Constructors and the Corps intended to avoid this problem and so they implemented a number of rigorous screening and training procedures. North Atlantic Constructors partnered with the Minnesota State Employment Agency to advertise for and vet applicants, most of whom were expected to come from the Upper Midwest, where cold weather construction was a reality. Men were vetted, trained, and tested before being hired. In the end five thousand of the twenty-five thousand men screened were hired; nearly 90 percent proved their worth on the job.[46]

Many workers did not share Priebe's positive overseas construction experience. Complaints by workers at far-flung construction sites filtered home. In June 1951 Congressman John F. Kennedy (D-MA) wrote directly to Pick demanding to know why men were being sent to Greenland without proper attire and were living in subpar housing facilities (the men were, indeed, being housed in Atwell tents until proper buildings could be constructed).[47] Priebe acknowledged a shortage of food in the early months of his work up north.[48] A 1952 Senate hearing, *Hiring for Work at Overseas Bases*, went into greater detail about the list of problems, ranging from contract violations to what Senator Johnson declared was "actual victimization."[49] The alleged misconduct included contractors refusing to pay for return trips home, subpar living conditions, and unreasonable finder's fees for work contracts. James H. Dillon, the president of the Construction Men's Association, an organization devoted to providing information and resources to men wanting overseas work, appeared before Congress and explained that many men felt their contracts were not being honored: promises of sixty-plus hours a week had turned into days spent idle, doing nothing and getting paid nothing while they sweltered in North Africa.[50]

If underpaid workers did not quite ignite the passions of congressional leaders, the whiff of malfeasance certainly did. Examples of men using military construction work as a conduit for "tourist junketing" circulated, as did stories of men so homesick they would not stay.[51] The Senate Subcommittee on Preparedness found that nearly 25 percent of workers sent to Morocco returned home before their contract was up. Drunkenness was widespread.[52] Senator Johnson declared it all added up to "a million dollars down the drain."[53]

There was more. Senators accused the Corps and its contracting partners of negligence in surveying sites, improperly planning for materials, and making errors in basic construction. The partial collapse of one of Morocco's runways was held up as proof. Worse yet, materials that had been shipped across the Atlantic were sitting idle in Casablanca. In 1952 it was discovered that some 27 million board feet of lumber had been shipped to Morocco but remained unused. The justification was that plans had shifted so rapidly that acquisition could not be stopped. Yet the notion of Washington State pine moldering on the shores of Casablanca infuriated congressmen.[54] Indeed, everywhere they looked in the early 1950s, congressional committees seemed to find mismanagement of resources in overseas base construction. In one instance senators discovered a pipeline in Morocco that led nowhere.[55] This is why Senator Johnson called for Pick's censure in 1952.[56]

The criticisms overlooked the reality on the ground in many parts of the world where Corps engineers were managing massive military projects with a keen eye toward fiscal responsibility. In many cases the Corps provided political cover for private companies. The criticism also masked the creativity of Corps officials. Indeed, in Libya and Saudi Arabia, Troxler was going out of his way to marshal local resources and repurpose unused surplus whenever possible. For example, realizing that the traditional wooden barracks of US military bases were not particularly practical in the desert—because of both local resources and local labor capabilities—Troxler adopted the practice of using the masonry, tile, and stone seen in the small houses scattered around Tripoli. The savings were considerable. Troxler reported that using masonry to construct a three-story airman's dormitory rather than wood saved nearly $100,000 per unit.[57]

The infusion of American dollars and wages into local economies was significant.[58] Military construction often became an economic magnet, sucking men and materials toward American projects. The construction of Wheelus Air Base in Libya demonstrates the powerful effect US military construction could have on a local economy, not only in terms of hiring local workers but also in spillover effects from having so many Americans living in the region. Americans spent money, they rented rooms, and the Corps upgraded roads, ports, and more. Libya had been decimated by World War II and was only slowly rebuilding and moving toward independence. Its economy was in shambles. As the lead US diplomat to Libya, Henry S. Villard, admitted in 1952, without US military spending, "Libya could not hope to exist as an economic unit."[59] So powerful was the draw of US defense dollars and opportunity that men came from hundreds of miles away seeking work. In Tripoli, a British district commissioner reported that by the spring of 1951 men were lining up outside of his office asking for a job "anywhere in the U.S.A. unit." Troxler estimated that Libyans received between 90 and 250 Libyan Lira per day of work (roughly 55 cents to $1.40 per day), a small fortune in local terms.[60]

In most cases it was the Corps of Engineers that mediated and administered these local interactions and realities. In the Middle East and North Africa, Troxler's office worked between the prime contractor for Wheelus, Crow-Steers-Shepherd, and local subcontractors and labor groups.[61] Troxler and his office purchased land and negotiated leases, mapped terrain, and determined best practices for working in the region. The engineers also had to intervene when local and American regulations collided. For example, in June 1951, Troxler needed to get competitive bidding regulations waived for native firms. Troxler admitted that "the entire concept of renegotiation is foreign to [the Libyan] system of jurisprudence and business practices." So when the Americans advertised for local companies to bid on work, no one submitted.[62] The same story played out in Morocco, where the French government refused to participate in competitive bidding.[63] In the end Troxler was able to waive protocol so that local firms could be hired without providing bids or estimates. Between 1951 and 1956—the peak years of construction—148 local subcontractors were used in Libya.[64]

Not that these tasks were without difficulty. Troxler was an astute critic of military construction practices from within. His reports to Corps headquarters are full of suggestions for how to make things more efficient, from using local practices and materials, to sharing materials and ideas across regional engineering divisions (for example, materials from Libya could be copied in Saudi Arabia), to the problems of labor and expertise. Troxler was particularly concerned that the United States simply did not have the personnel at home required for the overseas work he understood would continue throughout the 1950s, not just for bases but for infrastructure and development projects as well. He recognized that it was hard to hire good, skilled workers and engineers, partly because of a lack of interest, perhaps, but also because there was so much construction going on at home. Moreover, there was a general lack of expertise and knowledge about international construction work. "The expanding interests of the US on a global basis," he wrote, "require that a large segment of its construction industry be versed in the problems peculiar to overseas work."[65]

Troxler's reports highlight the ways that the Corps of Engineers sat at the center of a set of relationships that redefined markets and exchange. Not only did Troxler have to encourage US firms to enter into international construction work, but he also had to manage individual projects around the world. The two were related in that the Corps could use its established expertise in a specific location to entice US-based firms to enter. Importantly, the Corps and the US military provided their unprecedented logistical network to private firms and individuals. By agreeing to manage contrasting views of contracts and work, massaging labor needs and compensation, and smoothing over cross-cultural differences that could quickly lead to conflict, the Corps served as a vital sponsor and middleman as US construction expanded around the world. Indeed, recognizing the near certainty of overseas work, Troxler continued to press for new ways of thinking about the Corps's role. Given that no two places had precisely the same conditions, Troxler insisted that the Corps of Engineers needed more autonomy in making quick decisions on the ground about the appropriate allocation of resources, substitutions, and labor practices. He was advocating not for privatization of such overseas military functions but for a more nimble engineering agency that could adapt and move fluidly around as needed.

Corps reports and retrospectives from later years suggest that not all of Troxler's ideas were implemented. Problems of labor, resources, and contracting continued to bedevil Corps personnel, who remained deployed around the world throughout the twentieth century. In fact, the Middle East District seemed to experience the same sorts of conflicts and irritations throughout the 1970s and 1980s as the Corps did in the 1950s. The details are less important here than the overall story: once the Corps moved overseas to take on a management role for US construction firms—first for the US military and then for other projects as well—it never returned home. In fact, in the 1970s the Corps started managing projects *for* foreign governments, in this case programs for the Royal Saudi Navy and the Saudi Arabian National Guard.[66] By the late 1970s the Corps of Engineers was engaged in overseeing billions of dollars of construction work in Saudi Arabia. According to internal reports, the "district engineer had direct, often face-to-face contact with the Saudi ministers."[67] Serving as a center of expertise, logistical capacity, and know-how was vital in encouraging the expansion of US construction work overseas, even when it was no longer for the US government.

CHAPTER 7

Militarized Circuits: Kang Ki Dong, the US Military, and the Rise of Global High Tech

Patrick Chung

Kang Ki Dong's mind raced as he traversed the corridors of Motorola's facilities in Phoenix, Arizona.[1] Kang was a manager in the company's semiconductor division, then one of the world's leading producers of transistors and
integrated circuits (ICs). A few days before, Kang had been called into a
meeting by his supervisor with little warning or explanation, prompting fears
of being fired or even sent back to his native South Korea. At the meeting,
however, he was greeted by two US Air Force officers, who explained that
his expertise was needed for the top-secret Minuteman defense program. It
was 1965, three years since the first Minuteman ICBMs became operational.
Recent intelligence suggested that the Soviet Union had developed counter-
measures that could disable the circuitry of existing US missiles.[2] The air
force officers asked Kang to help develop radiation-hardened chips for use in
missiles.[3] Over the following months, Kang contributed his expertise to the
air force's far-reaching research and development (R&D) program that would
culminate in the unveiling of the Minuteman II ICBMs.[4]

For Kang, the Minuteman project was part of a lifelong relationship with
the US military. His interest in technology was sparked by the surplus electronics and educational reforms brought to South Korea by the US military
following World War II. As he sought further opportunities in the United
States, Kang and his research benefitted from US military largesse during
the Cold War arms race. With the know-how and connections developed

working for US military–backed academic and corporate institutions, Kang decided to start a company that would capitalize on the growing demand for semiconductors, produced by an industry with longstanding ties to the US military. Kang founded Korea Semiconductor Corporation (KSC), the first company in South Korea capable of producing its own advanced semiconductor devices.[5] KSC ran into financial difficulties as US military cutbacks and the oil crisis depressed the global economy during the 1970s. Facing bankruptcy, Kang sold his company to the Samsung Corporation. With the aid of Kang's expertise, Samsung made substantial technological advancements and became one of the world's most successful companies.[6]

Kang's story helps to reframe the history of global high-technology (high-tech) industries, from the perspective of the developing world.[7] Popular accounts have lionized the innovations of Silicon Valley firms and the entrepreneurial drive of their founders, while glossing over the central role of the US military in developing both cutting-edge technologies and the transnational production processes behind the transformation of high tech from a niche to a global industry.[8] Scholars of Cold War science and technology have made a compelling case for understanding the US high-tech industry as an outgrowth of what Stuart Leslie calls the "military-industrial-academic" complex.[9] A rich body of literature has demonstrated how military R&D programs supported the development of semiconductor technology, which enabled the rise of personal electronics by replacing cumbersome vacuum tubes with miniature silicon chips.[10] The US military's desire for high performance and reliable technology was a catalyst for many key innovations: from germanium point-contact and junction transistors during the late 1940s to diffused silicon transistors in the late 1950s to mesa and then planar IC chips during the 1960s.[11]

While existing studies have done much to explain the US military's contribution to the domestic semiconductor industry, they have paid less attention to its global dimensions. As historian Hyungsub Choi argues in his study of the US and Japanese semiconductor industries, "the full story becomes comprehensible only when we transpose the local and the global, by attending more to the local responses than to global forces."[12] Yet even Choi's focus on the United States and Japan does not fully explain how developing countries like South Korea became key sites of semiconductor production. Studies that have considered Korea specifically have focused on the actions taken by the Park Chung Hee government or *chaebŏls* (Korean conglomerates) like Samsung starting in the 1970s, when South Korea began its economic takeoff.[13]

These works fail to do enough to acknowledge the fact that the US military provided a key precondition for the success of South Korea's high-tech industry: the training of skilled engineers and workers like Kang Ki Dong.[14]

In tracing Kang's story, this chapter situates the rise of Korean high-tech industries within the longer history of US-led militarization of the Korean peninsula since World War II. It argues that the US military influenced the development of high-tech industries *on* both sides of the Pacific *from* both sides of the Pacific. During the early Cold War, US capital and expertise remade the South Korean education system. US foreign assistance programs emphasized technical education to develop the human capital necessary first for South Korea's rehabilitation and then for its economic development; such efforts provided opportunities for students like Kang to study and work at leading US research universities and corporations. These international students contributed their labor and expertise to the US Cold War military-industrial complex, taking part in crucial defense projects like the Minuteman ICBM project. By the 1970s, the circulation of men and women like Kang around the Pacific allowed US high-tech firms to open offshore assembly plants and form the transnational supply chains that enable the mass consumption of advanced electronics. In some cases, they established firms like KSC that promoted the growth of high-tech industries and Silicon Valleys around the world.[15]

The chapter begins with a discussion of Kang's time as a schoolchild in Korea in the aftermath of World War II, moves on to his participation as a student and engineer in the United States at the height of the Cold War, and concludes with his efforts to build a start-up as South Korea was about to take off during the age of globalization. Ultimately, these vignettes from Kang's life provide a lens for understanding the complex and evolving role of the US military in the transpacific dispersal of technologies, personnel, and capital that undergird the post–Cold War knowledge economy.

Black Markets and Ham Radio

Kang Ki Dong learned from an early age that warfare and opportunity went hand in hand. Kang was born in Japanese-occupied Korea on December 9, 1934. After studying agriculture at the Imperial University in Tokyo, Kang's father returned to Korea shortly before Japan's invasion of Manchuria (in 1937) to work for the colonial government. In exchange for ensuring the steady flow of rice to the Japanese Imperial Army, the elder Kang was able to provide a life of relative comfort for his family.[16] With the defeat of the Japanese and Korea's liberation in 1945, Kang and his family lost their privileged place in society. They were forced to flee their home in Daegu during the October Uprisings, a peasant revolt against policies of the newly installed US Army Military Government in Korea (USAMGIK).[17] The Kang family ultimately resettled in Seoul, headquarters of USAMGIK, where, just as his father had with the Japanese military, Kang Ki Dong would find educational and financial opportunity with the US military.

Like most Koreans, the young Kang experienced US military occupation most directly through consumer goods. The US military maintained posts and bases in much of the noncommunist world. To feed and house their far-flung troops, US military logisticians oversaw the flow of US consumer products around the world.[18] Few places were as bereft of such comforts as Korea, where Japanese colonial rule (1910–1945) had systematically drained the peninsula of resources. The establishment of USAMGIK provided a much-needed lifeline for Koreans; US troops not only bought but also provided goods and services. With enterprising servicemen often serving as conduits, goods flowed from army bases to black markets that emerged around US military bases.[19] Most Koreans bought necessities like rice, clothing, and medicines. However, luxury goods and the latest technological gadgets were available to those with the money and inclination.

Surplus military electronics sparked Kang's lifelong passion for electronics. As a middle school student in Seoul, Kang scoured the junk shops that sold second-hand US military electronics near the Chŏnggyechŏn, a stream that flowed in the center of the city.[20] Under USAMGIK, the area became the center of black market activities in Seoul where peddlers sold all manner of US goods.[21] Kang recalled saving and scrimping to buy spare radio parts as well as second-hand textbooks and magazines, all of which could invariably be traced back to the US military. During the tumult of the Korean War (1950–1953), Kang found solace and inspiration in black market US military electronics. Kang and his family fled Seoul after the North Korean army captured the city in the summer of 1950. They settled for a time near the K2 military base, from which Kang obtained a copy of *QST*, the magazine of the American Radio Relay League (the official ham radio organization in the United States).[22] He spent hours poring over technical details in the magazine. Over the course of the war, he became hooked by the feeling of connection and being on the technological cutting edge that ham radio provided.[23]

In ham radio, Kang found entry into a worldwide fraternity with a passion for technology and with a close association with the US military-industrial complex. Popularized after its use by militaries during World War I, ham radio allowed civilians to utilize and master state-of-the-art technology.[24] Like Kang, many "hams" spent hours collecting parts and tinkering.[25] Often more than mere hobbyists, ham radio operators in the United States frequently worked in the fields of radio communication or electrical engineering, both closely tied to the US military.[26] And as historian Christophe Lécuyer argues, ham radio enthusiasts were a valuable source of engineering talent for early Silicon Valley tech firms competing for military contracts.[27] Like his US counterparts, Kang started with an interest in ham radio and ended up pursuing formal study of electrical engineering, enrolling at South Korea's premier university, Seoul National University (SNU), at the end of the Korean War in 1954.

SNU brought Kang more closely into the orbit of the US military. Unlike black markets and second-hand magazines, the South Korean education system was planned and capitalized by USAMGIK. With the aim of removing the vestiges of Japanese colonial rule, education advisors and experts were brought in from the United States to modernize South Korea's schools, starting with its universities; SNU was established by USAMGIK in 1945 to serve as the country's flagship university.[28] Despite these efforts, the attitudes of USAMGIK officials prevented a complete overhaul of the colonial-era system. Like their Japanese predecessors, USAMGIK officials' racialized worldviews led them to deem Koreans incapable of engaging in advanced sciences and technology.[29] They concluded that skilled technicians and laborers rather than researchers and academics would best achieve US objectives in Korea. Proposals by Korean scientists to enhance the country's research capabilities were largely ignored. The situation was such that several prominent researchers left South Korean universities, including some who went to North Korea.[30]

The Korean War brought increased US investment in South Korean universities, though the change was quantitative and not qualitative. The country's educational facilities were in ruins by the end of combat in 1953.[31] It was only through the support of the US military and foreign assistance programs that Korean universities were able to hold classes and maintain laboratories. It is estimated that SNU's Engineering College lost 85 percent of its laboratory equipment during the conflict.[32] Between 1954 and 1967, the United States invested more than $30 million on education in South Korea.[33] Reflective of the immediate needs of reconstruction, US assistance programs targeted technical fields that would produce engineers, technicians, and skilled work-ers. As a result, US assistance programs in science and engineering did not emphasize innovation and instead focused on basic competency and voca-tional training.

Ambitious students like Kang bristled at the limitations of South Korea's educational system. Electrical engineering students at SNU recalled their department was more akin to a technical school than a true research univer-sity, focusing on practical applications like power generation rather than the more advanced research being conducted in the United States.[34] Kang recalled his disappointment at the lack of faculty expertise in emerging technologies. He recalled that his attempts to discuss the interworking of shortwave radios and transistors were met with blank stares by professors.[35] Frustrated, Kang shifted his attention away from classes to running the nation's first ham radio organization, the Korean Amateur Radio League.[36] In his senior year, Kang prepared to study abroad in the United States, where he could join those on the leading edge of technological change.

Despite its limitations, SNU provided a suitable launching pad for Kang. With the help of SNU professors and classmates, he was able to secure a stu-dent visa to pursue graduate studies in the United States. Kang's study in the United States was facilitated by an educational initiative funded by the US Mutual Security Program. Conceived by the US Foreign Operations Admin-istration, a partnership between SNU and the University of Minnesota was established with the aim of improving the technical education at SNU.[37] Pro-gram funding supported the improvement of SNU's facilities and educational exchanges of faculty between the two universities. By 1959, 80 percent of SNU's engineering faculty had had a period of study in the United States.[38] On their return, exchange scholars were to bring back the latest scientific and pedagogical techniques to Korea.[39] Further, the personal connections estab-lished by US-trained professors helped facilitate the migration of promising Korean students to the United States.

Kang's early life and education highlight the diffuse but omnipresent impact of the US military around the world following World War II. Cast-off parts and secondhand magazines from US military bases led Kang to ham radio, a passion that would lead to study in laboratories and classrooms funded by US defense dollars, first in South Korea and then in the United States. Despite the vast cultural and economic differences, Kang would find a common thread between Korean and US universities: the central role of US military funding.

Missiles and Microchips

Kang began graduate studies in the United States at a fortuitous time. Shortly before his arrival, the 1957 launch of Sputnik sent shockwaves across the world.[40] Opponents of the administration of President Dwight D. Eisenhower claimed Sputnik was evidence of Soviet technological superiority and proclaimed the existence of a "missile gap." While the Eisenhower administration denied these accusations publicly, it inaugurated increased federal spending on R&D with goal of ensuring US technological superiority.[41] The Kennedy administration went even further and upped R&D spending by military programs to more than 10 percent of the US federal budget.[42] Among the leading recipients of increased R&D funds were major research universities like Ohio State University (OSU), where Kang and a generation of international students became part of the US military-industrial-academic complex.

While overshadowed by the likes of Stanford and MIT, OSU fit the mold of a "cold war university."[43] OSU's relationship with the US military predated the Cold War. The OSU Research Foundation was founded in 1936 to coordinate contracted research. The foundation saw a huge uptick in government contracts during World War II, when departments ranging from physics to geography contributed research to the war effort.[44] During the postwar period, OSU continued to court US military funding. Located an hour away from Wright-Patterson Air Force Base, OSU maintained particularly close ties to the air force.[45] Air force personnel regularly attended classes at OSU and collaborated with OSU faculty.[46]

OSU became a center of semiconductor research due to its relationship with the air force. In 1946, the air force awarded the electrical engineering department a $230,000 grant to conduct research on "special electron tubes" (i.e., vacuum tubes).[47] The funds underwrote the construction in 1948 of the Electron Devices Laboratory, which would later become a center for semiconductor research under the direction of Marlin O. Thurston. Thurston served in the army and the air force before earning a PhD in electrical engineering from OSU.[48] After graduating he taught at the Air Force Institute of Technology at Wright-Patterson before joining OSU's electrical engineering department. Despite Thurston's ties to the air force, it was the Army Signal Corps that was his primary source of funding during the 1950s and 1960s.[49] Historians have emphasized the role of the Signal Corps in semiconductor research, because of its policy of knowledge sharing. Signal Corps R&D contracts related to semiconductor research during this era called for "the wide dissemination of technical reports." Recipients were required to share information and take part in government-sponsored conferences and symposia in order to accelerate the pace of innovation.[50] Through a series of Signal Corps contracts, Thurston and his graduate students conducted research related to the production of semiconductors. Among Thurston's earliest graduate students was Kang Ki Dong, who worked under Thurston between 1958 and 1962.

Throughout the early Cold War, the US military set the agenda for semiconductor research. The Department of Defense ICBM program and NASA's Apollo program were two of the largest sources of federal R&D funds, and both invested heavily in the development of smaller and more dependable electrical components. Through World War II, electrical systems depended on vacuum tubes to manipulate the flow of electricity. In vacuum tubes, electrons flow through a sealed compartment that is too fragile and difficult to miniaturize for military purposes. During the 1950s, all three military service branches began to replace vacuum tubes in their electrical systems with semiconductor transistors and later with IC chips.[51] Transistors were solid pieces of metal and thus could be made smaller and more resistant to shock and heat—a critical requirement for intercontinental or space rockets.[52] Government funding for semiconductor research nearly doubled between 1955 and 1961.[53] Under Thurston, Kang's research at OSU evolved in lockstep with US military demand for semiconductors.

Kang's research addressed an increasingly important aspect in semiconductor production, the manipulation of semiconductor surfaces. Kang's dissertation research examined the impact of oxidation and gas diffusion on silicon surfaces.[54] His work was related to recent breakthroughs at Fairchild Semiconductor, the pioneering Silicon Valley firm. In 1958, a year into Kang's PhD studies, Fairchild's Jean Hoerni developed a new process for producing silicon transistors.[55] Hoerni's method involved creating a single silicon crystal with both positively and negatively charged regions through the introduction of dopants via gas diffusion ("doping"); discretely charged regions are formed by rendering parts of the silicon surface inert via oxidation ("oxide masking") during the doping process. Kang was fully aware of the larger developments in the field. He began his dissertation by making an explicit connection between his work and the advance of semiconductor research, stating that his work addressed "one of the most important considerations in the transistor or diode fabrication technology."[56] Kang's dissertation and later research focused largely on the manipulation of silicon "surface states" during the production of semiconductors.

Working for Thurston opened doors for Kang—providing not only an entry into the field of semiconductor production but also a valuable introduction to the US military contracting system. After a strong performance in his second-year qualifying exams, Kang was invited to join Thurston's newly established semiconductor lab, funded by the Signal Corps.[57] As the first member of the lab, Kang became its de facto head; his responsibilities included hiring and recruiting members, buying equipment, and presenting finds. During his final years at OSU, he regularly submitted reports to the Signal Corps and presented the lab's findings to various military and corporate officials.[58] As a result, by the time of his graduation in 1962, Kang received numerous job offers from leading firms like IBM, General Electric, and Motorola.[59] Not only an expert in the science of semiconductors, he was also versed in the practical aspects of producing them and had already navigated the bureaucratic hurdles involved in working with the industry's most important customer, the US military.

Far from unique, Kang was part of a cohort of international scientists and engineers that contributed to the early development of semiconductor research. During the 1950s, the US government passed a series of reforms to immigration law that provided opportunities for foreign students and workers with science and engineering backgrounds.[60] The flow of foreign students studying science and engineering increased steadily.[61] Among the first wave of student immigrants were several key figures in the development of semiconductor research, including Dawon Kahng. In many ways, Kahng provided a path forward for Kang and other Korean electrical engineers. Born three years before Kang, Kahng graduated from the same high school and college as Kang in Korea. In the United States, he also attended OSU and studied under Thurston. Like Kang, Kahng specialized in silicon surface oxidation and gas diffusion.[62] Following graduation, Kahng collaborated with Mohamed Atalla, another foreign-born researcher, to produce the first field-effect transistor at Bell Laboratories in 1959.[63] Known as MOSFET (metal-oxide-semiconductor field-effect transistor), the new technology eased the fabrication of complex ICs and enabled the mass production of ICs.

The parallel paths of Kang Ki Dong and Dawon Kahng were no coincidence.[64] They highlight the networked nature of foreign study fostered by the US military over the course of the Cold War. With its admission requirements and empowerment of primary advisors, graduate study in the United States was open only to a select few from around the world—students at elite universities that employed professors with connections to US universities.[65] In Kang's case, he could access the contacts of his SNU professors who studied in the United States as well as fellow SNU alumni to navigate the US academic system.[66] Throughout his graduate studies and then his career in private industry, Kang would continue to draw on the connections and collaborations enabled by the US military. In fact, these networks would enable immigrants like Kang to play a key role in the globalization of semiconductor production during the 1970s, when high-tech firms sought out offshoring opportunities in the Pacific.

Consumption and Production

In 1967, *Home Furnishings Daily* proclaimed the "discovery" of South Korea by the US electronics industry. Noting the country's abundant supply of cheap labor, the trade magazine for home goods predicted that the Korean manufacturers would soon challenge more established competitors in Taiwan and Hong Kong.[67] That such analysis was coming from an outlet focused on consumer sales reflected shifts in the market for semiconductor devices. As semiconductor-powered electronics became ubiquitous in US households, manufacturers invested more in the production of cheaper, mass-market devices. Kang Ki Dong's career path was determined by the larger shifts in the semiconductor industry during the 1960s and 1970s. His career began at Motorola, where he focused on military projects. As the industry shifted toward mass production for the consumer market, Kang helped facilitate Motorola's offshoring of production to Korea. These experiences ultimately led Kang to start his own company. Thus, tracing Kang's path toward the founding of KSC in 1972 provides a lens with which to understand broader shifts in the semiconductor industry: from military to civilian consumption and from national to global production.

Military work was the focus of Kang's labors when he started at Motorola. Kang took a position as a manager at Motorola's newly expanded semiconductor production facility in Phoenix in 1962.[68] At the time, producing germanium transistors for the US military was a big part of Motorola's business.[69] The company's ties to the military went back to World War II, when it supplied the army with two-way radios (walkie-talkies), the development of which was spearheaded by Motorola's head of research, Dan Noble.[70] The company continued to aggressively seek out military contracts following the war. Going beyond theoretical research, Kang plied his expertise in overseeing the actual production of semiconductors.[71] His efforts paid immediate dividends for the company.

During Kang's time at Motorola, the company became a leader in the production of semiconductors for both military and commercial markets. He joined the company as it was transitioning away from producing germanium to silicon transistors.[72] Before his arrival, Motorola had struggled to implement the range of processes involved in the production of diffused silicon IC chips.[73] One of Kang's first assignments was to set up a manufacturing line for silicon devices like the ones he produced at OSU. Kang's early work at Motorola helped produce a more efficient method for producing PNP silicon transistors.[74] The company's 1963 annual report predicted that the "new process" would give Motorola a "leadership position" in the market for PNP transistors.[75] During subsequent years, Motorola successfully gained market share in silicon transistors and IC chips in the United States. Testifying to his critical role in Motorola's success, Kang was among the select few engineers asked by the air force to contribute to the Minuteman project.[76]

Kang's heritage became an asset as semiconductor production moved abroad. Kang was among a growing but still small number of Asian employees of US semiconductor firms as semiconductor production began to take hold in Asia during the 1960s. Motorola began seriously investigating the possibility of opening a semiconductor assembly plant in Asia in 1966.[77] The next year, Lester Hogan, the head of Motorola's Semiconductor Division, asked Kang to accompany him on a fact-finding mission to Asia as a cultural ambassador.[78] At the time, US semiconductor manufacturers were only beginning to seek out opportunities to build production facilities in developing countries. Previously, offshore plants were built in developed countries as a way to enter foreign markets.[79] Motorola ultimately chose South Korea because of its cheap workforce and the government's eagerness for foreign investment. Kang took the lead role in meetings with Korean government officials and businessmen to clarify the terms of Motorola's investment.[80] The company eventually received approval for a plan to commit $7.5 million for the manufacture of IC chips in a factory outside of Seoul.[81] Motorola Korea, a wholly owned subsidiary of Motorola, commenced operations in 1968 and was the country's largest electronics company by 1972.[82]

Motorola's decision to offshore production was part of an industrywide trend toward the production of cheaper consumer products. During the 1950s, the US military was the primary consumer of semiconductors. As a result, manufacturers focused on producing cutting-edge, high-cost products that met exacting military specifications.[83] The previous reliable military market began to deteriorate during the mid-1960s. Cutbacks in military R&D

spending, coupled with the proliferation of semiconductor producers, led enterprising firms like Fairchild and National Semiconductor to shift their attention away from the military to the consumer market.[84] Unlike military officials, civilians did not demand the state of the art and prioritized afford-ability. To cater to regular consumers, semiconductor manufacturers sought ways to lower costs. Industry executives turned their eyes overseas to places in Korea, where local governments subsidized foreign investment and labor was educated and cheap.[85]

In addition to Motorola, eight other US firms opened plants in South Korea during the late 1960s.[86] At the time, Korean line workers were the second-lowest paid in Asia, and Korean engineers were the lowest paid in Asia.[87] Lower labor costs enabled Motorola and other companies to meet the growing demand for its products while also dramatically lowering the price on its products. Between 1964 and 1972, the price for silicon transistors and ICs dropped sixfold and seventeenfold, respectively [88]

The US military played an indirect but critical role in South Korea's emer-gence as a semiconductor production hub. More than merely cheap labor, South Korean workers were highly educated and technologically competent. As US firms moved into the country, they drew on the science and engi-neering students who had benefited from the US military's investment in the country's educational system during the 1950s. At the same time, the South Korean government used US defense assistance funds to establish a series of science and technology R&D institutes staffed by repatriated Korean immi-grants who had settled in the United States and Europe.[89] The investments of US firms and the South Korean government built on the transnational flows of expertise initiated by the US military. The engineers and scientists who provided expertise as well as the technicians and skilled workers who pro-vided the manpower in Korea's emerging high-tech sector bore the imprint of US military investments in education on both sides of the Pacific.

While many of his compatriots chose to join government institutes or established corporations on returning to Korea, Kang decided to start his own semiconductor production company. Foreign investment did little to advance the technological capabilities of South Korean firms. Like Motorola, US firms established assembly facilities in Korea and other developing countries but few advanced production facilities with R&D capabilities.[90] Until the late 1960s, Korean electronics firms all assembled foreign-made parts.[91] None of these firms was capable of producing the latest semiconductor devices until Kang established KSC.[92] The company was backed by an array of contacts

Kang had made over the previous decade, including former classmates from SNU and contacts he established during his time in the United States.[93]

KSC was the only Korean firm on the cutting edge of the semiconductor industry. On October 4, 1974, KSC celebrated the opening of the most advanced semiconductor manufacturing plant in the country. The new plant was capable of producing IC chips using the same complementary metal-oxide semiconductor (CMOS) large-scale integration technology as leading semiconductor firms in the United States and Japan.[94] First developed by Fairchild and several of the companies it spawned, CMOS circuits were notable for extremely low power usage, which made it useful for portable devices like digital watches. It was only a few years earlier when Jean Hoerni produced the first mass-production CMOS circuit for the Japanese watchmaker Seiko.[95] Kang's grasp of CMOS technology was a huge asset and put the company ahead of its competitors, including Samsung Electronics.[96]

Despite its technological advantage, KSC would ultimately be doomed by a lack of investment capital. The company ran into financial difficulties almost immediately due to the oil shocks and subsequent pullback in the market for semiconductors during the mid-1970s. As a result, Kang decided to sell a majority stake in his company to Samsung Electronics in December 1974, a mere two months after opening KSC's plant.[97] At the time, the company's semiconductor division was less than a decade old and was far behind foreign competitors. It primarily assembled components produced by more advanced Japanese and American firms because it lacked the know-how to design and produce them. What Samsung did have was capital, which it used to exploit KSC's financial situation. Initially, Kang was allowed to continue overseeing KSC while sharing his knowledge with Samsung engineers. Under Kang, KSC achieved its greatest success, the production of a CMOS chip for use in digital watches sold by Samsung.[98]

While the CMOS chip was a huge milestone, and a financial success, it was not enough to save Kang. He left the company in 1976 after Samsung executives made clear he had no future there. He returned to the United States and was on the outside looking in as Samsung capitalized on the operational infrastructure he established and the skilled workers he helped train. Samsung became a leader in the production of memory chips during the 1980s and then the production of consumer electronics for the world market during the 1990s.[99] Kang concluded in a 2002 interview, decades removed from his time in the semiconductor industry, "Basically, [Samsung] got the semiconductor operation for nothing. . . . Otherwise, they may have had to pay hundreds or [a] hundred million dollars [sic] to reach that particular stage."[100]

What insights can be gleaned from Kang's assessment? Kang's claims about the monetary value of KSC's technology are not unfounded. In the decade following the KSC acquisition, Samsung and Korea's three other major semiconductor producers (Goldstar, Hyundai, and Daewoo) spent more than a million dollars on the importation and development of semiconductor technology.[101] At the same, KSC was only one of the sources of technology that fueled Samsung's success.[102] Silicon Valley firms continued to provide investment and technological transfers. US-trained engineers and scientists continued to staff the country's corporate and government labs. Notably, the channels by which new technology entered South Korea were the same transnational pathways established by the US military and traversed by Kang. Thus, while his ultimate contribution to Samsung is impossible to gauge accurately, Kang's life nevertheless is a testament to the impact the US military has on the global high-tech industry through its patronage and development of technological expertise.

Conclusion

In February 1983, Lee Byung-chul boldly declared that his company, the Samsung Corporation, would become the world leader in the production of cutting-edge very large-scale integration (VLSI) semiconductors.[103] Most within the electronics industry scoffed. By the end of the decade, however, the company had made substantial technological advancements and, consequently, considerable gains in the market for semiconductors and the products they power. Fulfilling Lee's promise, Samsung became the world's largest supplier of semiconductors in 2017.[104] More than that, the company is now one of the largest and most successful companies in the world. This chapter has shown that Samsung's unlikely transformation was part of a longer history of the US military and its contribution to the development of high-tech expertise in the Pacific.

Kang Ki Dong's life highlights the diverse ways in which the US military shaped the market for technological expertise over the course of the Cold War. Kang's interests, education, and professional trajectory were shaped directly by the global expansion of the US military after World War II and during the long Cold War. His early life and education were inextricably tied to the presence of the US military in South Korea. In particular, his experience "tinkering" with surplus US military parts led him to ham radio—a passion that then led him to study electrical engineering at SNU, using equipment provided by US military assistance programs. Following his arrival in the

United States, Kang learned and worked in an endless series of classrooms, meeting rooms, laboratories, and assembly plants funded by the US military buildup following Sputnik. From Ohio State to Motorola, Kang's professional experiences in the United States were driven by the military's demand for advanced electronics. Finally, Kang's attempts to produce semiconductors in South Korea would not have been possible without global dispersal of technologies, personnel, and capital initiated by the US military.

The contrasting fates of Kang and Samsung bring to mind President Eisenhower's farewell address. In warning the public of the dangers of the military-industrial complex, he observed that "the solitary inventor, tinkering in his shop, has been overshadowed by task forces of scientists in laboratories and test fields."[105] The demise of KSC, like so much of Kang's career, was a result of structural changes enacted, albeit indirectly, by the US military. The semiconductor industry's shift toward commercial production was sparked by the pullback in US military procurement in response to the Vietnam War.[106] The collapse in the military market had widespread consequences including a shift toward more flexible, transnational production. Within such a system, a solitary tinkerer like Kang was doomed to fail, while better-capitalized firms like Samsung were much more likely to succeed, and succeed on a large scale. Ultimately, Kang's story highlights the critical role that the US military played in the formation of today's global market for high-tech products. Through its deployment and demand for new technologies and its multifaceted engagements with technical experts, the US military established the ground rules by which success and failure are achieved.

More broadly, Kang's story suggests the utility of understanding the Cold War military-industrial complex as a global technopolitical system. Gabrielle Hecht defines "technopolitics" as the "strategic practice of designing or using technology to enact political goals."[107] In a variety of roles and contexts—from ham radio enthusiast to foreign PhD student, and from Motorola to a small start-up in a developing country—Kang was subject to the US military's imposition and promotion of technology both in the United States and abroad. At the same time, Kang was not without agency. Technology became a means through which Kang, as an individual, crisscrossed the globe in pursuit of education, employment, and economic opportunity. Similarly, on a larger scale, technology allowed nations like South Korea and companies like Samsung to make a place for themselves in a global economy dominated by richer and more powerful competitors.

CHAPTER 8

"Don't Discuss Jobs Outside This Room": Reconsidering Military Keynesianism in the 1970s

Timothy Barker

Ever since World War II ended the Great Depression, Americans have worried that their prosperity rested on military spending. But in February 1974, against the backdrop of the deepest recession since the 1930s, Secretary of Defense James R. Schlesinger stated the case with unusual bluntness. Schlesinger told the House Appropriations Committee "that there is an element of economic stimulus in this budget. I think that is sound economic policy."[1] This statement, reported in the *New York Times* under the headline "Military Budget Spurs Economy," echoed from the bulletin of Americans for Democratic Action to the newsletter of First National City Bank.[2] As late as 1982, Schlesinger's "excess of candor" was being cited in Congress as evidence of the economic origins of rising defense budgets.[3] The remark remains one of the most open articulations of military Keynesianism in American history.

Readers may have encountered the concept "military Keynesianism," but what exactly is it? We might distinguish two senses. First, take the following sentence from a US government publication: "It is generally agreed that the greatly enlarged public sector since World War II, resulting from heavy defense expenditures, has provided additional protection against depressions, since this sector is not responsive to contraction in the private sector and provides a sort of buffer or balance wheel in the economy."[4] This refers to a *functional* effect: military spending has tended to stabilize the economy over a period of decades, regardless of anyone's intentions.

In contrast, consider President Dwight D. Eisenhower's directive to "consider a stepped-up program of military production if something were needed to prime the pump."[5] This exemplifies the *instrumental* use of military spending to address specific economic problems (when Eisenhower spoke in February 1954, unemployment was nearly double what it had been six months earlier). Both the functional and instrumental examples share an underlying economic theory: a capitalist economy left to its own devices does not automatically generate the level of aggregate demand required for full employment of people and resources. This points to a corresponding political idea: the economy can be stabilized by government demand creation. When military spending is a large component of demand, as in the post–World War II United States, we can speak of military Keynesianism.

How is military Keynesianism different from more familiar terms? This is a question of historical specificity. For thousands of years, societies have chosen how to allocate resources between military or civilian purposes—swords and plowshares, guns and butter. The terms "garrison state" and "permanent war economy" were coined during the 1940s, but militarized societies existed long before.[6] State finance and large-scale military production have been combined throughout history: early "military-industrial complexes" include the Roman *fabricae* and the Venetian Arsenal.[7] By contrast, Keynesianism—military or otherwise—is a recent phenomenon.[8] Only in the 1920s and 1930s did governments come to regard "the economy" as something they could measure and manipulate.[9] This new way of thinking corresponded to institutional developments. The problems that Keynes attacked—idle industrial capacity, the business cycle (as distinct from climatic and agricultural rhythms), even unemployment in the modern sense—emerged from the history of late-nineteenth-century capitalism.[10] Likewise, Keynesian solutions— setting interest rates, adjusting taxes, and spending on a large scale—required forms of state capacity that had not always existed but had to be achieved historically.

The term "military Keynesianism" has been used by historical actors, most of them social critics and social scientists.[11] But leaving aside the exact phrase, the phenomenon has been discussed far more widely. Keynes himself described the coming of war as a test of his proposals, while Franklin Roosevelt welcomed military orders as a means to prosperity.[12] For workers, the planned wartime economy could be "an experience of opportunity rather than limitation," while unionists pointed to high wartime production to support arguments for increased purchasing power.[13] Conservatives invoked the specter of a "military WPA."[14] Investors skimming the business press read about "military pump priming" while government economists calculated its effects.[15] By the early 1950s, Americans of all kinds felt that the defense budget dominated economic outcomes and described this effect in terms borrowed from Keynes and the New Deal.

Despite the ubiquity of these discussions, historians of the United States have often mentioned military Keynesianism only in passing. Instead, the history of the post–New Deal political economy has been framed around the displacement of New Dealish "social Keynesianism" by a "commercial Keynesianism" centered on personal consumption, tax cuts, and suburban development.[16] Historians of the 1970s have focused their attention on the breakdown of an ostensible Keynesian consensus—a story in which military spending appears (if at all) as an off-stage source of economic problems.[17] Aspects of the militarized economy have received attention in other subfields. Scholars of American foreign relations have shown how investment bankers and Keynesian economists collaborated on the crucial planning memo NSC-68.[18] Historians of the New Right have interpreted the Sunbelt as a spatial legacy of military spending.[19] Social scientists outside of history departments have carefully calculated correlations between military spending and economic variables.[20]

Despite their insights, these literatures offer only a partial view of post-1945 American capitalism. A focus on commercial Keynesianism, for example, obscures the fact that aerospace, not auto, was the United States' largest manufacturing employer for much of the 1950s and all of the 1960s.[21] For all we now know about NSC-68 and Orange County, there has been little work on military Keynesianism after 1950 or outside of the Sunbelt.[22] Meanwhile, the historical literature on the 1970s has not offered a clear explanation of the causes and consequences of the decade's crisis. Even historians attuned to political economy rely on simple dichotomies: from "age of compression" to "age of inequality," the "great exception" versus the "Reagan restoration," "managed capitalism" against "laissez-faire."[23] In different ways, these schemas both overstate and understate historical continuity. On the one hand, neoliberalism is misleadingly conflated with distant predecessors ("inequality" and "laissez-faire" evoke the Gilded Age; "restoration" speaks for itself). On the other, the blunt distinctions sever the connective tissue that organically links neoliberalism to the midcentury mixed economy.[24]

In the usual narrative of the 1970s transition, two Republican presidents face each other across a chasm. Richard Nixon, the "last New Deal president," practiced a form of big government intervention that Reagan laid to rest.[25] According to a leading scholar of the New Deal order, Nixon wanted to "manage capitalism's growth in the public interest," while Reagan "unfettered" capitalism and sought to "eliminate" the federal government. In this account, both Eisenhower and Nixon were Keynesians, but no subsequent Republican has been.[26]

This chapter offers a different interpretation of the 1970s transition through a study of Richard Nixon's practice of military Keynesianism. The available sources from the Nixon administration reveal candid discussions of the economic uses of the defense budget.

In one discussion of military stimulus, Nixon warned his subordinates, "Don't discuss jobs outside this room. . . . Don't write any memos on this," an order which suggests that many of the discussions that might shed light on the history of military Keynesianism left no trace.[27] The traces Nixon did leave help us understand that the first half of the 1970s was the beginning of an era as much as the end of one. Far from representing the last gasp of a previously consensual Keynesianism, Nixon in fact invented a new Republican style of crudely instrumental deficit spending, an orientation that set him apart from predecessors like Eisenhower and linked him directly to successors like Reagan.

Throughout this transition, capitalism was not "unfettered" but managed in new ways, to new ends. Neoliberalism entailed not anarchy but the use of the state to create certain kinds of markets and protect them from certain political claims.[28] In this regard, it was not entirely different from the New Deal order, which also deployed new forms of state capacity to set rules for new markets and secure the conditions for private enterprise to flourish. As Amy Offner has written, neoliberalism "remade societies not by inverting their every feature but by extinguishing a few of their defining elements and breathing new life into others."[29] To understand how, there is no better place to look than the largest government program in history: the American military.

From Eisenhower to Nixon, 1948–1968

The history of military Keynesianism starts with the Cold War rearmament that took off after 1948. World War II had provided a powerful object lesson in full employment, but every important sector in American society was initially eager to drastically reduce military spending. This was seen as essential to fight inflation, expand consumer production, and—depending on your politics—fund tax cuts or new social programs. Well into 1950, President Harry S. Truman wanted to balance the budget by limiting annual defense spending to $13 billion. Within three years, the defense budget would be four times that size, partly financed by deficits. This transformation, like the World War II mobilization, rested on military emergency rather than economic consensus.[30]

President Eisenhower repeatedly tried to balance the budget by trimming defense. Historians who emphasize Eisenhower's embrace of the New Deal paradigm obscure his often pre-Keynesian fiscal politics. After the recession of 1958, the American economy operated well below capacity for years: unemployment did not return to its pre-1958 low until November 1965.[31] This stagnation was the result of a deliberate policy of restraint. Eisenhower was proud to achieve a budget surplus in 1960, at the cost of the third recession in six years. President John F. Kennedy, who inherited 7 percent unemployment, found himself struggling against the "mythologies" of the balanced budget.[32] Truman and Eisenhower alike opposed Kennedy's proposed tax cut on the grounds that it would enlarge the deficit.[33] Only after the "first Keynesian president" was assassinated did his stimulus plans become politically viable.[34]

Nobody understood Eisenhower's fiscal reticence better than Richard Nixon, who blamed his loss to Kennedy in 1960 on Eisenhower's refusal to accelerate defense spending.[35] But even though Nixon recognized the short-term benefits of defense stimulus (as even Eisenhower did, on other occasions) he remained wary of more ambitious plans. Nixon dismissed Kennedy–Johnson growthmanship as a "misguided crash program."[36] In 1968, his campaign literature drew the analogy—despised by Keynesians—between household budgets and government finances.[37] Still, his advisors noted his intense feelings about the 1960 defeat and predicted he would respond energetically to rising unemployment.[38]

Containing Inflation, 1969–1970

Nixon inherited an overheated boom and a war that had already cost $40 billion or $50 billion.[39] As prices rose and profits fell, business leaders and Republican politicians sought to restore stability, even at the cost of recession.[40] But the unemployment problem was more explosive than ever, given the recent wave of urban revolts. Any downturn would disproportionally hurt black workers.[41] Liberals and social movements wanted to plow the post-Vietnam "peace dividend" into antipoverty programs.[42] But even conservatives like Nixon worried that unemployment might make the cities ungovernable.[43]

In theory, warfare and welfare could expand together. But there were limits: tax increases were unpopular, while deficits threatened domestic price stability and international confidence in the dollar. The dollar problem reached crisis proportions in 1968, when rapid gold outflows forced President Lyndon B. Johnson to limit the further escalation of the Vietnam War.[44] As inflation continued into 1969, Federal Reserve chairman William M. Martin tightened money and credit, limiting the possibility of expansion.[45] The stage was set for conflict over the level and composition of government spending.

On taking power, Nixon decided to attack inflation through deficit reduction. Since "two-thirds of all controllable outlays in the budget are Defense outlays," this would require significant defense cuts.[46] Further pressure came from an increasingly antimilitarist Congress.[47] Nixon also used his veto to slash social spending.[48] For the last time until 1998, the federal budget showed a surplus. Between December 1969 and December 1970, unemployment jumped from 3.5 percent to 6 percent, the highest in almost a decade.[49] Like Eisenhower, Nixon was balancing the budget to cool off a Democratic war boom.

Goosing the Economy, 1970–1973

As recession set in, Nixon slyly suggested that unemployment was preferable to military Keynesianism. "What was wrong with 1968 and 1967? We had full employment. But at what cost? 300 Americans dead every week," he told the AFL-CIO.[50] Liberals found the implication disconcertingly reminiscent of Marxism.[51] By early 1970, Nixon realized the recession had gone farther than anticipated.[52] He began to ask his staff about stimulus.[53] As the midterm elections approached, Defense Secretary Melvin Laird argued internally that stepped-up procurement would increase employment as well as security.[54]

On November 3, 1970, Democrats held the Senate and picked up twelve House seats. Nixon pivoted. On November 9, Deputy Defense Secretary David Packard told a room full of defense and budget officials that "We should not cut down on items that affect the economy."[55] A few hours later, two participants in that meeting—National Security Advisor Henry Kissinger and Director of the Office of Management and Budget George Shultz—spoke on the phone about "pumping up [defense] expenditures to help the economy." Kissinger worried that "It proves every argument of every critic of society."[56] On November 11, Nixon told John Ehrlichman that "the economy must *boom* beginning July 1972."[57] Kissinger (despite his misgivings) asked military planners to identify programs to "serve as a means of economic pump priming."[58] The FY1972 budget (formulated in 1970–1971) marked "a significant turning point" away from post-Vietnam cuts, with total obligational authority jumping $4 billion from the previous fiscal year.[59]

Within the administration, an economic rationale for the defense hike had emerged. The crucial point, Laird argued, was that "Defense spending in the durable goods area will generate more lasting benefits to the health of the economy" than "transfer payments."[60] Packard similarly stressed the impact of defense on "the capital goods and research and development sectors—both of which are currently depressed."[61] In addition to antiwelfare ideology, these statements reflected an institutional reality. Transfer payments did not translate directly into business activity, but orders for military goods immediately activated the economy's industrial core. Government support for those volatile sectors might keep a slowdown from becoming a depression.

The preference for hardware over human beings applied within the defense budget as well. Laird distinguished procurement from "manpower-related costs," and Kissinger explained to Shultz that increasing military pay "does not help the economy" the way durable goods would.[62] Nixon became obsessed with cutting manpower. In 1968, personnel costs had taken up 41.8 percent of defense outlays, a figure that had reached 50.9 percent by 1971.[63] But Kissinger believed that Nixon's zeal was "not really budgetary" but reflected an ideological desire to thin the ranks of government employees.[64] Hardware procurement could lend state support to the economy while increasing the weight of the private sector.

In January 1971, Nixon came out as "a Keynesian in economics," which meant he would not balance the budget until full employment was achieved.[65] The administration's fiscal conservatives—Robert Mayo of Budget, David Kennedy of Treasury, and Paul McCracken of the Council of Economic Advisors (CEA)—departed. Their replacements were more enthusiastic about expansion.[66] The lodestar was the new treasury secretary, John Connally, a Texas Democrat whom Nixon called his "closest political adviser."[67] Connally, whose enthusiasm for tariffs scandalized northeastern Republicans, was equally frank about defense. This became clear in a debate with Senator William Proxmire (D-WI) about whether the government should save Lockheed from bankruptcy. When Proxmire protested Lockheed's poor production record, Connally asked, "What do we care whether they perform?" The real "rationale and justification" for the bailout was to "provide employment for 31,000 people throughout the country at a time when we desperately need that type of employment."[68]

The crisis in aerospace, of which Lockheed was just one victim, was another influence on Nixon's expansionist turn. As the Vietnam War wound down and commercial sales flagged, the industry faced severe problems with costs, performance, and indebtedness.[69] In Seattle, 62,000 Boeing jobs evaporated, generating 13 percent unemployment in 1971.[70] In Southern California, newspapers worried that "state unemployment compensation" would "not support . . . the way of life most engineers and scientists have adopted."[71] Nationwide, the industry shed 187,000 workers between 1968 and 1970, accounting for 38 percent of all manufacturing jobs lost in that period.[72] Lockheed also exemplified a pattern of escalating financial instability that now threatened major corporations beyond aerospace.[73]

Nixon, an Orange County native, had stocked his White House with aerospace insiders and raised incalculable sums from aerospace firms over more than two decades.[74] But even someone without these personal ties might have rescued this core sector. Even in the crisis year of 1971, aerospace generated 9.1 percent of durable goods employment and almost 10 percent of merchandise exports.[75] Fed officials worried that "the general financial situation could deteriorate as the result of problems in the aerospace industry."[76] In a phrase already heard in the 1970s, Lockheed was too big to fail.[77] Nixon's behind-the-scenes favors were just as significant. In December 1971, Kissinger reported that Packard and Nixon wanted an extra billion dollars to procure "politically essential" F-111 aircraft from Texas and California (by comparison, the Lockheed loan was only $250 million). When Shultz complained that the F-111 was useless, Kissinger reiterated that "the President's motives are entirely political."[78]

With the Apollo space program winding down, space interests sought support for a new shuttle. Nixon, who believed that "unemployment numbers" in "battleground states" gave "the space program . . . an importance out of proportion to its budget," announced the shuttle program in January 1972.[79] *Aviation Week* took the occasion to celebrate the president's shifting economic priorities. At first, Nixon had "gutted both the space program and defense as a means of accomplishing his initial goal of deflating the economy." But since mid-1971, "a new set of economic advisers" had steered him toward

Figure 8.1. President Richard Nixon with NASA Director James Fletcher on the day of the space shuttle announcement, January 5, 1972. Source: Richard Nixon Library via the National Archives, National Archives Identifier 27580097, https://catalog .archives.gov/id/27580097.

"economic stimulus."[80] While "the spectre of unemployment still stalks many areas," the editorial concluded, "a decision such as the space shuttle contract is more eloquent than any campaign speech."[81]

Federal Reserve chair Arthur Burns confided to his journal that "the President will do anything to be reelected."[82] But personal political gain was not the only reason Nixon and Burns rethought their economics. Rising unemployment had not ended inflation. A deeper recession might have worked, but this risked triggering civil disorder and financial collapse. In November 1970, Burns had diagnosed "an entirely new problem—namely, a sizable inflation in the midst of recession . . . new medicine is needed for the new illness."[83] The illness was "stagflation," the combination of rising prices and unemployment that would define the decade.[84] The medicine was the "Nixon shock" of August 1971, when Connally's Treasury Department stopped exchanging dollars for gold. The effect on the exchange rate, combined with an import surcharge, boosted American manufacturing.[85] Just as dramatically, Nixon froze wages and prices. The controls—the first in "peacetime" history—would continue in some form into 1974.[86]

With controls in place, Nixon believed he could pursue growth without inflation. CEA chair Herb Stein recalled one January 1972 meeting in which Nixon told his cabinet that "whereas he has regularly in the past urged them to be economical in their expenditures he was now urging them to get out and spend."[87] When Burns realized the budget "was much less stimulative than raw figures suggested," he urged Nixon to require regular progress reports on accelerated spending.[88] Nixon then told Haldeman he was "concerned that [Defense officials] aren't using the purchasing power we have to get the economy moving," and wanted "to really put the heat on them to force them to do it."[89] According to Stein, the Pentagon did more than any other department "to carry out the President's expansionist policy for the first half of 1972."[90]

Nixon was attracted to military Keynesianism for ideological as well as practical reasons. He believed that "To goose the economy, the private sector is the best place. In government the best place is the military, because it helps the country." By contrast, "public service jobs—that means nothing to the country."[91] By "helping the country," Nixon meant in part that defense spending purchased national security and international prestige. He was anxious that the United States had "become a second-rate power in defense."[92] Among other threats, he feared Soviet nuclear parity, the self-assertion of the Third World, and export competition from other industrial capitalist countries.[93]

Behind all this was a vague but heartfelt commitment to keeping America great. During Nixon's unsuccessful fight to save Boeing's proposed supersonic transit (SST) plane, Nixon said he was "utterly convinced that if we do not go ahead with this dramatic breakthrough, this nation will have lost its feel for greatness."[94] Since SST was ostensibly a civilian project, this showed Nixon's interest in industrial policy was not exclusively militarist. But SST fit with his other ideological commitments. As Boeing executives emphasized, the ultimate plan was to "get the program back out of the Government and into private enterprise."[95] Aerospace spending directed profits and employment through private channels. Conversely, Nixon believed that welfare "stagnates enterprise and perpetuates dependency."[96] It weakened the relationship between income and employment, a concern reflected in Nixon's efforts to deny striking workers access to unemployment insurance.[97] The increase of social spending as a share of national income threatened to crowd out private spending and defense capabilities. Nixon complained constantly about critics who would have America "get out of the world" in order "to clean up the ghettos."[98]

Nixon was not the only one with this set of views. In 1972, General Electric executive Jack S. Parker contrasted "unproductive" transfer payments with "productive" defense spending, which contributed directly to business activity.[99] Jerry Whipple, a United Auto Workers (UAW) official, dismissed proposals to build "houses instead of bombers." His members were proud to build the B-1 "for the good of the country," but they "can't have pride in making low-cost housing, when the low-income families just use them for putting garbage in the hall."[100] For both the corporate executive and the labor leader, military Keynesianism reconciled a commitment to existing structures of property and power with the recognition that the economy did not always take care of itself.

The size of this prodefense constituency was confirmed in Nixon's landslide reelection in 1972. His opponent, Democrat George McGovern, proposed reducing the defense budget by almost one-third to fund new social spending, including a guaranteed income.[101] Nixon seized on this as a weakness. House Republicans, aided by Laird's assistant William J. Baroody, Jr., circulated detailed reports on potential defense unemployment.[102] Campaign strategists proposed leaflets warning that "If McGovern wins, Los Angeles will have an unemployment rate that will match Seattle's and Southern California will be the West Virginia of the seventies." Another idea was to send fake hippies to protest at defense plants with signs reading, "The MIC is Thru in '72. Vote McGovern."[103]

These attacks complemented Nixon's outreach to organized labor.[104] The AFL-CIO did not endorse anyone in 1972, but its top leadership detested McGovern and tacitly supported Nixon. Unions had been a key constituency for military Keynesianism since the late 1940s.[105] Many unionists were ideological anticommunists, but the economic benefits were no secret. One union head welcomed the invasion of Cambodia by saying, "The effect of our war . . . is to keep the economic pipeline loaded with a turnover of dollars because people are employed manufacturing the things of war."[106] AFL-CIO chief George Meany (an old friend of Laird's) advised Nixon that "some people are talking about [defense] in terms of jobs . . . our people know jobs are involved—you don't have to tell them."[107] Pollsters found workers who told them that "our economy needs a war. Defense spending should be increased to make more jobs for people."[108]

As Vietnam became Nixon's war instead of Johnson's, liberal union leaders like the UAW's Walter Reuther finally came out as doves. Reuther's successor, Leonard Woodcock, backed McGovern.[109] But even the UAW was split. In 1972, members of the struggling aerospace locals deposed progressive West Coast UAW director Paul Schrade. As one worker said, "He's for the S.D.S. and against defense and we're for defense."[110] Schrade's successor, Jerry Whipple, called the B-1 bomber "a very necessary jobs program."[111] In November 1972, Nixon won 54 percent of the union vote—twenty-five points higher than his 1968 performance, though still below his 1972 popular vote margin.[112]

For Nixon, "blue-collar" meant white men.[113] Military dollars built bridges to Southern Democrats and facilitated racially differentiated stimulus. Kevin Phillips, an architect of the Southern strategy, also emphasized the potential of "the vast Southwestern Military-Industrial Complex."[114] Nixon kept an obsolete army base open because "they [Louisiana Democrats] are indispensable to us."[115] Meanwhile, urban military bases that provided employment for African Americans were closed.[116] The aerospace bailouts benefited workers who skewed white.[117] Veteran activist Bayard Rustin protested that jobless African Americans were told not to "be so particular" but no one told "the unemployed aerospace engineer ... to hire out as a dishwasher."[118] By November 1972, white unemployment had fallen to 4.7 percent, which was roughly the administration's definition of full employment.[119] The figure for black workers was 10 percent, a level white Americans had not seen since the Depression.[120]

Stop and Go, 1973–1976

Safely reelected, Nixon announced that "instead of operating primarily as a stimulus, the budget must now guard against inflation."[121] He returned to budget cutting, but defense was mostly spared. In late 1973, recession came once more and Nixon resumed his military Keynesianism. In December 1973, as Schlesinger admitted to Congress, billions were added to the defense budget as stimulus. Schlesinger's candor drew attention, but few seemed surprised by the practice itself. Michael Levy, a Conference Board economist, found it "not necessarily a bad way of priming the pump." Charles Schultze (later head of Jimmy Carter's CEA) worried only that the stimulus might be mistimed.[122]

In fact, Nixon and his aides discussed the problem of timing. At the December 1973 meetings, budget director (and major defense contractor) Roy Ash told Nixon, "We need to spend on things that have maximum impact on the economy in the short term" and estimated that a supplemental defense appropriation in January would hit in the summer.[123] When Nixon asked US Army Chief of Staff Creighton Abrams how to spend money so that it "would affect production," the general quickly answered, "Tanks."[124] Compared to welfare programs, much defense spending authority was discretionary, allowing for the sort of manipulation George Shultz once described: "We can move the outlays down by a billion and a half to two billion or we can move them up just by sheer outlay management."[125]

These were technical questions. Newly elected senator Joseph Biden (D-DE) had normative objections. Provoked by Schlesinger, he proposed an amendment clarifying that "it is not a proper function of the Department of Defense, in determining the amount of the budget for that department for any fiscal year, to make allowances for amounts needed to help stimulate or otherwise effect a change in the domestic economy."[126] Senator John Tower (R-TX) allowed that defense should not be contrived solely for economic reasons but reminded his colleagues, "The fact is that defense spending is an economic stimulus in various areas of the country." Tower asked Biden to clarify that his amendment was not intended to prohibit "legitimately needed military expenditure" that also happened to serve as stimulus. With this stipulated, even the Pentagon "had no objection" to the amendment.[127] The difficulty of identifying "pure" stimulus made it hard to outlaw military Keynesianism.

As unemployment rose to 9 percent, Congressional antimilitarism receded. One Hill staffer reported, "prospects of higher unemployment make increased defense spending particularly attractive" in 1974.[128] The next year, the *Wall Street Journal* reported that the Ford administration believed "the current recession may protect much of the military budget from deep cuts."[129] In 1976, Congress reversed its post-Vietnam practice of cutting Pentagon proposals, instead adding billions to the request.[130] Just as defense spending put a floor under the business cycle, the business cycle now put a floor under defense spending. New justifications, stressing the balance of trade or productivity gains, were found to fit the new crisis.[131] A decade of record-breaking defense budgets had begun.

Conclusion: Keynesianism After the New Deal Order

Historians view the 1970s as a hinge in modern American history. The decade divides welfarist consensus from an austere age of fracture, the New Deal order from the New Right. A key set piece in this narrative is the eclipse of Keynesianism, which fell into disrepute for its failure to explain stagflation and thus gave way to the new market fundamentalism articulated by Milton Friedman, promoted by business, and implemented by Reagan.

The 1970s was indeed a pivotal decade, and a frustrating one. But the 1970s malaise did not kill the practice of demand management.[132] Nixon's discovery of stagflation in 1970 did not discredit Keynesianism but motivated his turn toward stimulus. Unlike in the 1930s, historically unprecedented deficits continued through the mid-1970s, stopping the downturn from becoming a depression. Right-wing economists were ascendant, but those who made it to the White House still acknowledged Keynes's "diagnosis of recessions and depressions . . . the foundation of modern macroeconomics."[133]

After the brief Carter interlude, military Keynesianism flourished as record deficits drove the Reagan economic expansion.[134] In 1972, Reagan had defended Nixon's embrace of Keynes, asserting that no president could "shut off spending by the world's biggest buyer of goods & services (the US govt.) without risking a full scale depression."[135] Reagan's defense secretary, Caspar Weinberger, trumpeted the job-creating effects of defense, an appeal he had learned working against McGovern.[136] The tradition stretched forward to Dick Cheney, the Nixon staffer who later said, "Reagan proved deficits don't matter."[137] Donald Rumsfeld, who succeeded James Schlesinger in 1975, returned to the Pentagon during the 2001 recession and quickly asked for a list of defense items "that would be helpful in terms of jobs and stimulus."[138] In 2008, Reagan CEA chair Martin Feldstein argued that "Defense Spending Would Be Great Stimulus."[139]

Nixonian economic activism was plainly cynical. The practice was at odds with the economic theories espoused by the ascendant conservative movement. Does such opportunism have anything to do with Keynesianism proper? The term is appropriate for two reasons. First, no actual policy has ever been "purely" Keynesian. The New Economics of the 1960s was also shaped by instrumental considerations and justified by a theory (the neoclassical synthesis) that Keynes would not have recognized as his own.[140] Historians have cataloged the slips between theory and implementation, but few would deny that the Kennedy–Johnson program was somehow "Keynesian."[141]

Second, even conservative rationalizations retained distinct Keynesian elements. James Schlesinger studied with Alvin Hansen, published professionally on Keynes, and justified himself to Congress by pointing them to "the macroeconomic literature."[142] Some Nixon officials just spent like crazy, but others made technical estimates of how much spending would create "a deficit just about fitting the economy."[143] US Air Force General Robert Pursley, who was completing six years at the Pentagon in the role of military assistant to the secretary of defense, wrote to Laird, "As long as we are below full employment, a deficit can have positive effects."[144] Generals have always sought more resources, but Pursley's language crystallizes a much more specific way of seeing the economy. Likewise, Caspar Weinberger cited specific multiplier effects ("35,000 more jobs for every extra $1 billion you spend on national defense"). Weinberger's calculations were derived from an econometric model designed by Lawrence Klein, author of *The Keynesian Revolution* (1947).[145] In turn, Klein, a lifelong left-liberal, recognized Reagan as "the greatest Keynesian policy maker of all time."[146]

There were also clear differences. Most important was the retreat from full employment, a process already under way during the Nixon years but that accelerated in the late 1970s.[147] After the deep recession of 1979 to 1982, macroeconomic management would backstop profits, asset values, and credit conditions instead of labor markets.[148] Central bankers became the most important managers of the economy, but much of their new role (including Lockheed-style lender of last resort functions) had been carved out during the Vietnam years.[149] By breaking the air traffic controllers' union (PATCO) in 1981, the federal government threw its full weight behind the employers' offensive against labor. The image of PATCO leaders in shackles contrasted starkly with photos of Nixon in a hardhat. However, the difference was not that Nixon thought "labor should be strong."[150] When postal workers went out on a wildcat strike in 1970, Nixon deployed troops to replace them (like PATCO, the postal strike was technically illegal). When the strikers prevailed, it was not because of Nixon's worldview. Rather, the president was constrained by the nationwide mood of labor revolt and the soldiers' unwillingness or inability to take over tasks like sorting the mail.[151]

Most scholars now accept that the rise of neoliberalism meant the transformation of the state, not its withering away. By the same token, the neoliberal era has witnessed a mutation of older Keynesian practices, not their negation. Since its origins in the 1930s, functional finance has taken different forms and served different projects.[152] Keynes dreamed of a shorter work week and the socialization of investment. Nixon bought South Vietnam the fourth largest air force in the world.[153] But the Cambridge don and the crook from Orange County both recognized that private investment could not guarantee full employment. In our society, people need jobs but not everyone gets to have one. So long as that remains the case, we can expect to find "strong support for sustaining or increasing defense spending that provides an economic lifeline for working families and communities."[154] The challenge of the 1970s remains our own.

CHAPTER 9

Mediating the Economic Impacts of Service: Race and Veterans' Welfare After the War in Vietnam

Jessica L. Adler

In 1972, twenty-one-year-old James Peters was out of work and he was dejected. "I've been to every agency that deals with jobs," the Milwaukee, Wisconsin, native told reporter Mary Lou Ballweg. "People say that if you really want to work, you can find work, but it's not true because I've been everywhere."[1] When Peters deployed for a thirteen-month combat duty tour in Vietnam in early 1969, seasonally adjusted unemployment rates among people sixteen and older hovered at around 3.4 percent. By March 1972, Peters had been looking for a job for two years, and unemployment had increased to 5.8 percent.[2]

Ballweg's article focused on the special economic and employment challenges faced by "new veterans" who, during the increasingly challenging economic times, reportedly had relatively high unemployment rates of around 15 percent.[3] But Peters frankly distinguished his experiences from others, reporting, "I think it's just because I'm black."[4]

Peters's sentiment was borne out by data demonstrating that African Americans—veterans and nonveterans alike—faced unique economic challenges. Between 1975 and 1990, the overall unemployment rate among Black Americans remained between 10.2 and 21.2 percent. During the same decade and a half, it was 6.6 to 15.7 for Hispanic/Latino workers and between 4.2 and 9.7 percent for white workers.[5] In 1972, when Peters was interviewed, Black working-age adults had an unemployment rate of 11.2 percent, according to the US Census Bureau.[6] During the first quarter of the same year, the Urban League reported, Black veterans had unemployment rates of approximately 22 percent.[7]

Those realities—and James Peters's sentiments—were emblematic of a larger reckoning and transition. For generations, Black veterans had recognized that they faced higher economic hurdles than their white counterparts. But during and after the war in Vietnam, even as the larger social safety net came under siege, multiple stakeholders ensured that the unique circumstances and concerns of Black veterans were publicly acknowledged and addressed. Drawing from research produced by economists and sociologists in the 1960s and 1970s about the economic impacts of military service, statements of Black political leaders and activists, and government documents, this chapter shows that efforts to highlight racial inequality in labor market outcomes among Black former service members fostered a shift toward more expansive and egalitarian veterans' benefits after the war in Vietnam.

Studies of the economic impacts of military service by sociologists and economists have produced mixed findings, based on time period of focus, which datasets and variables are examined, and how veteran populations are defined. But one relatively consistent conclusion is that outcomes vary by race and ethnicity. For example, under a variety of circumstances, Black former service members historically had lower incomes and higher unemployment rates than white veterans but had higher incomes and lower unemployment rates than Black nonveterans. When explaining such findings, researchers have pointed to a variety of forces, including the potential long-term economic consequences of exposure to military training and the impacts of "dual entitlement": access to civilian and military benefits that offer additional safety nets.[8]

While social science literature has sought to explain the tremendous complexity of labor market access and economic outcomes among former service members, historians who write about military and veterans' social policy have worked to uncover how and why former service members won access to entitlements that offer a special layer of protection for one segment of the US population. In the late twentieth century, they have shown, veterans' benefits were hard fought in a political environment dominated by skepticism of the worthiness of the war in Vietnam. Scholars have argued that expansions in veterans' entitlements in the 1970s and 1980s were relatively stingy, prompted in no small part by an increasing tendency to represent martial citizenship as ideal citizenship.[9]

Placing economic data and debates in context with the historical development of veterans' activism and access to labor-related benefits, this chapter
has three broad implications. First, the role of veterans from marginalized
groups in advocating for veterans' entitlements after the war in Vietnam—
and the emergence of an impulse to represent those entitlements as a means
of increasing equity—has been underappreciated. Second, when assessing
the economic impacts of military service, scholars must consider not just the
influence of the service itself, but the potentially profound consequences of
gaining access to veterans' benefits, some of which may not be immediately
visible within a larger federal bureaucracy. Finally, this study shows that economic opportunity is created not simply by the establishment of entitlements,
but by the people and processes that shape entitlements to be egalitarian.

Conceptualizing Differential Economic Impacts of Service

When James Peters was interviewed in 1972, military veterans in the United
States had long had conditional access to unique state-sponsored benefits
intended to enhance their economic security. In the eighteenth and nineteenth
centuries, they could claim land grants, pensions, and disability compensation. By the World War I era, Congress had created a new federal agency—the
Veterans' Bureau, forerunner to the current Department of Veterans Affairs
(VA)—intended to manage a growing portfolio of benefits, including insurance, vocational training, and a nationwide network of health care facilities.
In the World War II years, the burgeoning veterans' welfare state was further
strengthened and entrenched with the passage of the landmark Servicemen's
Readjustment Act of 1944, often referred to as the GI Bill. Among other benefits, the legislation offered veterans financial aid for college and guarantees of
home loans—a key to the institutions and bureaucracies of American middle-
class life.[10]

The GI Bill and its legislative predecessors underscored the US government's consistent willingness to mark military service both as a superior
means of demonstrating commitment to citizenship and as an economic sacrifice. Legislation expanding veterans' benefits reflected and advanced the ideals that some citizens were more worthy than others and that former service
members did not receive "welfare"—they earned entitlements.[11] Following the
1973 creation of the all-volunteer force (AVF), a diverse military welfare state

operated alongside veterans' benefits, signaling to potential recruits that service could beget economic rewards and security.[12] Between 1940 and 2012, the VA's inflation-adjusted share of the federal budget increased at an average of 3.8 percent per year, with spikes during and after World War II, the war in Vietnam, and the conflicts in Iraq and Afghanistan. Overall, spending on the VA was fourteen times higher in inflation-adjusted dollars in 2012 than it was in 1940.[13]

While expansive, the vast veterans' welfare state was more accessible to some former service members than others through at least the mid-twentieth century. It is hardly surprising, perhaps, that access to veterans' benefits was historically tied to the race, ethnicity, and gender of potential recipients.[14] White, male veterans who were most welcomed and visible in politically powerful veterans' organizations, and who faced relatively few limits on freedoms in general society, had an easier time winning entitlements. Whether seeking Civil War disability compensation or access to professional training, home loans, and college tuition via the World War II–era GI Bill, people from marginalized groups faced special—sometimes insurmountable—challenges. For example, only some occupations, colleges, and neighborhoods were accessible to anyone other than white men—with or without the 1944 GI Bill. In short, veterans' benefits could offer people from marginalized groups a boost, but they reflected and failed to undo pervasive social and political inequality.[15]

Many African American veterans, aware of these inequities, were proud of their service; some were radicalized by it, deeply frustrated that even an honorable discharge could not guarantee access to equal citizenship and economic opportunity. As early as the Revolutionary War, Black veterans came together in civic bodies such as Masonic lodges and posts of veterans' organizations to form networks of self-support.[16] Following World War I and World War II, they assumed positions of leadership in increasingly visible civil rights organizations.[17] While many fought openly for rights and recognition, it was not until the Vietnam War era that reports of the particular experiences of Black veterans shaped how scholars, policymakers, and the general public understood the impact of war on individuals' lives.

In the mid-1960s, as the Vietnam War escalated, sentiments resembling those expressed by previous generations of African Americans—that military service could advance the civil rights struggle, and that it could foster economic opportunity—were present, but they were tempered by experience and a more pronounced sense of skepticism and radicalism. Advisor

to President Lyndon B. Johnson and soon-to-be chair of the Equal Employment Opportunity Commission Clifford Alexander, Jr., echoed the World
War II era "double victory" campaign when he told a Saigon-based *Time*
magazine reporter in 1967, "We are fighting over here against the Viet Cong
and at home against discrimination: together we can win in both places."
But *Time* featured the sentiments, too, of senior officers who maintained
that former service members' "anger could well be triggered if, on his return,
the Negro veteran of Viet Nam finds himself cast back into the ghetto and a
social immobility."[18] Between 1959 and 1969, African Americans, 11 percent
of the US population, constituted about 12 percent of those who served in
Vietnam. Widespread charges that they were disproportionately likely to be
placed in harm's way were supported by statistics: Black service members
made up 15 percent of Vietnam War casualties that occurred between 1959
and 1969.[19]

Sentiments of antimilitarism and anti-imperialism, which had long been
part of the African American activist tradition, were only strengthened by
growing awareness of the diverse and wide-ranging economic injustices arising from the conflict in Southeast Asia. Civil rights advocates, as well as those
who served in Vietnam, spoke out against the carnage of the war and against
a military draft apparatus that disproportionately targeted people from poor
communities and communities of color. The war was fought on the backs
of young people who lacked economic opportunities, leaders maintained,
and the money used to pay for it was being stripped from domestic social
programs. "America would never invest the necessary funds or energies in
rehabilitation of its poor," Martin Luther King, Jr. declared in a 1967 speech,
"so long as adventures like Vietnam continued to draw men and skills and
money like some demonic, destructive suction tube."[20] Black power and radical activists echoed these concerns, often using distinctly economic terms.
Some served as "draft counselors," who guided potential recruits on how to
avoid service in a military they viewed "as a racist institution that 'trapped'
African American men with 'the false promise of learning valuable skills and
travel to other places.'"[21]

As civil rights advocates trumpeted antimilitarism, a parallel conversation was taking place about the abolition of the draft and the creation of the
AVF. The conservative economists who favored and helped to design the AVF
justified it based on the ethos that "in a Free society we must allow people to
choose their own destiny."[22] In support of that ideal, members of the Gates
Commission, formed by Richard Nixon in 1969 to consider the formulation

of a new AVF, published papers making the case that the draft had negative economic consequences for veterans. Because of "abnormally low levels of first-term pay" in the military, wrote Gates Commission senior staff member and economist Walter Oi in the *American Economic Review,* "reluctant volunteers" and "draftees" faced significant annual income losses.[23] Using a term that informed conversations among Gates Commission staff members, a subsequent paper maintained that those who served incurred an "implicit tax": a "financial loss" resulting from the career delay that placed former service members "'behind' in civilian employment."[24]

Even as free market economists made arguments that military service had generally detrimental economic impacts, they maintained that it could enrich the most impoverished Americans. Milton Friedman noted in 1967 that some who opposed abolishing the draft argued that a volunteer army would reflect the inequities of larger society and "be staffed predominantly by Negroes, because a military career would be so much more attractive than the other alternatives open to them."[25] Friedman stopped short of denying that possibility but maintained, "We must handle our domestic problems as best we can and not use them as an excuse for denying Negroes opportunities in the military service. We should be proud of the armed forces for the fine job they have done in providing opportunities to the disadvantaged and for eliminating racial discrimination—not discriminate against the Negroes in manning the armed forces because we have done so much less well in civilian life."[26] According to free market ideology, military service represented opportunity for Black Americans and a hindrance to progress for whites. The market offered more freedom to some than others.

In the early 1970s, sociologists tested that theory by examining the long-term impacts of military service on the life course among subgroups of veterans. Early studies pointed out that previous research had focused mainly on whites and maintained that "given the grossly different life circumstances of individuals from minority versus majority backgrounds . . . the differential effect of military service on . . . status attainment" was worthy of investigation. Authors of a 1973 article concluded that among both Black and Mexican Americans, veterans had higher average incomes than their nonveteran counterparts. They attributed the difference to the fact that "the military can provide further education, acquisition of skills and valuable experience managing large-scale bureaucratic environments." Additionally, it "takes men from their ghetto and ethnic environments and more fully exposes them to the bureaucratic Anglo world." Qualifying their findings, the authors acknowledged that, following discharge, Mexican American veterans were able to "derive more advantage . . . measured in dollar differences" than African Americans. Both groups, the authors noted, "are subject to a variety of discriminatory practices, but these may be more severe and unyielding for blacks."[27] Inequities of the civilian world, the researchers suggested, might be tamed, but not eliminated, by military service.

In the charged environment of the 1970s, as antiwar, antimilitary, and Black power sentiments pervaded public discourse, researchers were wary of suggesting that military service be viewed as an ideal solution to social problems. Authors of a 1977 study demonstrating higher income among some Black veterans than their nonveteran counterparts noted that some aspects of service—for example, spending the bulk of one's enlistment learning and performing skills that had no application in the civilian world—"may work in a negative manner for Black veterans." The authors noted, "It is not our intention to suggest that military conscription is the proper course of action for black men to overcome their handicaps of discrimination and inequalities of opportunity."[28]

There was, in fact, hardly a consensus about the economic impacts of military service for Black veterans. Sociologist James M. Fendrich argued in 1972 that they were "uniquely caught in the causal nexus" of "the two major crises of the United States": the war in Vietnam and "interracial conflict." For that reason, he said, their "patterns of adjustment" might be unique. Focused on veterans in Jacksonville, Florida, Fendrich's study considered a range of variables: whether Black veterans were likely to feel alienated, to have a "positive Black identification," to achieve gainful employment, and generally "'[make] it in civilian life." He cited Department of Defense studies from 1969 and 1972 showing that 10.7 percent of Black veterans reported not being employed full-time, as opposed to 4.7 percent of white veterans, and that average earnings among Black veterans were less than those of white veterans, even when correcting for educational differences. Fendrich maintained not only that "the veterans' benefits and assistance available do not appear to be adequate in helping veterans become upwardly mobile," but also that "a large minority of the veterans are highly alienated" and "could become a vanguard for the black community, particularly if black disenchantment with white America intensifies."[29]

Fendrich was not alone in voicing skepticism that exposure to military service fostered net economic gains. A 1974 study published in the *American*

Sociological Review focused on earnings in the 1960s and concluded that "little evidence of positive effect of service can be found among Black veterans." The author called into question prior research suggesting that the military should be construed as a "bridging environment" that could offer a path out of poverty by providing exposure to travel, job training, and education benefits. "Direct approaches to underemployment and low income," said the 1974 article, "are probably more likely to benefit the poor than are indirect efforts to place them in bridging environments."[30]

In terms of historical implications, the quantitative results were almost beside the point. When scholars and government agencies like the Department of Defense acknowledged and studied the unique experiences of Black veterans, they bolstered a new and more complex understanding of post-service experiences and the labor market status of former service members. Unlike their predecessors, African American former servicemen in the 1970s could point to hard data as they brought attention to their lived realities and sought better economic outcomes.

Advocating for Black Veterans' Economic Security in the 1970s

Throughout the 1970s, individuals, civil rights groups, and elected officials helped draw attention to Black veterans' experiences with inequity. In congressional hearings and beyond, advocates maintained that egregious discrimination made the rights and economic benefits typically accrued via military service inaccessible to African Americans. Connecting their arguments with larger movements for political, social, and economic rights for both Vietnam veterans and Black Americans, they straddled the worlds of civil and veterans' rights activism.

Two important congressional bodies offered Black former service members public outlets for making their case about economic discrimination in the 1970s: the Senate Committee on Veterans' Affairs and the Congressional Black Caucus (CBC), originally formed in 1969 as the Democratic Select Committee. One of approximately 225 groups composed of legislators interested in advancing policies in a given area, the CBC aimed to "positively influence the course of events pertinent to African Americans and others of similar experience and situation, and to achieve greater equity for persons of African descent in the design and content of domestic and international programs and services."[31] Seven of the group's thirteen founding members were veterans. One, William Lacy Clay (D-MO), counted among his bevy of civil rights activities protesting segregation and discrimination at an army base where he was stationed during two years of military service in the mid-1950s.[32]

As part of its broader activities focused on economic security, community development, and civil rights, the CBC made explicit arguments about connections between military endeavors, discrimination, and financial well-being. In March 1971, the group addressed President Richard Nixon: "Since you assumed office, we have spent billions on war, while over 2 million Americans have been added to the ranks of unemployed, and 2.5 million more are on ever-mounting relief roles." In the area of veterans' affairs, the CBC demanded that the White House investigate "the status of blacks and other minorities in the Veterans Administration," since they were disproportionately classified in low pay grades, and "focus on closing the critically wide gap between the needs of black veterans and the inadequate and uncoordinated existing programs for the Veterans Administration, the Department of Labor, Housing and Urban Development, and other federal agencies."[33]

Racism in the Armed Forces, the CBC argued, led to lack of long-term economic opportunity for Black service members. In a 1971 investigation of the treatment of African Americans in the military, which built on a similarly focused report by the National Association for the Advancement of Colored People, the CBC focused on the perspectives of Black service members stationed in Germany, offering vivid accounts of unequal access to promotions and housing.[34] A key form of discrimination with wide-ranging economic consequences, discussed in and beyond the CBC report, was the so-called administrative discharge, or "bad paper": other-than-honorable discharges that could bar veterans from receiving benefits and raise serious questions for potential future employers.[35] Department of Defense policy stipulated that other-than-honorable discharges could be issued for anything from an "inability to expend effort constructively" and alcoholism to "financial irresponsibility" and "homosexual or other aberrant tendencies."[36] While service members had long faced the prospect of receiving this punitive classification for any array of offenses,[37] those released from service between 1970 and 1972 were at an increased risk. From 1965 to 1969, there were an average of 11,500 undesirable discharges annually. By 1972, the number had skyrocketed to more than 40,000.[38] Black and Hispanic service members reported to a task force in 1972 that they believed "administrative discharges were used to get rid of minority group service members considered 'outspoken' or 'militant.'"[39] A 1978 report noted that Black veterans made up about 10 percent of discharges between 1971 and 1975 but 20 percent of the undesirable, bad conduct, and dishonorable discharges.[40] The "systemically racist" military, an activist would later say, "used the administrative discharge like a club . . . a bad discharge discriminates against the recipient in that he is more likely to be unemployed and incarcerated upon his return to civilian life."[41]

Aside from the CBC, a second congressional body provided a forum for Black veterans' advocates in the 1970s and 1980s: the Senate Committee on Veterans' Affairs, which was headed from 1971 to 1981 by Vance Hartke (D-IN) and Alan Cranston (D-CA), both outspoken critics of the war in Vietnam. Throughout the 1970s, the committee hosted former service members who brought attention to an array of issues and problems they encountered, including insufficient benefits and a VA health system out of step with their needs.[42]

In Senate Veterans Affairs' Committee hearings about economic conditions facing former service members reentering civilian life, advocates consistently made the case that Black veterans faced particular challenges. During 1972 congressional hearings about veterans' education benefits widely viewed as miserly, Lewis C. Olive, Jr., director of military and veterans affairs for the National Urban League, pointed out that attending college when only some tuition and expenses were covered was challenging for single, childless veterans but virtually impossible for those who supported families. Black veterans, he noted, were disproportionately in the latter group; 61 percent were married, and 72 percent had children.[43] Advocates pointed out that noneconomic hurdles, too, could make African Americans less likely to claim veterans' benefits, especially those accessible through the VA: "The average white, middle class veteran, with a high school degree and some tolerance for bureaucracy, can get what he wants out of the VA," said David Heaphy, a veterans' counselor at LaGuardia Community College. "But for people who have had only negative experiences all the time with bureaucracy, who have only seen bureaucracy as a wall, they don't do so well."[44]

While representatives of major civil rights organizations drew attention to economic challenges faced by Black veterans, individual former service members and locally organized community groups also played important roles in raising awareness. One of the more visible of those groups was the National Association of Black Veterans (NABV), founded in 1969 in Milwaukee, Wisconsin. The organization's work, which extended well beyond veterans' issues, offered a window on to the interconnectedness of fights for social, political, and economic rights in the late twentieth century.[45] In 1972, the group led a march with fellow community organizations to protest a police officer's slaying of a nineteen-year-old Black woman, Jacqueline Ford. Though the cause ostensibly had little to do with veterans' matters, NABV representatives helped form a community-based committee in Milwaukee consisting of fellow prominent Black citizens that led multiple rallies and demanded a hearing with the police chief about "the long-standing threat of police brutality in the inner-city."[46] The NABV also offered educational programs led by veterans and intended for local youth, as well as drug counseling and counseling for incarcerated veterans.[47] The mission of the group was initially so diverse, in fact, that one attendee of its 1974 convention worried that its leaders may be "ignoring the fact that there are still more than 3,000 Black vets walking around this city without jobs."[48] But the NABV's wide-ranging activities reflected that many Black veterans tied individual veterans' economic problems to larger race-based injustices, and vice versa.

When Tom Wynn, national commander of the NABV, testified in front of Cranston's committee in 1980 during hearings about veterans' challenges with "readjustment and transition to civilian life," he maintained that addressing the particular economic circumstances of Black veterans was part of a larger movement for civil rights. "The Black veteran in this country has always had enormous problems that were his alone," he told the committee. [49] Wynn was a veteran of the Korean War, who had begun working with younger veterans at the Milwaukee campus of the University of Wisconsin in the early 1970s. His duties included helping service members receive early discharge to attend college and assisting veterans whose applications had been rejected by the university to seek other opportunities.[50] "Our major focus is the problems with racism and classism in the military as it relates to poor and minority persons in this country," Wynn told the senators. "Following the advice of Malcolm X, we intend to do for SELF" (emphasis in original).[51]

Weaving together explanations of various sources of inequity, Wynn discussed the Department of Defense Project 100,000 program, which enabled the army and the marine corps to adapt standards between 1966 and 1971 so

that more than 400,000 working class and poor people with limited education—approximately 160,000 of them African American—could be recruited
into combat units deployed to Vietnam. Sold to and embraced by the public
as a means of "social uplift" for urban youth,[52] Project 100,000 provided, as
Wynn put it, "an escape mechanism for nearly a million white reservists" to
remain safely at home.[53]

Wynn's testimony was remarkable because of the context it provided.
"Black veterans are encircled in a system that has perpetually denied him
human rights," he said.[54] The NABV leader's sentiments departed somewhat
from those of white veterans who testified during the same hearings; they also
expressed a tremendous sense of isolation but argued that their social, psycho-
logical, and economic challenges were due mainly to their service in Vietnam.
They requested specific services, programs, and benefits based on conditions
that stemmed from their time in the military. Wynn, too, maintained that
Black veterans faced challenges because of the nature of their service, but he
was concerned with demonstrating that their trials reflected a larger system
that "locks the disadvantaged into a socioeconomic poverty cycle."[55]

Implementing Policy Changes in the 1970s and 1980s

Social welfare initiatives of the 1970s and 1980s reflected a growing recognition of—and drive to undo—the disparate postservice economic situations
of veterans. Informed by data and veterans' advocates, policymakers and
bureaucrats incorporated veteran-focused initiatives into government programs overseen by multiple federal agencies—most prominently, the VA and
the Department of Labor (DOL). During the presidency of Ronald Reagan,
the idealization of small government ushered in slashes to welfare programs,
including those aimed at veterans. Still, by the 1990s, thanks in part to the
government's willingness to help shape views of the economic consequences
of military service, "minority veterans" were somewhat more protected from
poverty and political stigmatization than their nonveteran counterparts.

While legislators were hesitant throughout the 1970s to approve comprehensive benefits packages for those who served in the era of the war in
Vietnam, veterans' preference—and preference particularly for so-called
minority veterans—made its way into new federal jobs programs. Instituted
as unemployment and poverty were increasing, real wages were stagnating,
and corporations were undercutting labor rights virtually unchecked, DOL

aid programs were intended to stem catastrophe.[56] The Vietnam Era Veterans' Readjustment Assistance Act of 1974 underscored that some national initiatives would prioritize the needs of disadvantaged former service members. The law established veterans' employment preference under federal contracts and enhanced eligibility and priority of service for the DOL's employment and training opportunities.[57] In the waning days of his presidency in 1980, Jimmy Carter built on veteran-focused programs when he signed into law the Disabled Veterans' Outreach Program, which required the secretary of labor to appoint outreach specialists in state employment offices nationwide; preference for the positions was to be given to "disabled veterans of the Vietnam era."[58]

While legislation itself generally contained no mention of targeted demographic groups, a 1976 DOL report maintained that the agency was continuing "its program emphasis on the unemployment problems of younger, minority, and disabled veterans"—the populations consistently reported to be the most disadvantaged in the labor market. In 1976, the DOL noted, Black veterans ages twenty to twenty-four had an unemployment rate of more than 16 percent—twice as high as their white counterparts. That year, the report said, state employment service agencies placed 425,000 Vietnam Era veterans in jobs. A full 17.4 percent of those served by the DOL's Comprehensive Employment and Training Act were former service members.[59]

Though they were precariously funded and faced a variety of challenges, the DOL's veteran-focused initiatives marked an important shift. While disabled veterans had received special preference since the earliest days of the veterans' benefits administration, the addition of so-called minority veterans to those who were ostensibly most needy and deserving was new—the product of activism on the part of groups like the CBC and the NABV, and a reflection of a larger shift toward affirmative action in the 1970s and 1980s.[60] In an especially precarious postindustrial economy, it appeared, the federal government was willing to at least signal that veterans from marginalized groups deserved special recognition.

Veteran T. Morocco Coleman viewed the jobs programs as crucial, because they helped African American veterans create networks of support that could enhance economic opportunities. By the mid-1980s, Coleman was living homeless in Atlanta, Georgia. On a whim, he walked into a building that had a sign reading, "Department of Labor, Veterans' Employment." He looked, as he recalled, "broke down"—in combat boots and a field jacket,

with a beard and long hair. When the veterans' employment representative—
an older Black man who eventually became a mentor—addressed him as
"sir," he recalled thinking, "he sees my worth." Coleman would soon begin
working as an employment counselor himself, using community connections in order to find jobs for veterans and offering them guidance about how
they could access veterans' benefits. "I would go into . . . crackhouses . . . and
I would go and get those veterans out and tell them to come into the office,
sit there and wait. If it takes all day, I'm going to see you, I'm going to take
care of you."[61]

Coleman's recollections highlight that, in the early 1980s, veterans' benefits were beginning to fill holes created by structural racism and cuts in the
social safety net. The idealization of welfare state contraction or "retrenchment" during the presidency of Ronald Reagan ushered in slashes to welfare programs, including old-age pensions, housing assistance, and income
support.[62] Despite Reagan's increases in defense spending and trumpeting of
both militarism and veterans' nobility, the VA did not escape his administration's attack on presumed federal largesse; the agency's inflation-adjusted
budget authority decreased slightly between 1980 and 1990—constituting the
most protracted stagnation in VA funding since its inception.[63]

While Reagan and his advisors could be skeptical of veterans' programs
viewed as indicators of maladjustment (mental health counseling and disability benefits, for example), initiatives focused on jobs were somewhat
more favored.[64] A 1982 statute, for example, underscored the prioritization of
enabling veterans to become workers, pronouncing that "as long as employment and underemployment continue as serious problems among disabled
veterans and Vietnam-era veterans, alleviating unemployment and underemployment among such veterans is a national responsibility." The law established a job training program and stipulated that the secretary of labor assign
a director for veterans' employment to each state, along with "full-time cleri-
cal support to each such Director."[65]

Veterans visiting resource-strapped government offices like the one where
Coleman worked were more likely to receive assistance than people who had
never served, but their fates were impacted by the increasing precariousness
of the welfare state. "Consistent funding cut-backs by the federal government
over the last 10 years have strained the State Agencies to the breaking point,"
Coleman told members of Congress in 1992, when he was working as an outreach program specialist in Georgia. Veteran job specialists, he pointed out,

were being directed by managers to "carry out non-veteran program functions," which meant that less time and resources could be devoted to former service members, some of whom were more needy than others: "There is a problem in the delivery of service to African-American veterans," Coleman said. Many suffered from "PTSD [posttraumatic stress disorder], alcoholism, homelessness, the whole gamut."[66] Coleman, like earlier activists, argued that Black veterans were doubly vulnerable and that available resources were inadequate.

Veterans and their benefits were under increasing threat as federal funding for social welfare dried up and poverty increased. Homelessness, like joblessness, was a case in point. Between 1980 and 1990, the budget of the Department of Housing and Urban Development decreased from $29 billion to $17 billion, and aid in the form of housing subsidies decreased by about 40 percent. At the same time, cuts in Supplemental Security Income made it difficult for mentally ill people to pay rent, and changes in rules regarding Social Security disability benefits made support less accessible.[67] By 1986, elected officials reported that up to 350,000 people were homeless on any given night in the United States, and officials were disturbed to note that up to one-third were military veterans.[68]

As federal spending on welfare fell, veterans spoke out about tremendous need, sometimes presenting their claims as reflective of a lack of broader social protections. "My homelessness is not a result of Vietnam because I think, after four or five years, I sort of readjusted and accepted the fact that what has happened has happened, and the situation is as is," veteran Jesse Moses told members of Congress in 1987. "My homelessness is a result of being injured on the job and not receiving the compensation." Still, Moses reported that he had sustained injuries during a rocket attack in Vietnam and that he regretted that "the government for some reason seemingly has made it more difficult for us to enjoy the benefits that previous veterans have enjoyed." Ben Littlejohn, who completed two tours of duty in Vietnam and resided in the same Washington, DC, homeless shelter as Moses, connected his economic situation more directly to his military service. A back injury incurred during training, he said, made him unable to sustain a job, and the VA denied his disability claims. Littlejohn and Moses told senators that at least 40 percent of people in the DC shelter were Vietnam War veterans.[69]

In the 1980s, as the Reagan administration cut government budgets, and "inadequately enforced and otherwise undermined ... settled law in the field of civil rights," it was productive to focus on military service, rather than larger social circumstances, as the primary and root cause of depleted economic opportunities.[70] Such an approach had the potential to generate support from unlikely quarters. Long-time segregationist Strom Thurmond, for example, had railed against "welfare-statism" in the 1960s, maintaining that "every American" should understand that "any government big enough to give him everything he wants, must, necessarily, be big enough to take everything he's got, including his liberty."[71] Three decades later, presiding over the hearings where Moses and Littlejohn testified, Thurmond argued for the need to develop "a program to meet the shelter, employment, mental health, and other needs of homeless veterans."[72]

Sentiments like those helped bring about the 1987 creation of a VA-administered homeless chronically mentally ill (HCMI) program, offering case management and treatment to former service members. Operating within community-based organizations and VA medical centers, HCMI workers searched out veterans "in shelters and soup kitchens as well as on the streets" so they could receive "psychiatric assessment and treatment, substance abuse treatment, job counseling, and crisis intervention.[73] Within a year of its inception, the program had screened more than 10,500 former service members. They had a median age of 40 and more had served in the Vietnam era than in any other period. Among users of the program, three-fifths were white and one-third were Black.[74] Within a few years of the creation of the HCMI program, the National Coalition for Homeless Veterans had been created, and programs intended to address veteran homelessness had become part of the VA bureaucracy. In the same vein as the DOL jobs programs, economically troubled veterans were sought out and siphoned off from their nonveteran counterparts. While funding for veteran-focused anti-poverty programs was hardly generous or guaranteed in the late 1980s, it was at least defined as distinct and somewhat protected.

Although veteran and disability status constituted important means of accessing antipoverty programs in the hawkish, socially and fiscally conservative 1980s, advocates continued to devote themselves to drawing attention to the unique plight of Black veterans. In the 1980s, the CBC created the Veterans Braintrust, which served as an advisory body on issues of special concern to African American former service members. Annual gatherings and activities of the CBC Veterans Braintrust involved members of a VA-based African American working group, scholars, advocates, and others with special insights on issues facing Black and marginalized veterans.[75] In the 1990s, the CBC and its braintrust helped oversee congressional hearings entitled "Inner-City African American Veterans" and "African American Veterans and Community: Post-Traumatic Stress Disorder and Related Issues."[76]

In this later period, the tone changed, but the message remained relatively consistent. The explicit focus on structural racism and antimilitarism of the 1970s was somewhat muted, even as advocates and elected officials continued to argue that circumstances and inequities of larger society ensured that veterans who were from marginalized groups had distinctive experiences. When presenting legislation in 1991 intended to install a chief of minority affairs officer in the VA, Korean War veteran and CBC founding member Charles Rangel (D-NY), noted:

> Notwithstanding the percentage in the population, when the count is taken as to who is in combat, who is missing, and who is killed in action, unfortunately we find that minorities certainly are listed far higher in proportion than the percentage they represent in the population. That is not to say that the medals and the tributes that are paid to them are not honor enough to die for this country. But the problems we face are there when they come home after the parades, after the confetti, and after America seems to have forgotten. We have found that veterans of color, female veterans, and veterans who are Hawaiian natives as well as Alaskan Natives and Indians have found a more difficult time in adjusting to society because of lack of training and lack of support.[77]

Affirming Rangel's position, veterans' advocate Daniel Akaka (D-HI) argued that a chief minority affairs officer could "institutionalize concern for the special problems and needs of veterans from minority backgrounds."[78] Rangel and others framed their sentiments in terms of the needs of those who had served in the recent Persian Gulf War, arguing that the issue itself was timeless. "Each time our nation has been called into combat," Rangel said, "we expected that whether we were in the minority or in the majority, we would be there when our nation needed us."[79] The current proposal, he maintained, would benefit not just aging former service members but future veterans of the increasingly diverse AVF.

By 1995, the VA was home to both a Center for Minority Veterans and a Center for Women Veterans, each with their own advisory groups.[80] Two decades after social scientists and veterans' advocates underscored the disparate economic impacts of military service, veterans from marginalized groups had gained some institutional recognition and power. The question was no longer whether inequities existed, but how to address them.

Conclusion

At the turn of the twenty-first century, the federal government offered veterans a set of social and economic supports that superseded those afforded to other working-class Americans. No single factor explains myriad changes in the structure of veterans' benefits in the post–Vietnam War years, but emerging social science research about the economic lives of former service members, and the efforts of advocates for Black veterans, whose impressions shed light on varied postservice experiences, played important roles in the transitions. Veterans' benefits programs were never immune to funding cuts, but by the 1990s, they constituted an added layer of protection against poverty and racial discrimination prevalent in the civilian world.

Access to military and veterans' benefits, of course, was hardly a panacea. It did not fully reverse the economic impacts of living in a pervasively nonegalitarian society. In 2017, among white, Black, and Hispanic Americans, veterans had higher incomes than nonveterans—white veterans had higher incomes than white nonveterans, Black veterans had higher incomes than Black nonveterans, and likewise for Hispanic veterans and nonveterans. But the "veteran bump" did not raise Black and Hispanic veterans over white nonveterans; whites, veteran or not, had the highest incomes of all, followed by Hispanic veterans, Black veterans, Hispanic nonveterans, and Black nonveterans.[81] To use the words of a 1977 study, military service conditionally alleviated, but failed to eliminate, "handicaps of discrimination and inequalities of opportunity."[82]

More work is needed on how service members and veterans from marginalized groups experienced and shaped their access to labor markets, and on the complex historical factors that influence postservice economic opportunities. But homing in on the experience of Black veterans in the 1970s and 1980s shows that a variety of factors have historically influenced interpretations of the economic impacts of military service. At a moment of heightened civil rights activism, social scientists and economists presented new data about the diverse aftermaths of enlistment, drawing attention to ideas that had long been shared by Black service members and veterans: the possibility of economic advancement, for some, had at least as much to do with systemic racism as it did with exposure to military service. In the decades following the war in Vietnam, federal policy finally took into account the special circumstances of veterans from marginalized groups, even as it eschewed the parallel needs of their counterparts who had not served. In the case of economic opportunity for veterans, it is clear, the relationship between the military and the market has been mediated by the state, political and social activism, and a variety of other complex dynamics.

CONCLUSION

Jennifer Mittelstadt and Mark R. Wilson

At the start of the 2020s, as the COVID pandemic spread around the world, US defense officials were forced to grapple anew with difficult questions about the proper relationship between the military and the market. The crisis exposed tensions and trends in the military's relationships with defense firms and in its own strategies that had been developing over the previous decades. On the one hand, some of the shibboleths of privatization and corporate strategy came in for critical review. In July 2020, Ellen M. Lord, the undersecretary of defense for acquisition and sustainment, told an interviewer that "COVID has shone a bright spotlight" on weaknesses in supply chains for critical goods, including, for example, microelectronics, which were trapped in factories in Asia. In response, Lord said, the Department of Defense (DOD) would retreat from its reliance on global private firms and turn to American ones, in an effort to "make sure we re-shore as much as possible." The DOD now would aim to have at least one supplier of key items located within the boundaries of the United States. Defense authorities announced that they would also step back from just-in-time logistics strategies pursued for three decades by building up larger strategic stockpiles. But on the other hand, in the same interview, Lord emphasized that the military would nevertheless continue to seek opportunities to interface more seamlessly and quickly with commercial markets. Lord and her team would carry on pushing the military toward continued reliance on the private sector. She redoubled her commitment to implement an "adaptive acquisition framework," set forth in recent revisions to the Defense Department's Directive 5000.01, aimed at making military acquisition more agile, so as to better harness the rapid innovations coming out of key commercial sectors, such as the software industry.[1] As Lord's comments suggested, the military in the 2020s was ostensibly rethinking its approach to the market, but coming up with conclusions that reflected a continued reliance on private sector answers to military needs.

As they tried to reassess their approaches to private sector supply during the pandemic, military leaders were influenced not only by the COVID crisis but by new national strategic interpretations of the US role in the world that raised broader questions about the US strategy of privatization. DOD and uniformed military leaders embraced a growing consensus among mainstream Washington policymakers that the most pressing geopolitical challenge of the day was the economic and military ascendance of China. The growing US-China rivalry seemed to require a reevaluation of broader economic policies, as well as military-market relations in particular. Here, too, military leadership expressed commitments to onshoring economic activity but maintaining overall commitments to private sector reliance. Take for example the growing bipartisan consensus about the desirability of more protectionist trade and industrial policies, at least with regard to China. Immediately after taking office in January 2021, President Biden issued Executive Order 14005, strengthening the government's commitment to "Buy American" provisions—a move that echoed a similar order made by President Trump nearly four years before. During the COVID crisis, defense officials in the Trump administration had linked the current medical supply chain problems with a broader overreliance on China. For instance, in October 2020, Jeffrey Nadaner, the deputy assistant secretary of defense for industrial policy, warned of dependence on "adversarial" or "unreliable partners," including China, while declaring that the Trump administration rejected the outcomes of the "invisible hand" of the market in an international trade system it regarded as unfairly weighted against American interests.[2]

But in order to compete with China, did the United States need to adopt economic policies and military acquisition strategies that would eschew markets, in favor of more government command, heavier public subsidies, and more state-owned enterprise? The question echoed dilemmas from the Cold War era, in which military leaders and policymakers had struggled to harmonize defense and capitalism. At the start of the 2020s, probusiness conservatives answered in the same way they had for fifty years: they again touted the superiority of markets as a solution to US security needs. According to Daniel McGroarty, a former speechwriter in the George H. W. Bush administration, the United States should not attempt to become more state-centered and "China-like," in an effort to respond to supply chain problems with items such as rare earths, a key component in microelectronics. By "substituting its wisdom for the wisdom of the markets," the United States would be unwisely deviating from its most important comparative advantage over China. "That would be a bad plan," said McGroarty.[3] In the 2020s the military seems be struggling with the outcomes of its long-term privatization strategy, adapting it to new circumstances, but refusing to back away from a celebration of the private sector.

Today's ongoing debates about the military and the market must be understood in the context of a long-run history of struggles over public and private provision in the defense sector, which have been described in several chapters in this book, including the broader surveys of the terrain, by Jennifer Mittelstadt and Mark Wilson and by Dan Wirls. New debates have also arisen in additional areas examined by other contributors to this volume. Privatized housing, whose history in the early Cold War is recounted in the chapter by A. Junn Murphy, continues to generate debate within the military today. In 2020, two decades after US military housing was comprehensively privatized, military families complained of poor management by the private sector and substandard living conditions. In 2021, Congress was holding new hearings about these problems, as military leaders grappled with the problem of how to ensure sufficient public oversight of private developers.[4] Recent events similarly confirm the contemporary relevance of Kara Vuic's chapter, on the long-run history of the military and markets for sex. Increasingly, it would appear, the military is seeing its own uniformed personnel involved in those markets, not least as managers of illegal sex work. In 2020, for example, Congress demanded explanations and reform from the navy, following reports that entrepreneurial sailors were engaged in human trafficking in Bahrain.[5] Echoes of the past are also heard today in many of the other fields discussed in the chapters of this book, such as the politics of military budgets and the struggles of diverse groups of veterans to secure equitable benefits and jobs. In more ways than one, current questions regarding defense and market relations can be better understood through critical histories of the military and the market.

Besides speaking to present-day concerns, the chapters in this book also suggest the promise of new scholarship about the past. Although the chapters provide valuable historical perspectives on many important areas of military-market relationships, they should be understood not as a comprehensive synthesis or final word but rather as an invitation to additional research and writing. We hope that this book may inspire additional bold analyses of the intertwining of markets and war-making, across modern history. Together, the chapters in this volume suggest that the next generation of work in this area must continue to take a broad view of the military and the markets and firms with which it engages.

First and foremost, scholars will want to do more to explore the history of militaries and markets at the global level. Here, new scholarship may build on the transnational approaches taken in this volume by Patrick Chung and by Gretchen Heefner and extend the investigation even more widely. While this volume is focused on the historically unprecedented power and impact of the US military, in particular, we expect future research will look more closely at non-US militaries, and local and transnational markets across the globe as well. Future studies can do more to compare the behaviors of different national or imperial military forces. They might inquire into the impact of regional military deployments and bases, and the global networks of trade and labor that support them. New studies might investigate the extent to which military-market relations in given national contexts are affected by the structure of the broader national political economies, including the extent of the welfare state. How have military-market relations developed in places that import most of their weapons and materiel, or those that rely heavily on mercenaries? Comparative studies of global military networks might also explore the extent to which different configurations of military-market relationships may affect trade, diplomacy, and the reputation and effectiveness of armed forces.

Scholars will also want to continue to broaden the history of labor and consumption history of the US military, which have been illuminated in this book in the chapters by Sarah Weicksel and Kara Vuic. This volume only touches the surface of the immense role the US military has played in supervising both free and unfree labor, creating new labor markets, demanding goods and services for direct military use, and altering patterns of consumption beyond the formal boundaries of the military. In the future, scholars will undoubtedly want to explore the relationships between militaries and labor unions, regimes of labor created by or utilized by militaries, and the differences in labor conditions faced by uniformed personnel and contractors, both within national boundaries and overseas. Migration, immigration, and nation-to-nation relations should occupy important places in new inquiries, centering labor as a vital site of power and contestation in military-market relations. A focus on power and contestation also ought to shape inquiries into the histories of militaries and consumer markets, practices, and ideologies. It has become practically axiomatic that modern militaries mobilize with a significant "tail," comprised in no small part of consumer goods and services for personnel. Scholars need to know more about how such consumption shapes military approaches to preserving morale and well-being, how it serves as compensation, and what market actors and relationships characterize such military consumer culture.

The scholarship in this book confirms what has been suggested by a growing body of scholarship about the military and about capitalism and the political economy: that military and market structures, actors, and ideas often have been shaped by gendered and racialized ideologies and practices. Chapters in this volume by A. Junn Murphy, Kara Vuic, and Jessica Adler demonstrate the close interpenetration of gender, race, the military, and markets. Additional research has miles to go in recovering these histories. In what ways are expectations about military morale and service personnel support influenced by gendered ideas about consumption and labor? How has the racialization of both military service and civilian labor markets, nationally and globally, affected the patterns of military labor and contracted labor? How is the increasing privatization and outsourcing of military production, real estate, and services of all kinds related to notions of independence, maximization of utility, and evaluation of core versus noncore functions that are themselves products of a highly racialized and masculinized corporate and economic culture?

It should be no surprise that the military—as a state institution and function—has been contoured by inequalities of gender and race, because military-market relations constitute important parts of wider national policy regimes and welfare states. This volume's chapters by Tim Barker, Jessica Adler, and A. Junn Murphy point to the need to consider military-market histories as closely tied to federal fiscal and social welfare regimes. While there has been growing scholarship on military social welfare, and on the relationship between social welfare and capitalist markets in a neoliberal age, there is a need for additional scholarship that brings these two realms together. Neither military personnel nor military leadership and institutions operate outside of the political, economic, and social policies of their nations, and it is important to know more about how these actors interact with both civilian and military state structures and programs. Likewise, contractors and other market-side actors in military settings also rely on and help shape national fiscal and social policies.

The book has suggested the complexities of the ways that military institutions, leaders, and policymakers and market actors and institutions have worked together and apart, in cooperation and conflict, to manage problems defined as pertaining to war and defense and economics. The histories related in this volume demonstrate that military leaders and US policymakers cannot act effectively without reflecting on the many ways in which the US military both affects and is affected by a wide variety of market institutions, actors, ideas, and practices. As the Defense Department's present-day reexamination of its preparation for global pandemics and for relations with China suggest, there is plenty of room for critical discussion of the military's recent past and present configurations. Histories of the military and the market offer the opportunity to inform these discussions with open-mindedness and sharp critical questions. Better knowledge of the relevant history can help current leaders today debunk myths, assumptions, and so-called common knowledge that has emerged over the past fifty years about the nature of military-market relations. Critical historical inquiry can help leaders consider anew how best military-market configurations should be configured.

Perhaps the most pressing question raised by the collective contributions to this book is whether the US military should continue to embrace and extend its profound shift in the direction of reliance on the private sector. Are we, as some observers have suggested, heading toward an essentially fully privatized mercenary force? Is it acceptable for the military to rely wholly on for-profit firms for weapons, services, and logistics? Has military service become essentially nothing more than an ordinary labor market exchange, without even a vestige of political obligation and connection to citizenship? Does it matter if it is? If military leaders and observers determine that they wish to reverse certain aspects of privatization, are military leaders, policymakers, and elected officials in a position to change this? What would be required to return some military services or production to the public sector? Which should be prioritized and why?

Military leaders might also ask about the internal transformation of their own systems of thought and management. Should the years-long trend toward modeling the military on a corporation—using corporate strategies of management—continue? The global COVID pandemic and the US national strategy toward China clearly offer openings for reconsidering some of the prevailing patterns of management. For example, might recent geopolitical developments require new thinking about "core" versus "noncore" military capacities and functions, perhaps with less deference to the ways in which those have been defined by for-profit entities? The contents of this book suggest that military leaders and policymakers with knowledge of the long-run record, as they face pressing challenges in this century, may arrive at new answers to these questions.

NOTES

Introduction

1. Devon L. Suits, "Army Launches Enlisted Assignment for Select Career Fields," Army News Service (February 27, 2020), https://www.army.mil/article/233145/army_launches_enlisted _assignment_market_for_select_career_fields (accessed January 2021); Casey Wardynski, David S. Lyle, and Michael J. Colarusso, *Towards a US Army Officer Corps Strategy for Success: Employing Talent* (Carlisle, PA: US Army War College, Strategic Studies Institute, 2010), https:// apps.dtic.mil/dtic/tr/fulltext/u2/a519580.pdf (accessed January 2021).

2. Gordon E. Bannerman, *Merchants and the Military in Eighteenth-Century Britain: British Army Contracts and Domestic Supply, 1739–1763* (London: Pickering & Chatto, 2008); Roger Knight and Martin Howard Wilcox, *Sustaining the Fleet, 1793–1815: War, the British Navy and the Contractor State* (Woodbridge, UK: Boydell & Brewer, 2010).

3. Stuart D. Brandes, *Warhogs: A History of War Profits in America* (Lexington: University Press of Kentucky, 1997); Mark R. Wilson, *The Business of Civil War: Military Mobilization and the State, 1861–1865* (Baltimore: Johns Hopkins University Press, 2006).

4. Ajay K. Mehrotra, "Lawyers, Guns, and Public Moneys: The US Treasury, World War I, and the Administration of the Modern Fiscal State," *Law and History Review* 28, no. 1 (2010): 173–225; Anthony J. Arnold, "'A Paradise for Profiteers'? The Importance and Treatment of Profits During the First World War," *Accounting History Review* 24, no. 2–3 (2014): 61–81; Neil Rollings, "Whitehall and the Control of Prices and Profits in a Major War, 1919–1939," *Historical Journal* (2001): 517–40; Christine Grandy, "'Avarice' and 'Evil Doers': Profiteers, Politicians, and Popular Fiction in the 1920s," *Journal of British Studies* 50, no. 3 (2011): 667–89; Mark R. Wilson, *Destructive Creation: American Business and the Winning of World War II* (Philadelphia: University of Pennsylvania Press, 2016).

5. Seymour Melman, *Pentagon Capitalism: The Political Economy of War* (New York: McGraw Hill, 1970); Alex Roland, "The Military-Industrial Complex: Lobby and Trope," in *The Long War: A New History of US National Security Policy since World War II*, ed. Andrew J. Bacevich (New York: Columbia University Press, 2007), 335–70.

6. William D. Hartung, *How Much Are You Making on the War, Daddy? A Quick and Dirty Guide to Profiteering in the Bush Administration* (New York: Nation Books, 2003); *Why We Fight*, dir. Eugene Jarecki (Sony Pictures, 2006); Dina Rasor and Robert Bauman, *Betraying Our Troops: The Destructive Consequences of Privatizing War* (New York: St. Martin's Press, 2007); Robert Higgs, *Delusions of Power: New Explorations of the State, War, and Economy* (Oakland, CA: Independent Institute, 2012); Paul A. C. Koistinen, *State of War: The Political Economy of American Warfare, 1945–2011* (Lawrence: University Press of Kansas, 2012).

7. Merton J. Peck and Frederic M. Scherer, *The Weapons Acquisition Process: An Economic Analysis* (Boston: Harvard Business School, 1962); Alain C. Enthoven and K. Wayne Smith, *How Much Is Enough? Shaping the Defense Program, 1961–1969* (New York: Harper & Row, 1971; Santa Monica, CA: RAND Corporation, 2005).

8. Elliott V. Converse III, *Rearming for the Cold War, 1945–1960* (Washington, DC: Historical Office, Office of the Secretary of Defense, 2012); Walter S. Poole, *Adapting to Flexible Response, 1960–1968* (Washington, DC: Historical Office, Office of the Secretary of Defense, 2013); J. Ronald Fox, *Defense Acquisition Reform, 1960–2009: An Elusive Goal* (Washington, DC: Center of Military History, 2011); Aaron L. Friedberg, *In the Shadow of the Garrison State: America's Anti-Statism and Its Cold War Grand Strategy* (Princeton, NJ: Princeton University Press, 2000); Linda Weiss, *America, Inc.?: Innovation and Enterprise in the National Security State* (Ithaca, NY: Cornell University Press, 2014); Peter Levine, *Defense Management Reform: How to Make the Pentagon Work Better and Cost Less* (Stanford, CA: Stanford University Press, 2020).

9. P. W. Singer, *Corporate Warriors: The Rise of the Privatized Military Industry* (Ithaca, NY: Cornell University Press, 2003); Deborah D. Avant, *The Market for Force: The Consequences of Privatizing Security* (New York: Cambridge University Press, 2005); Pratap Chatterjee, *Halliburton's Army: How a Well-Connected Texas Oil Company Revolutionized the Way America Makes War* (New York: Nation Books, 2009); Christopher Kinsey and Malcolm Hugh Patterson, eds., *Contractors and War: The Transformation of United States' Expeditionary Operations* (Palo Alto, CA: Stanford University Press, 2012).

10. For example, Kara Dixon Vuic, *Officer, Nurse, Woman: The Army Nurse Corps in the Vietnam War* (Baltimore: Johns Hopkins University Press, 2010); Aaron B. O'Connell, *Underdogs: The Making of the Modern Marine Corps* (Cambridge, MA: Harvard University Press, 2012); Olivier Burtin, "A Nation of Veterans: The American Legion and the Politics of Veterans' Citizenship" (PhD diss., Princeton University, 2017); Stuart Schrader, *Badges without Borders: How Global Counterinsurgency Transformed American Policing* (Chicago: University of Chicago Press, 2019); David Fitzgerald, *Militarization and the American Century: War, the United States and the World since 1941* (London: Bloomsbury Academic, 2021); Jana K. Lipman, *In Camps: Vietnamese Refugees, Asylum Seekers, and Repatriates* (Berkeley: University of California Press, 2020); Amy J. Rutenberg, *Rough Draft: Cold War Military Manpower Policy and the Origins of Vietnam-Era Draft Resistance* (Ithaca, NY: Cornell University Press, 2019); A. Junn Murphy, "Making Managers in the US Military: The Case of the Army Management School, 1945–1970," *Management & Organizational History* 15, no. 2 (May 2020): 154–168.

11. For example, Julia C. Ott, *When Wall Street Met Main Street: The Quest for an Investors' Democracy* (Cambridge, MA: Harvard University Press, 2011); Jonathan Levy, *Freaks of Fortune: The Emerging World of Capitalism and Risk in America* (Cambridge, MA: Harvard University Press, 2012); N. D. B. Connolly, *A World More Concrete: Real Estate and the Making of Jim Crow South Florida* (Chicago: University of Chicago Press, 2015); Justene Hill Edwards, *Unfree Markets: The Slaves' Economy and the Rise of Capitalism in South Carolina* (New York: Columbia University Press, 2021); Rakesh Khurana, *From Higher Aims to Hired Hands: The Social Transformation of American Business Schools and the Unfulfilled Promise of Management as a Profession* (Princeton, NJ: Princeton University Press, 2007); Angus Burgin, *The Great Persuasion: Reinventing Free Markets since the Depression* (Cambridge, MA: Harvard University Press, 2015).

12. A few social scientists have attempted to offer broad theoretical essays emphasizing historical transformation, pointing to an emergence of "post-Fordist" or "marketized" armed

forces, around the world, in recent decades. See, for example, Anthony King, "The Post-Fordist Military," *Journal of Political and Military Sociology* 34, no. 2 (2006): 359–74; Yagil Levy, "The Essence of the 'Market Army,'" *Public Administration Review* 70, no. 3 (2010): 378–89. Historians unsurprisingly have also led the way in new work historicizing military and market questions. See, for example, Beth Bailey, *America's Army: Making the All-Volunteer Force* (Cambridge, MA: Harvard University Press, 2009); Meredith Lair, *Armed with Abundance: Consumerism and Soldiering in the Vietnam War* (Chapel Hill: University of North Carolina Press, 2011); Jennifer Mittelstadt, *The Rise of the Military Welfare State* (Cambridge, MA: Harvard University Press, 2015); Wilson, *Destructive Creation*; Patrick Chung, "From Korea to Vietnam: Local Labor, Multinational Capital, and the Evolution of US Military Logistics, 1950–97," *Radical History Review* 133 (2019): 31–55; Betsy A. Beasley, "The Strange Career of Donald Rumsfeld: Military Logistics and the Routes from Vietnam to Iraq," *Radical History Review* 133 (2019): 56–77.

13. Jaime Amanda Martinez, *Confederate Slave Impressment in the Upper South* (Chapel Hill: University of North Carolina Press, 2013); Jeffrey A. Engel, ed., *Local Consequences of the Global Cold War* (Stanford, CA: Stanford University Press, 2007); Mark L. Gillem, *America Town: Building the Outposts of Empire* (Minneapolis: University of Minnesota Press, 2007); Catherine Lutz, ed., *The Bases of Empire: The Global Struggle Against US Military Posts* (New York: New York University Press, 2009); Maria Hhn and Seung Sook Moon, eds., *Over There: Living with US Military Empire from World War Two to the Present* (Chapel Hill, NC: Duke University Press, 2010); Jonathan M. Hansen, *Guantánamo: An American History* (New York: Hill & Wang, 2011); David Vine, *Base Nation: How US Military Bases Abroad Harm America and the World* (New York: Metropolitan Books, 2015); Daniel E. Bender and Jana K. Lipman, eds., *Making the Empire Work: Labor and United States Imperialism* (New York: New York University Press, 2015); Gretchen Heefner, "'A Slice of their Sovereignty': Negotiating the US Empire of Bases, Wheelus Field, Libya, 1950–1954", *Diplomatic History* 41, no. 1 (January 2017): 50–77; Kara Dixon Vuic, *The Girls Next Door: Bringing the Home Front to the Front Lines* (Cambridge, MA: Harvard University Press, 2019); Adam Moore, *Empire's Labor: The Global Army that Supports US Wars* (Ithaca, NY: Cornell University Press, 2019); Christopher Capozzola, *Bound by War: How the United States and the Philippines Built America's First Pacific Century* (New York: Basic Books, 2020).

Chapter 1

1. "Semiannual Report of the Secretary of the Navy, January 1, 1953 to June 30, 1953," in *Semiannual Report of the Secretary of Defense* (Washington, DC: Government Printing Office, 1953), 174–75.

2. Ibid., 205, 210, 227.

3. Joshua E. Klimas, "Balancing Consensus, Consent, and Competence: Richard Russell, the Senate Armed Services Committee, & Oversight of America's Defense, 1955–1968" (PhD diss., Ohio State University, 2007), 15; Gary Gerstle, *Liberty and Coercion: The Paradox of American Government from the Founding to the Present* (Princeton, NJ: Princeton University Press, 2015), 255–56.

4. In general, the literature on these subjects does a good deal to describe operations, doctrine, technology, organizational reform, the unusual economics of defense contracting, and procurement techniques, while paying less attention to important long-run qualitative transformations, entangled with broader political struggles, such as the one we discuss in this chapter. We cannot possibly cite much of the vast literature here, but for examples of broad surveys of

US military history, see Allan R. Millett, Peter Maslowski, and William B. Feis, *For the Common Defense: A Military History of the United States from 1607 to 2012* (New York: Free Press, 2012); Richard W. Stewart, ed., *American Military History, Volume II: The United States Army in a Global Era, 1917–2008*, 2nd ed. (Washington, DC: Center of Military History, 2010); and Paula G. Thornhill, *Demystifying the American Military: Institutions, Evolutions, and Challenges since 1789* (Annapolis, MD: Naval Institute Press, 2019). Overviews of the seemingly endless work of "defense acquisition reform" include J. Ronald Fox, *Defense Acquisition Reform, 1960–2009: An Elusive Goal* (Washington, DC: Government Printing Office, 2012); and Peter Levine, *Defense Management Reform: How to Make the Pentagon Work Better and Cost Less* (Stanford, CA: Stanford University Press, 2020).

5. Beth Bailey, *America's Army: Making the All-Volunteer Force* (Cambridge, MA: Harvard University Press, 2009); Jennifer Mittelstadt, *The Rise of the Military Welfare State* (Cambridge, MA: Harvard University Press, 2015); P. W. Singer, *Corporate Warriors: The Rise of the Privatized Military Industry* (Ithaca, NY: Cornell University Press, 2003); Deborah D. Avant, *The Market for Force: The Consequences of Privatizing Security* (New York: Cambridge University Press, 2005).

6. Of course, there are exceptions to this generalization. For a valuable account of privatization in the 1950s defense sector, but with a different interpretative perspective than the one we offer here, see Aaron L. Friedberg, *In the Shadow of the Garrison State: America's Anti-Statism and Its Cold War Grand Strategy* (Princeton, NJ: Princeton University Press, 2000), esp. 245–95. For accounts of the post–World War II defense sector that point to the importance of the privatization trend, see, e.g., Paul A. C. Koistinen, *State of War: The Political Economy of American Warfare, 1945–2011* (Lawrence: University Press of Kansas, 2012); Ann R. Markusen, "The Case Against Privatizing National Security," *Governance* 16, no. 4 (2003): 471–501; Daniel Wirls, *Irrational Security: The Politics of Defense from Reagan to Obama* (Baltimore: Johns Hopkins University Press, 2010); Mittelstadt, *Military Welfare State*.

7. David Harvey, *A Brief History of Neoliberalism* (New York: Oxford University Press, 2005); Kim Phillips-Fein, "The History of Neoliberalism," in *Shaped by the State: Toward a New Political History of the Twentieth Century*, ed. Brent Cebul, Lily Geismer, and Mason B. Williams (Chicago: University of Chicago Press, 2019), 347–62.

8. Gary Gerstle, "The Rise and Fall (?) of America's Neoliberal Order," *Transactions of the Royal Historical Society* 28 (2018): 241–64.

9. Among the many, diverse studies that suggest the deep, pre-1970s roots of the neoliberal transformation of the US political economy are Jennifer Klein, *For All These Rights: Business, Labor, and the Shaping of America's Public-Private Welfare State* (Princeton, NJ: Princeton University Press, 2003); Kim Phillips-Fein, *Invisible Hands: The Making of the Conservative Movement from the New Deal to Reagan* (New York: W. W. Norton, 2009); Michael A. McCarthy, *Dismantling Solidarity: Capitalist Politics and American Pensions Since the New Deal* (Ithaca, NY: Cornell University Press, 2017); Amy C. Offner, *Sorting Out the Mixed Economy: The Rise and Fall of Welfare and Developmental States in the Americas* (Princeton, NJ: Princeton University Press, 2019); Michael Glass and Sean Vanatta, "The Frail Bonds of Liberalism: Pensions, Schools, and the Unraveling of Fiscal Mutualism in Midcentury New York," *Capitalism: A Journal of History and Economics* 2, no. 2 (Summer 2021): 427–72.

10. For example, Offner, *Sorting Out the Mixed Economy*; Quinn Slobodian, *Globalists: The End of Empire and the Birth of Neoliberalism* (Cambridge, MA: Harvard University Press, 2018).

11. Ken Alder, *Engineering the Revolution: Arms and Enlightenment in France, 1763–1815* (Princeton, NJ: Princeton University Press, 1997); Gareth Cole, *Arming the Royal Navy, 1793–1815: The Office of Ordnance and the State* (London: Routledge, 2016).

12. Carter Goodrich, "State In, State Out: A Pattern of Development Policy," *Journal of Economic Issues* 2, no. 4 (Oct. 1968): 365–83; Richard R. John, *Spreading the News: The American Postal System from Franklin to Morse* (Cambridge, MA: Harvard University Press, 1995); John Lauritz Larson, *Internal Improvement: National Public Works and the Promise of Popular Government in the Early United States* (Chapel Hill: University of North Carolina Press, 2001); Gautham Rao, "Administering Entitlement: Governance, Public Healthcare, and the Early American State," *Law and Social Inquiry* 37, no. 3 (2012): 627–56.

13. Mark R. Wilson, *The Business of Civil War: Military Mobilization and the State, 1861–1865* (Baltimore: Johns Hopkins University Press, 2006); Stephen K. Stein, *From Torpedoes to Aviation: Washington Irving Chambers & Technological Innovation in the New Navy, 1876 to 1912* (Tuscaloosa: University of Alabama Press, 2007); Paul E. Pedisich, *Congress Buys a Navy: Politics, Economics, and the Rise of American Naval Power, 1881–1921* (Annapolis, MD: Naval Institute Press, 2016), esp. 129–30, 188–202.

14. Paul A. C. Koistinen, *Mobilizing for Modern War: The Political Economy of American Warfare, 1865–1919* (Lawrence: University Press of Kansas, 1997), 26–57; Peter A. Schulman, "'Science Can Never Demobilize': The United States Navy and Petroleum Geology, 1898–1924," *History and Technology* 19, no. 4 (2003): 365–85; Daniel R. Beaver, *Modernizing the American War Department: Change and Continuity in a Turbulent Era, 1885–1920* (Kent, OH: Kent State University Press, 2006); Phyllis A. Zimmerman, *The Neck of the Bottle: George W. Goethals and the Reorganization of the US Army Supply System, 1917–1918* (College Station: Texas A&M University Press, 1992); Terrence J. Gough, "The Battle of Washington: Soldiers and Businessmen in World War I" (PhD diss., University of Virginia, 1997).

15. Mark R. Wilson, *Destructive Creation: American Business and the Winning of World War II* (Philadelphia: University of Pennsylvania Press, 2016).

16. Beaver, *Modernizing the American War Department*, 15–16.

17. *Report of the Special Committee Appointed to Investigate Government Competition with Private Enterprise*, House Report No. 1985, 77nd Cong., 2nd sess. (Washington, DC: Government Printing Office, 1933).

18. For a valuable account of privatization in the 1950s defense sector that covers some of the same ground as the following paragraphs, but with a different interpretative perspective, see Friedberg, *In the Shadow of the Garrison State*, 245–95.

19. "How to Save $7.5 Billion a Year: A Condensation," *Facts Forum News* (May 1956): 31–38, copy in folder 13 (Hoover Report), box 12, General Information: Pre-1970 Series, Phyllis Schafly Collection, Eagle Forum Archives, St. Louis, MO; Commission on the Organization of the Executive Branch of Government, *Business Enterprises: A Report to Congress* (Washington, DC: Government Printing Office, 1955).

20. How to Save $7.5 Billion a Year—and Reduce Your Personal Income Tax by 25 Per Cent!," *Human Events* 13, no. 2 (January 14, 1956): n.p., copy in folder 13 (Hoover Report), box 12, General Information: Pre-1970 Series, Phyllis Schafly Collection. See Lawrence B. Glickman, *Free Enterprise: An American Idea* (New Haven, CT: Yale University Press, 2019).

21. The 1955 language appears in L. Elaine Halchin, *The Federal Activities Inventory Reform Act and Circular A-76*, Congressional Research Service, Order Code RL31024 (April 2007).

22. Folder Cabinet Meeting of January 7, 1955, box 4, Cabinet Series, DDE Papers as President, Dwight D. Eisenhower Presidential Library, Abilene, KS.

23. White House press release, 27 Oct. 1956, folder OF 102-Q Government Competition with Private Enterprise, box 384, WHCF Official File, Eisenhower Library.

24. J. P. Pike to Carl Hayden, 8 Aug. 1955, copy in folder 6, box 106, Series IX (Legislative), Richard B. Russell Collection, Richard B. Russell Library, University of Georgia, Athens.

25. Logistics Management Institute, *Reconnaissance Study of Service Contract Methodology*, Task 69-9, Contract SD-271 (Washington, DC: Logistics Management Institute, 1969), 4.

26. Halchin, *Federal Activities Inventory Reform Act and Circular A-76*.

27. "Memorandum Announcing Revised Guidelines Governing Development by the Government of Products or Services for Its Own Use," Public Papers of the Presidents of the United States, Book I, 1967, https://www.presidency.ucsb.edu/documents/memorandum-announcing-revised-guidelines-governing-development-the-government-products-or.

28. Alain C. Enthoven and K. Wayne Smith, *How Much Is Enough? Shaping the Defense Program, 1961–1969* (New York: Harper & Row, 1971; Santa Monica, CA: RAND Corporation, 2005); John A. Byrne, *The Whiz Kids: The Founding Fathers of American Business—and the Legacy They Left Us* (New York: Doubleday, 1993); Lawrence S. Kaplan, Roland D. Landa, and Edward J. Drea, *The McNamara Ascendancy, 1961–1965* (Washington, DC: Historical Office, Office of the Secretary of Defense, 2006).

29. Undated 1965 memo, "LU," Office of the Assistant Secretary of Defense for Installations and Logistics, to McNamara, on "Base System Analyses-Industrial Facilities," folder Base Systems Analyses 1965, entry 13230-A, Robert S. McNamara Papers, Record Group 200, National Archives, College Park, MD.

30. McNamara to LBJ, 7 July 1964, folder ND 11 11/22/63-11/8/64, box 174, ND Series, White House Central Files, LBJ Presidential Library, Austin, TX; Walter S. Poole, *Adapting to Flexible Response, 1960–1968* (Washington, DC: Historical Office, Office of the Secretary of Defense, 2013).

31. DOD press release, March 6, 1970, folder Base Closures, 1970–71, box A56, Melvin R. Laird Papers, Gerald R. Ford Presidential Library, Ann Arbor, MI.

32. Commander J. J. Meyer, Jr., "Our Nation's Shipyards," *US Naval Institute Proceedings* 90, no. 11 (November 1964): 34–45; Commander F. E. Smetheram, "Comment and Discussion: 'Our Nation's Shipyards,'" *US Naval Institute Proceedings* 91, no. 3 (March 1965): 102–3; Commander R. C. Austin, "Comment and Discussion: 'Our Nation's Shipyards,'" *US Naval Institute Proceedings* 91, no. 4 (April 1965): 106–8.

33. Brig. Gen. D. A. Raymond, "A Brick and Mortar View of Construction in South Vietnam," *Defense Management Journal* 3, no. 4 (Fall 1967): 17–21; Scot MacDonald, "Overseas Military Construction: How Should It Be Done?" *Armed Forces Management* (June 1967): 51–56. See also James M. Carter, *Inventing Vietnam: The United States and State Building, 1954–1968* (New York: Cambridge University Press, 2008); Meredith H. Lair, *Armed with Abundance: Consumerism & Soldiering in the Vietnam War* (Chapel Hill: University of North Carolina Press, 2011).

34. John T. Warner and Beth J. Asch, "The Record and Prospects of the All-Volunteer Military in the United States," *Journal of Economic Perspectives* 15, no. 2 (Spring 2001): 190; Beth Bailey, *America's Army: Making the All-Volunteer Force* (Cambridge, MA: Harvard University Press, 2009), 21–33.

35. *The Report of the President's Commission on an All-Volunteer Armed Force* (Washington, DC: Government Printing Office, 1970), 63.

36. Harold Moore, "On Pay and Benefits" a 'Balanced Approach,'" *Army Magazine* 26, no. 10 (October 1976): 101.

37. Elizabeth Wickenden, *The Military Program and Social Welfare* (New York: National Committee on Social Work in Defense Mobilization, 1955), 23–25. For the full history of these social welfare programs see Mittelstadt, *Rise of the Military Welfare State*.

38. Mike Causey, "Private Contract Worker Push Revives," *Washington Post*, February 7, 1974; OMB, "Presidential Management Initiatives," Memorandum to Cabinet Members and Heads of Major Agencies, July 27, 1976, quoted in Martin Binkin, *Shaping the Defense Civilian Work Force: Economics, Politics and National Security* (Washington, DC: Brookings Institution, 1978), 23.

39. US General Accounting Office, *How to Improve Procedures for Deciding Between Contractor and In-House Military BAE Support Services*, LCD-76-347 (1977), https://www.gao.gov/products/lcd-76-347.

40. Department of the Army, *Historical Summary: Fiscal Year 1973* (Washington, DC: Government Printing Office, 1977), 95–96, 112, 144; Department of the Army, *Historical Summary: Fiscal Year 1975* (Washington, DC: Government Printing Office, 2000), 104; Department of the Army, *Historical Summary: Fiscal Year 1978* (Washington, DC: Government Printing Office, 1980), 138, 145–146; Department of the Army, *Historical Summary: Fiscal Year 1979* (Washington, DC: Government Printing Office, 1982), 87–88, 112–13.

41. Charles Shrader, *History of Operations Research in the United States Army*, Volume 3: *1973–1995* (Washington, DC: Center of Military History, 2009).

42. Department of the Army, *Historical Summary: Fiscal Year 1977* (Washington, DC: Government Printing Office, 1979), 28.

43. Pamela G. Hollie, "Northrop Finds Profit in Full-Service Pacts," *New York Times*, May 26, 1979; Northrop news release, "Northrop Awarded $28.8 Million Contract for Vance Air Force Base Support," 4 Oct. 1982, folder 3, box 26, Northrop Grumman Corporation Records, Huntington Library, San Marino, CA.

44. President's Private Sector Survey on Cost Control (Grace Commission), *A Report to the President* (Washington, DC: Government Printing Office, 1984), 3: 7, 16–17, 81.

45. Grace Commission, *Report to the President*, 3: 159.

46. Halchin, *Federal Activities Inventory Reform Act and Circular A-76*; Michal Laurie Tingle, "Privatization and the Reagan Administration: Ideology and Application," *Yale Law & Policy Review* 6, no. 1 (1988): 235.

47. John Handy and Dennis O'Connor, "A-76 Competitions: 'How Winners Win,'" *Defense Management Journal* 21, no. 3 (1985): 2–9.

48. In the 1990s, the cap was raised to 50 percent, creating the now well-known "50-50 rule." Michael Boito, Cynthia R. Cook, and John C. Graser, *Contractor Logistics Support in the US Air Force* (Santa Monica, CA: RAND Corporation, 2009), 10–12, https://www.rand.org/content/dam/rand/pubs/monographs/2009/RAND_MG779.pdf.

49. Secretary of Defense Caspar W. Weinberger, *Annual Report to the Congress, on the FY 1988/FY 1989 Budget and FY 1988–92 Defense Programs* (Washington, DC: Government Printing Office, 1987), 121, 331; Grace Commission, *Report to the President*, 3: 159.

50. During and after World War II, the US military, which previously recruited mostly single males, increasingly drafted married men with families—so much so that military "dependents"—spouses and children—came to outnumber military personnel. Sondra Albano, "Military Recognition of Family Concerns: Revolutionary War to 1993," *Armed Forces & Society* 20, no. 2 (Winter 1994): 283–302.

51. List from Zahava D. Doering and Bette S. Mahoney, *Briefing Notes: A Discussion of Military Dependents' Issues* (Arlington, VA: Defense Manpower Data Center, 1986), 29.

52. See especially P. W. Singer, *Corporate Warriors: The Rise of the Privatized Military Industry* (Ithaca, NY: Cornell University Press, 2003), chapter 9; Pratap Chatterjee, *Halliburton's*

Army: How a Well-Connected Texas Oil Company Revolutionized the Way America Makes War (New York: Nation Books, 2009).

53. US Army Materiel Command Historical Office, "A Brief History of AMC, 1962–2000" (Redstone Arsenal, AL: US Army Materiel Command, 2013), 4; Department of the Army, *Historical Summary: Fiscal Year 1990/1991* (Washington, DC: Government Printing Office, 1991), 121.

54. "A Brief History of AMC," 5.

55. Department of the Army, *Historical Summary: Fiscal Year 1989* (Washington, DC: Government Printing Office, 1989), 187–88.

56. "Supplemental History Report to the Transition Team for General Ross," 23 December, 1991, folder Transition Team Report (Vol A-1), 31 January, 1992 (2 of 3), box 8, Jimmy D. Ross papers, Military History Institute, US Army Heritage and Education Center, Carlisle, PA [hereafter MHI], 5; *Historical Summary Fiscal Year 1990/1991*, 122; Department of the Army, *Historical Summary: Fiscal Year 1992* (Washington, DC: Government Printing Office, 1992), 94; Department of the Army, *Historical Summary: Fiscal Year 1995* (Washington, DC: Government Printing Office, 1995), 90; Angel R. Martinez Lorente, Frank Dewhurst, and Barrie G. Dale, "Total Quality Management: Origins and Evolution of the Term," *TQM Magazine* 10, no. 5 (1998): 378–86; Ahmad K. Elshennawy and Kimberly M. McCarthy. "Implementing Total Quality Management at the US Department of Defense," *Total Quality Management* 3, no. 1 (1992): 31–46; John Rhea, "Total Quality Management: Myths and Realities," *National Defense* (Jan. 1990): 25–27.

57. Dennis Reimer, "VCSA Speech Book: Garrison Commanders' Conference Remarks, December 9, 1991, folder 870-5f, 9 Dec 1992 [*sic*], Garrison Commanders Conference, box 48, series VI, Dennis J. Reimer papers, MHI, 16, 17.

58. For the range of these activities, see folder 5: General Management Correspondence, June 1998 (1 of 2), box 12; and PowerPoint presentation, folder 870–56: CSA, Captains of Industry, March 7, 1997, box 33; W. K. Sutey to Reimer, memo, March 31, 1997; "National Security Leadership Course: Department of Defense Executive Management Development and Training Program," brochure, both in folder 870–5f: CSA, Office Call, Hon Sean O'Keefe, Maxwell School, Syracuse University, April 2, 1997, box 71; Peter Senge to Reimer, March 31, 1997, and Reimer to Senge, April 14, 1997, both letters in folder 5: General Management Correspondence, April 1997 (2 of 4), box 9, all in Reimer papers, MHI.

59. Institute for Defense and Business, "The First Annual General William G. T. Tuttle, Jr., USA (Ret.) Award for Business Acumen in Defense and Government," *PR Newswire,* www.prnewswire.com/news-releases/the-first-annual-general-william-gt-tuttle-jr-usa-ret-award-for-business-acumen-in-defense-and-government-115269869.html; *Historical Summary Fiscal Year 1990/1991*, 121–22; Bill Tuttle to Reimer, July 16, 1998, folder 5: General Management Correspondence July 1998 (1 of 2), box 12, Reimer papers, MHI.

60. Mark D. Sherry, *The Army Command Post and Defense Reshaping, 1987–1997* (Washington, DC: Government Printing Office, 2008), 146.

61. Lieutenant Colonel James L. Fletcher, "Medical Supply Readiness: Maximizing and Globalizing the DOD Partnership with Industry," US Army Strategy Research Project, US Army War College, Carlisle Barracks, 1998, https://apps.dtic.mil/dtic/tr/fulltext/u2/a345544.pdf.

62. Indeed, Osborne referred approvingly to the Hoover Commissions in public discussions. "Press Briefing on *Reinventing Government* by David Osborne and John Sharp, September 7, 1993," Public Papers of the President, William Jefferson Clinton, The American Presidency

Project, University of California Santa Barbara, http://www.presidency.ucsb.edu/ws/index.php ?pid=60041.

63. At the heart of the Clinton-Gore exercise in "reinventing government" lay the practice of "outsourcing," the corporate term used to describe the contracting out of so called noncore functions of firms—or government—to (other) private entities. See, for example, "Remarks by the President and the Vice President at Reinventing Government Anniversary Event," (14 Sept. 1994), in National Performance Review papers, University of North Texas: http://govinfo.library .unt.edu/npr/index.htm

64. William Perry to Les Aspin, 8 April 1993, folder 14, box 31, Part 4, Les Aspin Papers, Wisconsin Historical Society; Paul Taibi, Executive Summary, "Outsourcing and Privatization of Defense Infrastructure" (Washington, DC: BENS, 1997), 5, https://apps.dtic.mil/sti/pdfs /ADA530702.pdf; American Consulting Engineers Council, "The Last Word: ACEC Endorses HR 716, Asks DOD to be Leader in Government Outsourcing," 13, no. 7, March 17, 1996, Internet Archive (Way Back Machine), accessed April 2014.

65. "US Army Materiel Command, End of Tour Oral History Interviews: Lieutenant General James M. Link," interviewed 11–12 July 2000, MHI.

66. Jesse Ellman et al., *Defense Contract Trends: US Department of Defense Contract Spending and the Supporting Industrial Base* (Washington, DC: Center for Strategic and International Studies, 2011), 7–8, 27.

67. Maj. Michael T. Braman, "Privatization of Military Repair Depots" (Air Command and Staff College, 1997).

68. Donald H. Rumsfeld, "Bureaucracy to Battlefield," 10 Sept. 2001, PDF of transcript available at http://papers.rumsfeld.com/library (accessed December 2017); for video, see https://www.c-span.org/video/?165947-1/defense-business-practices.

69. A fuller discussion of the post-2001 wars in Afghanistan and Iraq is outside the scope of this article. Works by journalists and historians that emphasize the role of contractors include Naomi Klein, *The Shock Doctrine: The Rise of Disaster Capitalism* (New York: Metropolitan Books, 2007); Allison Stanger, *One Nation Under Contract: The Outsourcing of American Power and the Future of Foreign Policy* (New Haven, CT: Yale University Press, 2009); Christopher Kinsey and Malcolm Hugh Patterson, eds., *Contractors and War: The Transformation of United States' Expeditionary Operations* (Palo Alto, CA: Stanford University Press, 2012). See also Wirls, *Irrational Security*.

70. Dana Priest and Anne Hull, Soldiers Face Neglect at Army's Top Medical Facility," *Washington Post*, February 18, 2007; Steve Vogel and Renae Merle, "Privatized Walter Reed Workforce Gets Scrutiny," *Washington Post*, March 10, 2007; Charles S. Clark, "Ban on A-76 Competitions for Outsourcing Extended in Omnibus Bill," *Government Executive* (December 22, 2011), https://www.govexec.com/defense/2011/12/ban-on-a-76-competitions-for-outsourcing-extended-in -omnibus-bill/35708/.

71. US General Accounting Office, "Defense Logistics: Air Force Report on Contractor Support Is Narrowly Focused" (2000), https://www.gao.gov/products/nsiad-00-115; author interview with former US Secretary of Defense, May 16, 2018.

72. For accounts emphasizing associationalism and hybridity, see Brian Balogh, *The Associational State: American Governance in the Twentieth Century* (Philadelphia: University of Pennsylvania Press, 2015); Linda Weiss, *America Inc.?: Innovation and Enterprise in the National Security State* (Ithaca, NY: Cornell University Press, 2014); Eugene Gholz and Harvey M. Sapolsky, "The Defense Innovation Machine: Why the US Will Remain on the Cutting

Edge," *Journal of Strategic Studies* (published online June 2021), DOI:10.1080/01402390.2021.1917392.

Chapter 2

For their generous feedback on earlier drafts, the author would like to thank Elizabeth Blackmar, Emilie Connolly, Joan Flores-Villalobos, Beth Bailey, the Project on the Political Economy of Security at Boston University, the Business History Seminar at Harvard Business School, and this volume's two anonymous reviewers.

1. US House Committee on Armed Services, *Report of Special Subcommittee on Acquisition of Wherry Housing*, 86th Cong., 1st sess. (Washington, DC: Government Printing Office, 1959), 1937.

2. *Report of Special Subcommittee on Acquisition of Wherry Housing*, 1944–45.

3. *Report of Special Subcommittee on Acquisition of Wherry Housing*, 1835.

4. Elizabeth A. Fones-Wolf, *Selling Free Enterprise: The Business Assault on Labor and Liberalism, 1945–60* (Urbana: University of Illinois Press, 1994); Wendy L. Wall, *Inventing the "American Way": The Politics of Consensus from the New Deal to the Civil Rights Movement* (New York: Oxford University Press, 2008); Kim Phillips-Fein, *Invisible Hands: The Making of the Conservative Movement from the New Deal to Reagan* (New York: W. W. Norton, 2009); Lawrence B. Glickman, *Free Enterprise: An American History* (New Haven, CT: Yale University Press, 2019).

5. US Department of Defense, *Annual Report of the Secretary of Defense and the Annual Reports of the Secretary of the Army, Secretary of the Navy, Secretary of the Air Force, July 1, 1959, to June 30, 1960* (Washington, DC: Government Printing Office, 1961), 55.

6. The programs discussed in this essay dealt with construction in the United States, Alaska, and Hawai'i, but the provision of family housing for US service members stationed overseas in foreign and other US territories is a fascinating subject worthy of dedicated research. Like overseas US base infrastructure more generally, family housing in foreign territories was arranged through diplomatic agreements. Its construction was in part funded by the export of surplus agricultural commodities. For research on the US military's global network of bases, see Chalmers Johnson, *The Sorrows of Empire: Militarism, Secrecy, and the End of the Republic* (New York: Metropolitan Books, 2005); Mark L. Gillem, *America Town: Building the Outposts of Empire* (Minneapolis: University of Minnesota Press, 2007); Catherine Lutz, ed., *The Bases of Empire: The Global Struggle Against US Military Posts* (New York: New York University Press, 2009); Maria Höhn and Seungsook Moon, eds., *Over There: Living with the US Military Empire from World War Two to the Present* (Durham, NC: Duke University Press, 2010); Gretchen Heefner, "'A Slice of Their Sovereignty': Negotiating the US Empire of Bases, Wheelus Field, Libya, 1950–1954," *Diplomatic History* 41, no. 1 (January 2017): 50–77.

7. Jennifer Mittelstadt, *The Rise of the Military Welfare State* (Cambridge, MA: Harvard University Press, 2015); Beth L. Bailey, *America's Army: Making the All-Volunteer Force* (Cambridge, MA: Belknap Press of Harvard University Press, 2009).

8. Aaron L. Friedberg, *In the Shadow of the Garrison State: America's Anti-Statism and Its Cold War Grand Strategy* (Princeton, NJ: Princeton University Press, 2000); Mark R. Wilson, "Farewell to Progressivism: The Second World War and the Privatization of the 'Military-Industrial Complex,'" in *Capital Gains: Business and Politics in Twentieth-Century America*, eds. Richard R. John and Kim Phillips-Fein (Philadelphia: University of Pennsylvania Press, 2017), 80–94; Paul A. C. Koistinen, *State of War: The Political Economy of American Warfare, 1945–2011* (Lawrence: University Press of Kansas, 2012).

9. The civilian public housing estimate is based on the 509,367 reported units built under the Housing Act of 1949 and administered by the Public Housing Authority by the end of 1964. US Department of Housing and Urban Development, *Annual Report 1965* (Washington, DC: Government Printing Office, 1965), 167; Virge J. Temme, "'For Want of a Home . . .': A Historic Context for Wherry and Capehart Military Family Housing" (Aberdeen Proving Ground, MD: US Army Environmental Center, 1998), 4.

10. Jennifer Mittelstadt, *From Welfare to Workfare: The Unintended Consequences of Liberal Reform, 1945–1965* (Chapel Hill: University of North Carolina Press, 2005); Karen M. Tani, *States of Dependency: Welfare, Rights, and American Governance, 1935–1972* (New York: Cambridge University Press, 2016); Alice Kessler-Harris, *In Pursuit of Equity: Women, Men, and the Quest for Economic Citizenship in 20th Century America* (New York: Oxford University Press, 2001); Ira Katznelson, *When Affirmative Action Was White: An Untold History of Racial Inequality in Twentieth-Century America* (New York: W. W. Norton, 2005).

11. Tithi Bhattacharya, ed., *Social Reproduction Theory: Remapping Class, Recentering Oppression* (London: Pluto Press, 2017); Eileen Boris, "Reproduction as Production: Thinking with the ILO to Move Beyond Dichotomy," *Journal of Labor and Society* 22, no. 2 (December 15, 2019): 283–98; Mariarosa Dalla Costa and Selma James, *The Power of Women and the Subversion of the Community* (Bristol, UK: Falling Wall Press, 1975); Evelyn Nakano Glenn, "From Servitude to Service Work: Historical Continuities in the Racial Division of Paid Reproductive Labor," *Signs: Journal of Women in Culture and Society* 18, no. 1 (October 1992): 1–43.

12. Alice Kessler-Harris, "In the Nation's Image: The Gendered Limits of Social Citizenship in the Depression Era," *Journal of American History* 86, no. 3 (December 1999): 1251–79; Linda Gordon, *Pitied but Not Entitled: Single Mothers and the History of Welfare, 1890–1935* (Cambridge, MA: Harvard University Press, 1995); Margot Canaday, *The Straight State: Sexuality and Citizenship in Twentieth-Century America* (Princeton, NJ: Princeton University Press, 2009); Gwendolyn Mink, *The Wages of Motherhood: Inequality in the Welfare State, 1917–1942* (Ithaca, NY: Cornell University Press, 1995); Suzanne Mettler, *Dividing Citizens: Gender and Federalism in New Deal Public Policy* (Ithaca, NY: Cornell University Press, 1998).

13. William C. Baldwin, *Four Housing Privatization Programs: A History of the Wherry, Capehart, Section 801, & Section 802 Family Housing Programs in the Army* (Alexandria, VA: Office of History, US Army Corps of Engineers, 1996).

14. For recent work highlighting complex and counterintuitive dynamics of public-private partnerships, see Elizabeth Hinton, *From the War on Poverty to the War on Crime: The Making of Mass Incarceration in America* (Cambridge, MA: Harvard University Press, 2016); Amy C. Offner, *Sorting Out the Mixed Economy: The Rise and Fall of Welfare and Developmental States in the Americas* (Princeton, NJ: Princeton University Press, 2019); Keeanga-Yamahtta Taylor, *Race for Profit: How Banks and the Real Estate Industry Undermined Black Homeownership* (Chapel Hill: University of North Carolina Press, 2019).

15. For analyses of hidden structures of state investment, see Christopher Howard, *The Hidden Welfare State: Tax Expenditures and Social Policy in the United States* (Princeton, NJ: Princeton University Press, 1997); Suzanne Mettler, *The Submerged State: How Invisible Government Policies Undermine American Democracy* (Chicago: University of Chicago Press, 2011); Mariana Mazzucato, *The Entrepreneurial State: Debunking Public vs. Private Sector Myths* (London: Anthem Press, 2013); Monica Prasad, *The Land of Too Much: American Abundance and the Paradox of Poverty* (Cambridge, MA: Harvard University Press, 2012); Sarah L. Quinn, *American Bonds: How Credit Markets Shaped a Nation* (Princeton, NJ: Princeton University Press, 2019).

16. Ruth Wilson Gilmore, *Golden Gulag: Prisons, Surplus, Crisis, and Opposition in Globalizing California* (Berkeley: University of California Press, 2007); Tim Barker, "Macroeconomic Consequences of Peace: American Radical Economists and the Problem of Military Keynesianism, 1938–1975," *Research in the History of Economic Thought and Methodology* 37 (2019): 11–29; Lisa McGirr, *Suburban Warriors: The Origins of the New American Right* (Princeton, NJ: Princeton University Press, 2001); Seymour Melman, *Pentagon Capitalism: The Political Economy of War* (New York: McGraw Hill, 1970).

17. The military has a long and robust history of taking on many functions of social reproduction for its own members, expressed in the military concepts of "subsistence" and later "sustainment," which referred to the logistics and personnel services needed to reproduce its own labor force. Mark R. Wilson, *The Business of Civil War: Military Mobilization and the State, 1861–1865* (Baltimore: Johns Hopkins University Press, 2006).

18. Manpower levels rebounded in the 1950s with the adoption of the NSC-68 strategy for defense buildup and the Korean War. US Department of Defense, Washington Headquarters Services, Directorate for Information, Operations and Reports, *Department of Defense: Selected Manpower Statistics, Fiscal Year 1997* (Washington, DC: Government Printing Office, 1997), 51.

19. While the demographics of the military were changing in many ways, changes in its gender composition were limited. The Women's Armed Services Integration Act of 1948 opened all military branches to women, but it also limited the number of women to 2 percent of the enlisted population and restricted opportunities for promotion. More women began joining the military in the 1970s, after gender restrictions were reformed. Tanya L. Roth, "'An Attractive Career for Women': Opportunities, Limitations, and Women's Integration in the Cold War Military," in *Integrating the US Military: African Americans, Women, and Gays Since World War II*, eds. Douglas Walter Bristol, Jr., and Heather Marie Stur (Baltimore: Johns Hopkins University Press, 2017), 74–95.

20. Elaine Tyler May, *Homeward Bound: American Families in the Cold War Era* (New York: Basic Books, 1988).

21. US House Committee on Banking and Currency, *Housing Amendments of 1955: Hearings Before the Committee on Banking and Currency*, 84th Cong., 1st sess. (Washington, DC: Government Printing Office, 1955), 116.

22. Temme, "For Want of a Home," 14.

23. T. B. Larkin, "For Want of a House," *Army Information Digest* 5, no. 4 (April 1950): 11–12.

24. *Report of Special Subcommittee on Acquisition of Wherry Housing*, 1950–51.

25. Laura McEnaney, *Postwar: Waging Peace in Chicago* (Philadelphia: University of Pennsylvania Press, 2018); Lizabeth Cohen, *A Consumers' Republic: The Politics of Mass Consumption in Postwar America* (New York: Knopf, 2003).

26. George Lipsitz, *Rainbow at Midnight: Labor and Culture in the 1940s* (Urbana: University of Illinois Press, 1994), 20.

27. "$40,000,000 Construction Sought Here: Servicemen Housed in Chicken Coops, House Group Told. Chicken Coops House Troops," *Washington Post*, July 14, 1949; "Play and Housing Held Forces' Need: President's Committee Reports These Are Top Problems of Men in Services," *New York Times*, April 30, 1949.

28. Agnes E. Meyer, "Military and Civilians in a Housing Tug-of-War," *Washington Post*, June 5, 1949.

29. Temme, "For Want of a Home," 13.

30. Temme, 22.

31. N. D. B. Connolly, *A World More Concrete: Real Estate and the Remaking of Jim Crow South Florida* (Chicago: University of Chicago Press, 2014); David M. Freund, *Colored Property: State Policy and White Racial Politics in Suburban America* (Chicago: University of Chicago Press, 2007); Arnold R. Hirsch, *Making the Second Ghetto: Race and Housing in Chicago, 1940–1960* (New York: Cambridge University Press, 1983); Kenneth T. Jackson, *Crabgrass Frontier: The Suburbanization of the United States* (New York: Oxford University Press, 1985); Richard Rothstein, *The Color of Law: A Forgotten History of How Our Government Segregated America* (New York: Liveright, 2017).

32. Katznelson, *When Affirmative Action Was White*, 140; Louis Lee Woods II, "Almost 'No Negro Veteran ... Could Get A Loan': African Americans, the GI Bill, and the NAACP Campaign Against Residential Segregation, 1917–1960," *Journal of African American History* 98, no. 3 (2013): 392–417.

33. Freund, *Colored Property*; Cohen, *A Consumers' Republic*; Quinn, *American Bonds*; David Stein, "Containing Keynesianism in an Age of Civil Rights: Jim Crow Monetary Policy and the Struggle for Guaranteed Jobs, 1956–1979," in *Beyond the New Deal Order: US Politics from the Great Depression to the Great Recession*, ed. Gary Gerstle, Nelson Lichtenstein, and Alice O'Connor (Philadelphia: University of Pennsylvania Press, 2019).

34. Exec. Order No. 9,981, 13 Fed. Reg. 4313 (July 26, 1948); Douglas Walter Bristol and Heather Marie Stur, *Integrating the US Military: Race, Gender, and Sexual Orientation since World War II* (Baltimore: Johns Hopkins University Press, 2017); Morris J. MacGregor, *Integration of the Armed Forces, 1940–1965* (Washington, DC: US Army Center of Military History, 1981); Ulysses Lee, *The Employment of Negro Troops* (Washington, DC: Office of the Chief of Military History, US Army, 1966).

35. Catherine Lutz, *Homefront: A Military City and the American Twentieth Century* (Boston: Beacon Press, 2001); Carol Lynn McKibben, *Racial Beachhead: Diversity and Democracy in a Military Town* (Palo Alto, CA: Stanford University Press, 2011); Andrew H. Myers, *Black, White, & Olive Drab: Racial Integration at Fort Jackson, South Carolina, and the Civil Rights Movement* (Charlottesville: University of Virginia Press, 2006); Ryan Reft, "The Metropolitan Military: Navy Families and Housing in the American Sunbelt, 1941–2000" (PhD diss., University of California, San Diego, 2014); James T. Sparrow, "Behind the Atomic Curtain: School Desegregation and Territoriality in the Early Cold War," *Tocqueville Review* 33, no. 2 (December 29, 2012): 115–39; Brian McAllister Linn, *Elvis's Army: Cold War GIs and the Atomic Battlefield* (Cambridge, MA: Harvard University Press, 2016); Bristol and Stur, *Integrating the US Military*.

36. In the decades following formal integration, African American service members continued to face discrimination in off-base housing, schools, and amenities and faced racist abuse and violence, occupational segregation, and inequities in promotion. Kimberley L. Phillips, *War! What Is It Good for? Black Freedom Struggles & the US Military from World War II to Iraq* (Chapel Hill: University of North Carolina Press, 2012); James E. Westheider, *Fighting on Two Fronts: African Americans and the Vietnam War* (New York: New York University Press, 1997); United States Commission on Civil Rights, *Report of the United States Commission on Civil Rights* (Washington, DC: Government Printing Office, 1963); "McNamara Thinks Military Should Work with Communities on Racism," *Atlanta Daily World*, October 10, 1963.

37. Norman Lloyd, "Housing Called Service Health Problem No. 1: Shortage Also Strikes at Morale," *Chicago Daily Tribune*, April 4, 1949.

38. Temme, "For Want of a Home," 30.

39. Kenneth W. Condit, *The Joint Chiefs of Staff and National Policy, 1947–1949* (Washington, DC: Office of Joint History, Office of the Chairman of the Joint Chiefs of Staff, 1996), 100.

40. Congress expanded access to family housing and private housing allowances to enlisted service members ranking E-4 and above with the Career Compensation Act of 1949, as amended in 1950. Enlisted grades 1 through 3 were not eligible even if they had families, meaning most enlisted service members would become eligible after reenlisting and completing a second term of service. Access to military family housing for junior enlisted service members was extended in the mid-1980s but subject to limited availability. *An Act to Provide Allowances for Dependents of Enlisted Members of the Uniformed Services, to Suspend Certain Provisions of the Career Compensation Act of 1949, and for Other Purposes*, Pub. L. 81-771, *US Statutes at Large* 64 (1950): 794–97; Congressional Budget Office, *Military Family Housing in the United States* (Washington, DC: Congressional Budget Office, 1993).

41. "Troop housing" refers to barracks and bachelors' quarters, that is, not family housing. Industrial facilities are not represented in Figure 1 because they fell out of the reported categories (the top ten) in the mid-1960s. For the same reason, the figure for storage facilities in 1978 is missing from the report. *Real and Personal Property of the Department of Defense* (Washington, DC: US Department of Defense, 1955–80).

42. Mark R. Wilson, *Destructive Creation: American Business and the Winning of World War II* (Philadelphia: University of Pennsylvania Press, 2016), 62.

43. Congressional Budget Office, *Military Family Housing in the United States.*

44. Baldwin, *Four Housing Privatization Programs*; Reft, "The Metropolitan Military," 2014; Kathryn M. Kuranda et al., *Housing an Army: The Wherry and Capehart Era Solutions to the Postwar Family Housing Shortage (1949–1962): A Historic Context Prepared for the Department of the Army* (Frederick, MD: R. Christopher Goodwin & Associates, 2003); Kathryn M. Kuranda et al., *Housing an Air Force and a Navy: The Wherry and Capehart Era Solutions to the Postwar Family Housing Shortage (1949–1962)* (Frederick, MD: R. Christopher Goodwin & Associates, 2007).

45. Lindsay Schakenbach Regele, *Manufacturing Advantage: War, the State, and the Origins of American Industry, 1776–1848* (Baltimore: Johns Hopkins University Press, 2018); Wilson, *The Business of Civil War*; Katherine C. Epstein, *Torpedo: Inventing the Military-Industrial Complex in the United States and Great Britain* (Cambridge, MA: Harvard University Press, 2014).

46. An exceptional period of construction under the Lanham Act produced nearly a million units of government housing during WWII. This housing accommodated some service members but primarily served civilian defense workers at new production sites activated around the country for the war emergency. Lanham Act housing units were required by law to be disposed of after the war, partly because of the threat they posed to private real estate interests. They were generally of temporary construction and many were transferred local public housing authorities, demolished, or sold to private buyers. Kuranda et al., *Housing an Air Force and a Navy*, 63; Ryan Reft, "The Privatization of Military Family Housing in Linda Vista, 1944–1956," *California History* 92, no. 1 (May 2015): 53–72.

47. Echoing controversies over profit renegotiation with military contractors in WWII, the Wherry program was undone by controversy over developers extracting more profit than Congress intended. See Mark R. Wilson, "'Taking a Nickel Out of the Cash Register': Statutory Renegotiation of Military Contracts and the Politics of Profit Control in the United States During World War II," *Law and History Review* 28, no. 2 (May 2010): 343–83; Stuart D. Brandes, *Warhogs: A History of War Profits in America* (Lexington: University Press of Kentucky, 2015).

48. The major exception to this is the work of Ryan Reft on the local politics of military housing, especially the racial ideologies that shaped responses to military housing policy; Reft, "The Metropolitan Military," 2014; Reft, "The Privatization of Military Family Housing in Linda Vista, 1944–1956"; Ryan Reft, "The Metropolitan Military: Homeownership Resistance to Military Family Housing in Southern California, 1979–1990," *Journal of Urban History* 43, no. 5 (2017): 767–94.

49. P. W. Singer, *Corporate Warriors: The Rise of the Privatized Military Industry* (Ithaca, NY: Cornell University Press, 2003).

50. Wilson, "Farewell to Progressivism"; Wilson, *Destructive Creation*.

51. The two hundred thousand figure includes just the Wherry and Capehart units that are the focus of this essay. By 1993, the Department of Defense owned approximately three hundred thousand units in the United States, the balance acquired through direct appropriations funding. Matthew C. Godfrey et al., *A History of the US Army's Residential Communities Initiative, 1995–2010: Privatizing Military Family Housing* (Washington, DC: Government Printing Office, 2012); Congressional Budget Office, *Military Family Housing in the United States*, 2.

52. Wilson, *Destructive Creation*, 242–43; Fones-Wolf, *Selling Free Enterprise*; Phillips-Fein, *Invisible Hands*.

53. US Congress, Senate, *A Bill to Encourage Construction of Rental Housing at or in Areas Adjacent to Military and Naval Installations*, S 1184, 81st Cong., 1st sess., introduced in Senate March 5, 1949.

54. John L. Steele, "Amerasia Hearing Testimony Revealed; Witness 'Popular' with GOP He Says: Larsen Testifies He Regarded Lieut. Roth as a Communist," *Washington Post*, June 18, 1950; Randolph W. Baxter, "'Homo-Hunting'in the Early Cold War: Senator Kenneth Wherry and the Homophobic Side of McCarthyism," *Nebraska History* 84 (Fall 2003): 118–32; David K. Johnson, *The Lavender Scare: The Cold War Persecution of Gays and Lesbians in the Federal Government* (Chicago: University of Chicago Press, 2004), 79–99.

55. Notably, Wherry's antigovernment and antiwelfare positions did not extend to the issue of farm price subsidies. William S. White, "Portrait of a 'Fundamentalist': To Kenneth Wherry, GOP Floor Leader and the Fair Deal's Most Vigorous Foe in the Senate, Even Taft at Times Is Radical," *New York Times*, January 15, 1950, 14; Johnson, *The Lavender Scare*, 96–97.

56. Wherry developers had the option to secure and build on private land, but about 90 percent of Wherry housing was built on military land. Baldwin, *Four Housing Privatization Programs*.

57. *Report of Special Subcommittee on Acquisition of Wherry Housing*, 1956.

58. The Wherry Act was modeled in particular on Section 608 of the National Housing Act, which used FHA mortgage insurance to stimulate the construction of rental housing units for private citizens. *Report of Special Subcommittee on Acquisition of Wherry Housing*, 1952.

59. US House, Committee on Armed Services, *Military and Naval Construction: Hearings Before the Committee on Armed Services*, 83rd Cong., 2nd sess. (Washington, DC: Government Printing Office, 1954), 5383.

60. *An Act to Encourage Construction of Rental Housing on or in Areas Adjacent to Army, Navy, Marine Corps, and Air Force Installations, and for Other Purposes*, Pub. L. 81-211, US Statutes at Large 63 (1949): 570–77.

61. Kuranda et al., *Housing an Air Force and a Navy*, 67.

62. Quoted in Temme, "For Want of a Home," 46.

63. Larkin, "For Want of a House," 14; Temme, "For Want of a Home," 47.

64. Kathleen J. Frydl, *The G.I. Bill* (New York: Cambridge University Press, 2009); Jackson, *Crabgrass Frontier*; Katznelson, *When Affirmative Action Was White*; Ann Markusen et al., *The Rise of the Gunbelt: The Military Remapping of Industrial America* (New York: Oxford University Press, 1991); Roger W. Lotchin, *Fortress California, 1910–1961: From Warfare to Welfare* (New York: Oxford University Press, 1992); Michael S. Sherry, *In the Shadow of War: The United States Since the 1930's* (New Haven, CT: Yale University Press, 1995); Michael Brenes, *For Might and Right: Cold War Defense Spending and the Remaking of American Democracy* (Amherst: University of Massachusetts Press, 2020); Sarah Jo Peterson, *Planning the Home Front: Building Bombers and Communities at Willow Run* (Chicago: University of Chicago Press, 2013).

65. Alan Rabinowitz, "McNamara Biggest Landlord," *Boston Globe*, December 10, 1961.

66. Temme, "For Want of a Home," 52.

67. "Housing Plan Probe Asked," *Baltimore Sun*, April 22, 1955; Judge Glock, "How the Federal Housing Administration Tried to Save America's Cities, 1934–1960," *Journal of Policy History* 28, no. 2 (2016): 290–317.

68. Kuranda et al., *Housing an Air Force and a Navy*, 82.

69. "Senators Find F.H.A. Culpable in Scandals," *New York Times*, December 20, 1954; "Housing Probe Brings Firing of 21 Officials," *Chicago Daily Tribune*, October 24, 1954; "Blame Fixed in Housing Scandal," *New York Herald Tribune*, December 20, 1954.

70. "Builder Reveals $908,000 'Windfall' on a $2,000 Investment in Dayton," *Wall Street Journal*, July 20, 1954.

71. "1,000 Cases of Housing Frauds Filed," *Hartford Courant*, April 11, 1955.

72. "Housing Probe Brings Firing of 21 Officials."

73. In 1953, Congress amended the Housing Act (PL 83-94) to address windfall profits by adding a "recapture" clause that required new builders to return (to the lender) any mortgage funds not used in construction. *Report of Special Subcommittee on Acquisition of Wherry Housing Projects*, 1957.

74. *Housing Amendments of 1955: Hearings Before the Committee on Banking and Currency*, 122.

75. *Report of Special Subcommittee on Acquisition of Wherry Housing Projects*, 1954.

76. US Senate, Committee on Banking and Currency, Subcommittee on Housing, *Housing Act of 1955: Hearings Before a Subcommittee of the Committee on Banking and Currency*, 84th Cong., 1st sess. (Washington, DC: Government Printing Office, 1955), 479.

77. US Congress, Senate, *84 S. 2126 Amendment in the Senate*, S 2126, 84th Cong., 1st sess., introduced in Senate June 1, 1955.

78. The Capehart plan was adopted even though the assistant secretary of defense for property and installations Franklin G. Floete expressed the Defense Department's preference for appropriated funds construction. *Housing Amendments of 1955: Hearings Before the Committee on Banking and Currency*, 117–19.

79. "Agency Studying Military Housing Projects Reports Waste, Negligence at Army Post," *Wall Street Journal*, April 16, 1959.

80. Housing Act of 1956, Pub. L. No. 84-1020, 70 Stat. 1091 (1956).

81. Paul H. Symbol, "Family Housing for the Army," *Army Information Digest* 12, no. 7 (July 1957): 20.

82. Housing Amendments of 1955, Pub. L. No. 84-345, 69 Stat. 635 (1955): 635–654.

83. Temme, "For Want of a Home," 52–56.

84. US Senate, Committee on Armed Services, *Military Public Works Construction: Hearings Before the Subcommittee on Real Estate and Military Construction*, 84th Cong., 1st sess. (Washington, DC: Government Printing Office, 1955), 720.

85. *Housing Act of 1955: Hearings Before a Subcommittee of the Committee on Banking and Currency*, 124.

86. *Military Public Works Construction: Hearings Before the Subcommittee on Real Estate and Military Construction*, 717, 722.

87. Chamber of Commerce of the United States of America, *Policy Declarations of the Chamber of Commerce of the United States* (Washington, DC: Chamber of Commerce, 1949), 6–7; Wilson, *Destructive Creation*, 23.

88. Wilson, *Destructive Creation*, 271–75.

89. US House, Committee on Armed Services, *Authorizing Construction for the Military Departments*, 85th Cong., 1st sess., H.R. Rep. No. 638, (1957), at 31.

90. The bill included what Assistant Secretary of Defense for Property and Installations Franklin G. Floete called a provision permitting the military services "to take over any given Wherry project that the sponsor feels he wishes to get rid of." *Housing Amendments of 1955: Hearings Before the Committee on Banking and Currency*, 123.

91. *Report of Special Subcommittee on Acquisition of Wherry Housing Projects*, 1960–61.

92. Housing Act of 1956, Pub. L. No. 84-1020, 70 Stat. 1091 (1956).

93. *Military Public Works Construction: Hearings Before the Subcommittee on Real Estate and Military Construction*, 719.

94. *Military Public Works Construction: Hearings Before the Subcommittee on Real Estate and Military Construction*, 724.

95. US Congress, Senate, Committee on Armed Services, *Military Construction Authorization: Hearings Before the Subcommittee on Military Construction*, 85th Cong., 1st sess. (Washington, DC: Government Printing Office, 1957), 761–63.

96. The price could not exceed "the Federal Housing Administration Commissioner's estimate of the replacement cost of such housing and related property . . . reduced by an appropriate allowance for physical depreciation"; *An Act to Authorize Certain Construction at Military Installations, and for Other Purposes*, Public Law 84-968, *US Statutes at Large* 70 (1956): 991–1019.

97. The army acquired about half of its 22,248 units through condemnation and just 3,300 through negotiation. The air force, on the other hand, acquired most of its units through negotiation (23,000 of 37,103). The navy fell in between; Temme, "For Want of a Home," 67–69.

98. The military had acquired 70 percent of units by summer 1959 (58,339 of 83,742 constructed) and planned to acquire another 10,000. Wherry housing acquisition was financed with a new revolving fund for the purpose, established with $50 million initial capital to be replenished by quarters allowances. *Report of Special Subcommittee on Acquisition of Wherry Housing*, 1961.

99. *Report of Special Subcommittee on Acquisition of Wherry Housing*, 1966, 1971.

100. Kuranda et al., *Housing an Air Force and a Navy*, 68; Symbol, "Family Housing for the Army," 16.

101. Symbol, "Family Housing for the Army," 16.

102. *Report of Special Subcommittee on Acquisition of Wherry Housing Projects*, 1967.

103. Reft, "The Metropolitan Military," 2014.

104. "Hayes Blames Army Wives for Housing Breakdown," *El Paso Herald Post*, March 21, 1961; quoted in Temme, "For Want of a Home," 72.

105. Between 1960 and 1977, a relatively modest 93,000 additional military family housing units were built through direct appropriation. Reft, "The Metropolitan Military," 2017, 771.

106. Rabinowitz, "McNamara Biggest Landlord."

107. The Egyptian government compensated foreign shareholders 28.3 million Egyptian pounds or approximately $79 million at 1956 exchange rates; "Byrd Discloses New Windfalls," *Washington Post*, April 22, 1955; Bent Hansen and Khairy Tourk, "The Profitability of the Suez Canal as a Private Enterprise, 1859–1956," *Journal of Economic History* 38, no. 4 (1978): 938–958; Lawrence H. Officer, "Exchange Rates Between the United States Dollar and Forty-One Currencies," MeasuringWorth, 2021, http://www.measuringworth.com/exchangeglobal/.

108. The Capehart mortgage ceiling was increased by the Housing Act of 1956 (PL 84-1020), after initially being set at $1.36 billion in 1955 (PL 84-345). The value of mortgages actually issued for Capehart projects was more than $1.8 billion. *Report of Special Subcommittee on Acquisition of Wherry Housing*, 1958; US House, Committee on Appropriations, *Military Construction Appropriation Bill, 1969*, 90th Cong., 2nd sess., H.R. Rep. No. 1754 (1968), at 25.

109. US House, Committee on Banking and Currency, *Housing Act of 1957*, 85th Cong., 1st sess., H.R. Rep. No. 313 (1957), at 9.

110. Congressional Budget Office, *Military Family Housing in the United States*.

111. Approximately one quarter to one third of military families lived in housing owned and operated by the military from the time of their completion in the early 1960s to the eve of their privatization in the 1990s. Congressional Budget Office, 5–7.

112. The kind of welfare that military family housing policy created was formally colorblind but functionally racialized in the same way that American welfare policy was more broadly. As late as 1964, the commissioned officer corps of all of the military services were effectively all white, with African Americans making up 3.4% of the officer corps in the army, 1.5% in the air force, 0.4% in the marine corps, and just 0.3% in the navy. African Americans were also underrepresented in the higher enlisted ranks. Since access to military family housing required a rank of E-4 or above, what could have been a rare source of quality housing open to African American service members and their families was functionally often unavailable to them. Charles C. Moskos, "Racial Integration in the Armed Forces," *American Journal of Sociology* 72, no. 2 (September 1, 1966): 137; Jill S. Quadagno, *The Transformation of Old Age Security: Class and Politics in the American Welfare State* (Chicago: University of Chicago Press, 1988); Ira Katznelson, *Fear Itself: The New Deal and the Origins of Our Time* (New York: Liveright, 2013).

113. Mittelstadt, *The Rise of the Military Welfare State*; Bailey, *America's Army*.

114. Chester Hartman and Robin Drayer, "A Research Note: Military-Family Housing: The Other Public-Housing Program," *Housing and Society* 17, no. 3 (January 1, 1990): 67–78.

Chapter 3

I want to acknowledge the able and timely research assistance provided by Jessica Matlock, Aleksandra Singer, and Kylah Staley.

1. Mark Danner, "Taking Stock of the Forever War," *New York Times Magazine*, September 11, 2005; Dexter Filkins, *The Forever War* (New York: Knopf, 2008); Mark Danner, *Spiral: Trapped in the Forever War* (New York: Simon & Schuster, 2016).

2. Dwight D. Eisenhower, "The Farewell Address," January 17, 1961, https://www.eisenhower.archives.gov/research/online_documents/farewell_address.html; C. Wright Mills, *The Power Elite* (New York: Oxford University Press, 1956); James Ledbetter, *Unwarranted Influence:*

Dwight D. Eisenhower and the Military-Industrial Complex (New Haven, CT: Yale University Press, 2011).

3. B. Franklin Cooling, *Gray Steel and Blue Water Navy: The Formative Years of America's Military-Industrial Complex, 1881–1917* (Hamden, CT: Archon Books, 1979); Paul A. C. Koistinen, "The 'Industrial-Military Complex' in Historical Perspective: The Inter-War Years," *Journal of American History* 56, no. 4 (1970): 819–39; Alex Roland, "The Military-Industrial Complex: Lobby and Trope," in *The Long War: A New History of US National Security Policy Since World War II*, ed. Andrew J. Bacevich (New York: Columbia University Press, 2007), 335–70; Paul A. C. Koistinen, *State of War: The Political Economy of American Warfare, 1945–2011* (Lawrence: University Press of Kansas, 2012).

4. Steven J. Rosen, "Testing the Theory of the Military-Industrial Complex," in *Testing the Theory of the Military-Industrial Complex*, ed. Steven J. Rosen (Lexington, MA: Lexington Books, 1973), 2.

5. Gordon Adams, *The Politics of Defense Contracting: The Iron Triangle* (New Brunswick, NJ: Transaction Books, 1981).

6. J. Paul Dunne and Elisabeth Skons, "The Military-Industrial Complex," in *The Global Arms Trade: A Handbook* (New York: Routledge, 2014), 281–92; Vernon V. Aspaturian, "The Soviet Military-Industrial Complex: Does It Exist?," in *Testing the Theory of the Military-Industrial Complex*, 103–133; Alex Mintz, "The Military-Industrial Complex: American Concepts and Israeli Realities," *Journal of Conflict Resolution* 29, no. 4 (1985): 623–39; Masako Ikegami, *The Military-Industrial Complex: The Cases of Sweden and Japan* (Aldershot, UK: Dartmouth, 1992); Ron Matthews and Curie Maharani, "The Defense Iron Triangle Revisited," in *The Modern Defense Industry: Political, Economic, and Technological Issues*, ed. Richard A. Bitzinger (Santa Barbara, CA: Praeger, 2000), 38–59.

7. Rosen, "Testing the Theory of the Military-Industrial Complex," 3.

8. Jerome Slater and Terry Nardin, "The Concept of a Military-Industrial Complex," in *Testing the Theory of the Military-Industrial Complex*, 28.

9. Ben Fine, "The Military-Industrial Complex: An Analytical Assessment," *Cyprus Journal of Economics* 6, no. 1 (1993): 36.

10. For another such assessment, see Alex Roland, *Delta of Power: The Military Industrial Complex* (Baltimore: Johns Hopkins University Press, 2021).

11. Nick Turse, *The Complex: How the Military Invades Our Everyday Lives* (New York: Metropolitan Books, 2008); Ronald W. Cox, "The Military-Industrial Complex and US Military Spending After 9/11," *Class, Race, and Corporate Power* 2, no. 1 (2014): 1–20; John Bellamy Foster and Robert W. McChesney, "Surveillance Capitalism: Monopoly-Finance Capital, the Military-Industrial Complex, and the Digital Age," *Monthly Review* 66, no. 3 (July 2014): 1–31.

12. Linda Weiss, *America Inc?: Innovation and Enterprise in the National Security State* (Ithaca, NY: Cornell University Press, 2014).

13. Michael T. Klare, *Rogue States and Nuclear Outlaws: America's Search for a New Foreign Policy* (New York: Hill & Wang, 1995); Daniel Wirls, *Irrational Security: The Politics of Defense from Reagan to Obama* (Baltimore: Johns Hopkins University Press, 2010).

14. Adjusted for inflation, the Reagan military buildup exceeded both wars in both the single peak year of spending and in the total spending over nine-year periods encompassing each era (1950–1958, 1963–1971, 1981–1989). Office of Management and Budget, *Historical Tables*, Table 6.1: Composition of Outlays: 1940–2024, https://www.whitehouse.gov/omb/historical-tables/.

15. Daniel Wirls, *Buildup: The Politics of Defense in the Reagan Era* (Ithaca, NY: Cornell University Press, 1992).

16. Office of Management and Budget, *Historical Tables*, Table 3.2: Outlays by Function and Subfunction: 1962–2024.

17. Gerald I. Susman and Sean O'Keefe, eds., *The Defense Industry in the Post-Cold War Era: Corporate Strategies and Public Policy Perspectives* (New York: Pergamon, 1998); Ann R. Markusen and Sean S. Costigan, eds., *Arming the Future: A Defense Industry for the 21st Century* (New York: Council on Foreign Relations Press, 1999); Rachel Weber, *Swords into Dow Shares: Governing the Decline of the Military-Industrial Complex* (Boulder, CO: Westview Press, 2001); Elisabeth Skons, "The US Defence Industry After the Cold War," in *The Global Arms Trade: A Handbook*, ed. Andrew T. H. Tan (New York: Routledge, 2010), 235–49.

18. John Tirpak, "The Distillation of the Defense Industry," *Air Force Magazine* (July 1998), https://www.airforcemag.com/article/0798industry/.

19. To be precise, the Pentagon partially funded restructuring costs of particular mergers, some of which were pegged to large bonuses for the executives involved, while thousands of ordinary workers lost their jobs. Bernie Sanders, "Payoffs for Layoffs Have to Stop," *Los Angeles Times*, July 11, 1996; David E. Cooper, *Defense Industry Restructuring: Cost and Savings Issues*, GAO/T-NSIAD-97-141 (Washington, DC: US General Accounting Office, 1997), https://www.govinfo.gov/content/pkg/GAOREPORTS-T-NSIAD-97-141/pdf/GAOREPORTS-T-NSIAD-97-141.pdf; Weber, *Swords into Dow Shares*, 92.

20. For the history and analysis of various aspects of privatization in national security—particularly logistics and private security—see P. W. Singer, *Corporate Warriors: The Rise of the Privatized Military Industry* (Ithaca, NY: Cornell University Press, 2003); Dina Rasor, Robert Bauman, and Jonathan Alter, *Betraying Our Troops: The Destructive Results of Privatizing War* (New York: Palgrave Macmillan, 2007); Allison Stanger, *One Nation Under Contract* (New Haven, CT: Yale University Press, 2009); Ann Hagedorn, *The Invisible Soldiers: How America Outsourced Our Security* (New York: Simon & Schuster, 2014).

21. David Harvey, *A Brief History of Neoliberalism* (New York: Oxford University Press, 2007); Manfred B. Steger and Ravi K. Roy, *Neoliberalism: A Very Short Introduction* (New York: Oxford University Press, 2010).

22. Deborah C. Kidwell, *Public War, Private Fight? The United States and Private Military Companies* (Fort Leavenworth, KS: Combat Studies Institute Press, US Army Command and General Staff College, 2005).

23. Camille M. Nichols, "The Logistics Civil Augmentation Program," *Military Review* 76, no. 2 (1996): 65–72.

24. For a detailed analysis of some of these changes with the army's creation and provision of what historian Jennifer Mittelstadt calls the "military welfare state," especially in the 1980s and 1990s, see her *The Rise of the Military Welfare State* (Cambridge, MA: Harvard University Press, 2015).

25. Weiss, *America Inc.?*, 2. See also, Mariana Mazzucato, *The Entrepreneurial State: Debunking Public vs. Private Sector Myths* (New York: PublicAffairs, 2015).

26. Weiss, *America Inc.?*, 51–74.

27. Weiss, *America Inc.?*, 82–84. This is in contrast to the classic concepts of a spin-off, a technology or innovation developed for the military that eventually finds a commercial application, and a spin-on, a commercial innovation that ends up having a direct military application.

28. Wirls, *Irrational Security*, 91–167.

29. Here I use the term IT as a substitute for "automatic data processing," the term used by the Federal Procurement Data System, which covers services and equipment in that area.

30. The Federal Procurement Data System stopped producing its standard *Federal Procurement Report* in 2007. I was unable to find or replicate for later years the categories used in the reports through 2007.

31. Moshe Schwartz, John F. Sargent, Jr., and Christopher T. Mann, *Defense Acquisitions: How and Where DOD Spends Its Contracting Dollars*, Congressional Research Service, R44010 (July 2018), https://sgp.fas.org/crs/natsec/R44010.pdf

32. The original SAIC became Leidos in 2013 and spun off part of its original operation as a separate company named Science Applications International Corporation (which I list in the table as SAIC). In 2016 Leidos merged with Lockheed Martin's Information Systems and Global Services business.

33. Department of Homeland Security, "Creation of the Department of Homeland Security," https://www.dhs.gov/creation-department-homeland-security.

34. DHS is also at the heart of another transformation that affects the contracting complex. The creation of DHS and other policies after 9/11 altered what Matthew Waxman has called national security federalism, the traditional division of labor and, in part, wall of separation between national security and local law enforcement. DHS has been part of a vertical expansion and extension of national security policies and resources to the state and local levels. Matthew C. Waxman, "National Security Federalism in the Age of Terror," *Stanford Law Review* 64, no. 2 (March 2012): 289–350.

35. It would be fair to include some portion of other agencies as well, including NASA, the NSF, and the National Institutes of Health (NIH). Many NSF and NIH programs have had national security purposes and serve as another element of military R&D. NASA is a civilian agency but sprang from the military in the late 1950s under Eisenhower. And despite its civilian gloss, NASA has always overlapped with and supplemented national security policy. See, inter alia, Walter A. McDougall, . . . *The Heavens and the Earth: A Political History of the Space Age* (New York: Basic Books, 1985). There has always been a strong overlap between the top DOD contractors and NASA. In 2018, six of the top ten DOD and seventeen of the top fifty DOD are in the top fifty of NASA.

36. Office of Management and Budget, *Historical Tables*, Table 3.2: Outlays by Function and Subfunction: 1962–2024.

37. The term "Walmarts of War" has an uncertain provenance. One documented use applies it more specifically to private security firms such as Dyncorp or MPRI that offered a wide array of services in and around zones of conflict. See Hagedorn, *The Invisible Soldiers*, 145. I see the term as applicable to the diversified major contractors, such as Lockheed Martin.

38. General Dynamics, https://www.gd.com/about-gd/our-history. The company website provided the facts and dates for what follows in this paragraph.

39. Anthony Capaccio and Ben Brody, "Pentagon Goes Winner-Take-All for Cloud Award Worth Billions," March 7, 2018, https://www.bloomberg.com/news/articles/2018-03-07/amazon-oracle-microsoft-jockey-for-pentagon-s-cloud-business; Rachel Sandler, "Pentagon Awards JEDI Contract to Microsoft—Again—in Blow to Amazon," *Forbes*, September 4, 2020, https://www.forbes.com/sites/rachelsandler/2020/09/04/pentagon-awards-jedi-contract-to-microsoft-again-in-blow-to-amazon/#3565eb5a505f; Kate Conger and David E. Sanger, "Pentagon Cancels a Disputed $10 Billion Technology Contract," *New York Times*, July 6, 2021.

40. The MITRE Corporation, *Corporate Social Responsibility Report 2017*, 31, https://www.mitre.org/sites/default/files/publications/2017-MITRE-CSR-Report.pdf.

41. 65.3 percent with the VA and 29.7 percent with the DOD.

42. McKesson Corporation, "McKesson Reports Fiscal 2018 Fourth-Quarter and Full-Year Results" (May 2018), https://www.mckesson.com/about-mckesson/newsroom/press-releases/2018/mckesson-reports-fy2018-4th-quarter-and-full-year-results.

43. Office of Management and Budget, *Historical Tables*, Table 3.2: Outlays by Function and Subfunction: 1962–2026.

44. Erin Bagalman, "The Number of Veterans That Use VA Health Care Services: A Fact Sheet" Congressional Research Service, R43579 (June 3, 2014).

45. Richard A. Oppel, Jr., "Veterans Secretary Ousts Health Care Official Amid Criticism," *New York Times*, May 16, 2014; US Department of Veterans' Affairs, Office of Inspector General, *Veterans Health Administration, Interim Report: Review of Patient Wait Times, Scheduling Practices, and Alleged Patient Deaths at the Phoenix Health Care System* (Washington, DC: Veterans Health Administration, May 28, 2014), https://www.va.gov/oig/pubs/vaoig-14-02603-178.pdf.

46. Brendan W. McGarry, "The Defense Budget and the Budget Control Act: Frequently Asked Questions," Congressional Research Service, R44039 (September 30, 2019).

47. Department of Veterans Affairs, FY 2020 President's Budget Request, March 11, 2019, https://www.va.gov/budget/docs/summary/fy2020VAsBudgetRolloutBriefing.pdf.

48. Loren Thompson, "Eisenhower's 'Military-Industrial Complex' Shrinks to 1% of Economy," *Forbes*, May 8, 2017, https://www.forbes.com/sites/lorenthompson/2017/05/08/eisenhowers-military-industrial-complex-shrinks-to-1-of-economy/#294c7c7bed1f.

49. Charles J. Dunlap, "The Military-Industrial Complex," *Daedalus* 140, no. 3 (2011): 140.

50. William Lynn III, "The End of the Military-Industrial Complex: How the Pentagon Is Adapting to Globalization," *Foreign Affairs* (Nov./Dec. 2014): 104.

51. Lynn, "End of the Military-Industrial Complex," 105.

52. Dunlap, "Military-Industrial Complex," 138.

53. Thompson, "Eisenhower's 'Military-Industrial Complex' Shrinks to 1% of Economy." Notice that Thompson reduces Pentagon spending to just procurement and research to get the 1 percent while including the entire 17 percent of health care, which is mostly services and salaries.

54. "Medical-Industrial Complex," Encyclopedia.com, accessed May 3, 2019, https://www.encyclopedia.com/social-sciences/encyclopedias-almanacs-transcripts-and-maps/medical-industrial-complex; Barbara Ehrenreich and John Ehrenreich, *The American Health Empire* (New York: Random House, 1970); Charles Wolf, Jr., "Military-Industiral Simplicities, Complexities, and Realities," in *The Military-Industrial Complex: A Reassessment*, ed. Sam C. Sarkesian (Beverly Hills, CA: SAGE Publications, 1972), 25–52; Arnold S. Relman, "The New Medical-Industrial Complex," *New England Journal of Medicine* 303, no. 17 (Oct. 23, 1980): 963–70; Robert J. Buchanan, "The Financial Status of the New Medical-Industrial Complex," *Inquiry* 19, no. 4 (1982): 308–16; Elisabeth Rosenthal, *An American Sickness: How Healthcare Became Big Business and How You Can Take It Back* (New York: Penguin Press, 2017).

55. Joint Chiefs of Staff, *Joint Concept for Integrated Campaigning* (March 16, 2018), vi, https://www.jcs.mil/Portals/36/Documents/Doctrine/concepts/joint_concept_integrated_campaign.pdf?ver=2018-03-28-102833-257.

56. Bruce G. Brunton, "Institutional Origins of the Military-Industrial Complex," *Journal of Economic Issues* 22, no. 2 (1988): 599.

57. Elisabeth Braw, "Stop Worrying and Learn to Love the Military-Industrial Complex," *Wall Street Journal*, January 2, 2019.

58. Fine, "The Military-Industrial Complex: An Analytical Assessment," 28.

59. For one of the most sophisticated and comprehensive efforts, and one that spans from the Cold War to the post-9/11 era, see Rebecca U. Thorpe, *The American Warfare State: The Domestic Politics of Military Spending* (Chicago: University of Chicago Press, 2014).

Chapter 4

I thank the staff of the American Antiquarian Society, especially Ashley Cataldo, Vince Golden, Lauren Hewes, and Nan Wolverton, for their help in navigating research for this article. Thanks are also due to Margaret Abruzzo, Leora Auslander, Kathleen Conzen, Heike Jablonski, and Katie Knowles. Support for this research was provided through a Jay and Deborah Last Fellowship in American Visual Culture at the American Antiquarian Society.

1. James Fitzsimmons to William Willoughby, December 2, 1864, folders 13 and 17, William Augustus Willoughby Papers, 1861–1864, American Antiquarian Society, Worcester, MA [hereafter Willoughby Papers].

2. Clarence R. Geier, David G. Orr, and Matthew B. Reeves, eds. *Huts and History: The Historical Archaeology of Military Encampment During the American Civil War* (Gainesville: University Press of Florida, 2006); Clarence R. Geier, Douglas D. Scott, and Lawrence E. Babits, eds. *From These Honored Dead: Historical Archaeology of the American Civil War* (Gainesville: University Press of Florida, 2014).

3. Sarah Leigh Jones, "'A Grand and Ceaseless Thoroughfare': The Social and Cultural Experience of Shopping on Chestnut Street, Philadelphia, 1820–1860" (master's thesis, University of Delaware, 2008); Stuart M. Blumin, *The Emergence of the Middle Class: Social Experience in the American City, 1760–1900* (New York: Cambridge University Press, 1989); Brian Luskey and Wendy A. Woloson, *Capitalism by Gaslight: Illuminating the Economy of Nineteenth-Century America* (Philadelphia: University of Pennsylvania Press, 2015); Joanna Cohen, *Luxurious Citizens: The Politics of Consumption in Nineteenth Century America* (Philadelphia: University of Pennsylvania Press, 2017); Elizabeth White Nelson, *Market Sentiments: Middle-Class Culture in Nineteenth-Century America* (Washington, DC: Smithsonian Books, 2004); Dell Upton, *Another City: Urban Life and Urban Spaces in the New American Republic* (New Haven, CT: Yale University Press, 2008).

4. Cohen, *Luxurious Citizens*, 182.

5. Joanna Cohen, "'You have no flag out yet?' Commercial Connections and Patriotic Emotion in the Civil War North," *Journal of the Civil War Era* 9, no. 2 (September 2019): 378–409; Lawrence A. Kreiser, Jr., *Marketing the Blue & Gray: Newspaper Advertising and the American Civil War* (Baton Rouge: Louisiana State University Press, 2019).

6. On the history of suttling, see David M. Delo, *Peddlers and Post-Traders: The Army Sutler on the Frontier* (Helena, MT: Kingfisher Books, 1998); Francis A. Lord, *Civil War Sutlers and Their Wares* (New York: Thomas Yoseloff, 1969); Donald P. Spear, "The Sutler in the Union Army," *Civil War History* 16, no. 2 (June 1970): 121–38; Alfred J. Tapson, "The Sutler and the Soldier," *Military Affairs* 21, no. 4 (Winter 1957): 175–81.

7. Mark R. Wilson, *The Business of Civil War: Military Mobilization and the State, 1861–1865* (Baltimore: Johns Hopkins University Press, 2006); Judith Giesberg, *Army at Home: Women and the Civil War on the Northern Home Front* (Chapel Hill: University of North Carolina Press, 2009).

8. Drew Gilpin Faust, *Mothers of Invention: Women of the Slaveholding South in the American Civil War* (Chapel Hill: University of North Carolina Press, 1996); Jeannie Attie, *Patriotic Toil: Northern Women and the American Civil War* (Ithaca, NY: Cornell University Press, 1998); Nina Silber, *Daughters of the Union: Northern Women Fight the Civil War* (Cambridge, MA: Harvard University Press, 2005); Thavolia Glymph, *Out of the House of Bondage: The Transformation of the Plantation Household* (New York: Cambridge University Press, 2008); Stephanie McCurry, *Confederate Reckoning: The Political Transformation of the Civil War South* (Cambridge, MA: Harvard University Press, 2010).

9. LeeAnn Whites, "Forty Shirts and a Wagonload of Wheat: Women, the Domestic Supply Line, and the War on the Western Border," *Journal of the Civil War Era* 1, no. 1 (March 2011): 56–78.

10. Jeanne Boydston, *Home and Work: Housework, Wages, and the Ideology of Labor in the Early Republic* (New York: Oxford University Press, 1990); Christine Stansell, *City of Women: Sex and Class in New York, 1789–1860* (1982; Urbana: University of Illinois Press, 1987).

11. For an example of soldiers' indulgences, see Judith Giesberg, *Sex and the Civil War: Soldiers, Pornography, and the Making of American Morality* (Chapel Hill: University of North Carolina Press, 2017).

12. See, for instance, Bell Wiley, *The Life of Johnny Reb: The Common Soldier of the Confederacy* (Indianapolis, IN: Bobbs-Merrill, 1943); Bell Wiley, *The Life of Billy Yank: The Common Soldier of the Union* (Indianapolis, IN: Bobbs-Merrill, 1952); Joseph T. Glatthaar, *The March to the Sea and Beyond: Sherman's Troops in the Savannah and Carolinas Campaigns* (New York: New York University Press, 1985); Gerald F. Linderman, *Embattled Courage: The Experience of Combat in the American Civil War* (New York: The Free Press, 1987); Earl J. Hess, *Liberty, Virtue, and Progress: Northerners and Their War for the Union* (New York: New York University Press, 1988); Reid Mitchell, *Civil War Soldiers: Their Expectations and Their Experiences* (New York: Viking, 1988); James M. McPherson, *For Cause and Comrades: Why Men Fought in the Civil War* (New York: Oxford University Press, 1997); Michael C. C. Adams. *Living Hell: The Dark Side of the Civil War* (Baltimore: Johns Hopkins University Press, 2014).

13. Clayton R. Newell and Charles R. Shrader, *Of Duty Well and Faithfully Done: A History of the Regular Army in the Civil War* (Lincoln: University of Nebraska Press, 2011), 139, 143.

14. Wilson, *Business of Civil War*, 2, 4–6.

15. Judith Ann Giesberg, *Civil War Sisterhood: The US Sanitary Commission and Women's Politics in Transition* (Boston: Northeastern University Press, 2000).

16. Attie, *Patriotic Toil*, 90

17. Joan E. Cashin, "Trophies of War: Material Culture in the Civil War Era," *Journal of the Civil War Era* 1, no. 3 (September 2011): 342; Joan E. Cashin, *War Stuff: The Struggle for Human and Material Resources during the American Civil War* (New York: Cambridge University Press, 2018).

18. David Lane, *A Soldier's Diary: The Story of a Volunteer, 1862–1865* (n.p., 1905), 133–134.

19. *Congressional Globe*, 37th Cong., 2nd sess. (1862), 1144.

20. Brian P. Luskey, *Men Is Cheap: Exposing the Frauds of Free Labor in Civil War America* (Chapel Hill: University of North Carolina Press, 2020), 105.

21. William Willoughby to Nancy Willoughby (cited hereafter as William to Nancy), June 14, 1862, in folders 2 and 14, Willoughby Papers.

22. Luskey, *Men Is Cheap*, 90.

23. Timothy J. Regan, in *The Lost Civil War Diaries: The Diaries of Corporal Timothy J. Regan*, eds. David C. Newton and Kenneth J. Pluskat (Victoria, BC: Trafford Publishing, 2003), 119.

24. Luskey, *Men Is Cheap*, 90.

25. On armor vests, see Sarah Jones Weicksel, "Armor, Manhood, and the Politics of Mortality," in *Astride Two Worlds: Technology and the American Civil War*, ed. Barton Hacker (Washington, DC: Smithsonian Institution Scholarly Press, 2016), 157–90.

26. Luskey, *Men Is Cheap*, 105.

27. *Revised United States Army Regulations of 1861* (Washington, DC: Government Printing Office, 1863), 37–38, 510, 530.

28. *A Report to the Secretary of War of the Operations of the Sanitary Commission* (December 1861): 32.

29. *Congressional Globe*, 37th Cong., 2nd sess. (1862), 1146.

30. *Congressional Globe*, 37th Cong., 2nd sess. (1862), 1148.

31. Peter S. Carmichael, *The War for the Common Soldier: How Men Thought, Fought, and Survived in Civil War Armies* (Chapel Hill: University of North Carolina Press, 2018), 184.

32. 1860 United States Census, New Haven, Connecticut, accessed February 2, 2020, https://ancestry.com.

33. Hugh Willoughby, ed., *Civil War Letters of a Connecticut Volunteer: Three Years of Letters Home from Camps and Battlefields, Written by William Augustus Willoughby to His Wife Nancy Royce Willoughby* (2015), 4, ctvolunteerscivilwarletters.com.

34. William to Nancy, undated [August 1862], folders 2 and 14, Willoughby Papers.

35. William to Nancy, January 4, 1863, folders 4 and 14, Willoughby Papers.

36. William to Nancy, August 1, 1862, folders 2 and 14, Willoughby Papers.

37. Carmichael, *War for the Common Soldier*, 52.

38. J. Matthew Gallman, *Mastering Wartime: A Social History of Philadelphia During the Civil War* (1990; Philadelphia: University of Pennsylvania Press, 2000), 29–33.

39. William to Nancy, December 25, 1863, folders 9 and 16, Willoughby Papers.

40. Carmichael, *War for the Common Soldier*, 32.

41. William to Nancy, December 20, 1863, folders 9 and 16, Willoughby Papers.

42. William to Nancy, August 5, 1862, folders 2 and 14, Willoughby Papers.

43. William to Nancy, August 24, 1862, folders 2 and 14, Willoughby Papers.

44. Richard R. John, *Spreading the News: The American Postal System from Franklin to Morse* (Cambridge, MA: Harvard University Press, 1995); David Henkin, *The Postal Age: The Emergence of Modern Communications in Nineteenth-Century America* (Chicago: University of Chicago Press, 2008), 138.

45. John, *Spreading the News*, 255.

46. "Army Express," *New York Herald*, June 2, 1861.

47. "Adams Express Company," *Corinth [Mississippi] War Eagle*, August 7, 1862.

48. January 3, 1862, Adams Express Company Journal, 1855–1863, University of Kentucky Special Collections Research Center, Lexington, KY.

49. William to Nancy, November 16, 1862, folders 3 and 14, Willoughby Papers.

50. William to Nancy, July 22, 1862, folders 2 and 14, Willoughby Papers.

51. William to Nancy, May 1, 1862, folders 1 and 14, Willoughby Papers.

52. William to Nancy, November 16, 1863, folders 9 and 16, Willoughby Papers.

53. William to Nancy, December 20, 1863, folders 9 and 16, Willoughby Papers.

54. William to Nancy, March 8, 1863, folders 5 and 15, Willoughby Papers.

55. William to Nancy, November 16, 1863, folders 9 and 16, Willoughby Papers.

56. William to Nancy, August 9, 1864, folders 12 and 17, Willoughby Papers.

57. William to Nancy, March 8, 1863, folders 5 and 15, Willoughby Papers.

58. William to Nancy, November 16, 1863, folders 9 and 16, Willoughby Papers.

59. William to Nancy, August 22, 1863, folders 7 and 15, Willoughby Papers.

60. William to Nancy, November 16, 1863, folders 9 and 16, Willoughby Papers.

61. Lane, *A Soldier's Diary*, 133–134.

62. William to Nancy, August 23, 1863, folders 7 and 15, Willoughby Papers.

63. William to Nancy, December 10, 1863, folders 9 and 16, Willoughby Papers.

64. William to Nancy, June 11, 1864, folders 11 and 17, Willoughby Papers.

65. Cohen, *Luxurious Citizens*, 5.

66. William to Nancy, November 16, 1863, folders 9 and 16, Willoughby Papers.

67. William to Nancy, December 20, 1863, folders 9 and 16, Willoughby Papers.

68. Carl A. Zimring, *Cash for Your Trash: Scrap Recycling in America* (Piscataway, NJ: Rutgers University Press, 2005), 20; A. J. Valente, *Rag Paper Manufacture in the United States, 1801–1900: A History, with Directories of Mills and Owners* (Jefferson, NC: McFarland and Company, 2010), 107.

69. William to Nancy, April 12, 1863, folders 5 and 15, Willoughby Papers.

70. Daniel Boardman to William Willoughby, October 5, 1864, folders 12 and 17, Willoughby Papers.

71. Thomas Fowler to William Willoughby, December 3, 1864, folders 12 and 17, Willoughby Papers.

72. Thomas Fowler to William Willoughby, December 3, 1864, folders 12 and 17, Willoughby Papers.

73. James Fitzsimmons to William Willoughby, December 2, 1864, folders 12 and 17, Willoughby Papers.

74. For another example of market dynamics in an unexpected setting, see R. A. Radford, "The Economic Organisation of a P.O.W. Camp," *Economica* 12, no. 48 (November 1945): 189–201.

75. William to Nancy, February 4, 1864, folders 10 and 16, Willoughby Papers.

76. William Willoughby Diary, October 11, 1864, folder 19, Willoughby Papers.

77. Willoughby Diary, October 8–9, 1864, folder 19, Willoughby Papers.

78. In 1870, the Willoughbys' personal estate was valued at $300. *Benham's New Haven Directory* (New Haven, CT: 1865), 339; *Benham's Business Directory* (New Haven, CT: 1866), 408; *Benham's New Haven City Directory* (New Haven, CT: 1875), 258; *Benham's New Haven City Directory* (New Haven, CT: Price, Lee & Co., 1880), 292; *1870 United States Federal Census*, New Haven, Connecticut and *1880 United States Federal Census*, New Haven, Connecticut, accessed February 2, 2020, https://ancestry.com.

79. *Congressional Globe*, 37th Cong., 2nd sess. (1862), 1148.

80. Spear, "Sutler in the Union Army," 138.

81. The Exchange, https://www.aafes.com/exchange-stores/ (accessed October 12, 2020).

82. Malte Zierenberg, *Berlin's Black Market: 1939–1950* (Basingstoke: Palgrave Macmillan, 2015), 178.

83. Meredith H. Lair, *Armed with Abundance: Consumerism and Soldiering in the Vietnam War* (Chapel Hill: University of North Carolina Press, 2011), 204.

84. Meghan T., November 2019. Email correspondence with author.

85. Ashley Gilbertson, "A Taste of Home in Foil Packets and Powder," *New York Times*, September 4, 2010.

86. Robert Fairfax to Mother, August 29, 1861, Fairfax Letters, Brockenbrough Library, The American Civil War Museum, Richmond, VA.

87. Fitzsimmons to Willoughby, December 2, 1864, folders 13 and 17, Willoughby Papers.

Chapter 5

1. Lt. Col. Jesse H. Denton, interview by LTC Allan R. Wetzel, Senior Officer, Oral History Program, 1983, Military History Institute, United States Army Heritage and Education Center, Carlisle Barracks, PA, L-54-59 [hereafter MHI].

2. Cynthia Enloe, *The Morning After: Sexual Politics at the End of the Cold War* (Berkeley: University of California Press, 1993), 151.

3. Holly A. Mayer, *Belonging to the Army: Camp Followers and Community During the American Revolution* (Columbia: University of South Carolina Press, 1996); Edward M. Coffman, *The Old Army: A Portrait of the American Army in Peacetime, 1784–1898* (New York: Oxford University Press, 1986); Thomas P. Lowry, *The Story the Soldiers Wouldn't Tell: Sex in the Civil War* (Mechanicsburg, PA: Stackpole Books, 1994). The phrase "camp follower" originally referred to the many women and men who provided an array of services to the military, but it is commonly used to imply that a woman affiliated with the military is a prostitute.

4. Anne M. Butler, *Daughters of Joy, Sisters of Misery: Prostitutes in the American West, 1860–1890* (Urbana: University of Illinois Press, 1985), 124.

5. Andrew Byers, *The Sexual Economy of War: Discipline and Desire in the US Army* (Ithaca, NY: Cornell University Press, 2019), chapter 1, quote on 26.

6. Byers, *The Sexual Economy of War*, chapter 2. Also see Paul A. Kramer, "The Military-Sexual Complex: Prostitution, Disease and the Boundaries of Empire During the Philippine-American War," *Asia-Pacific Journal: Japan Focus* 9, no. 2 (July 2011), https://apjjf.org/2011/9/30/Paul-A.-Kramer/3574/article.html.

7. Byers, *Sexual Economy of War*, quote on 62, also 60–63.

8. Allan M. Brandt, *No Magic Bullet: A Social History of Venereal Disease in the United States since 1880* (New York: Oxford University Press, 1985), 53–56.

9. Frederick Palmer, *Newton D. Baker: America at War* (New York: Dodd, Mead, 1931), 1: 298. Also see Raymond B. Fosdick, *Chronicle of a Generation: An Autobiography* (New York: Harper and Brothers, 1958), 135–41.

10. M. J. Exner, "Prostitution in Its Relation to the Army on the Mexican Border," Publication No. 91 (New York: American Social Hygiene Association, 1917), quote on 8, Social Hygiene Pamphlets, Armed Services World War I-Related Records, YMCA Archive, University of Minnesota, Minneapolis.

11. Frank E. Vandiver, *Black Jack: The Life and Times of John J. Pershing* (College Station: Texas A&M University Press, 1977), 2: 662.

12. See M. J. Exner, "A Square Deal" (New York: Association Press, 1919), 12–13, Social Hygiene Pamphlets, Armed Services World War I-Related Records, YMCA Archive; John Dickinson, *The Building of an Army: A Detailed Account of Legislation, Administration and Opinion in the United States, 1915–1920* (New York: The Century Company, 1922), 203.

13. Selective Service Act of 1917, Pub. L. 65–12, 40 Stat. 76 (1917).

14. Brandt, *No Magic Bullet*, 70–77.

15. "Vice District to Be Closed," *Fort Worth Star-Telegram*, March 5, 1917; "Court Order to Break up 'Acre' Sought by Jamieson," *Fort Worth Star-Telegram*, March 20, 1917; "Drivers of Cars That Carry Immoral Women Now Liable," *Fort Worth Star-Telegram*, August 11, 1918.

16. Hugh Young, *A Surgeon's Autobiography* (New York: Harcourt, Brace, 1940), 329; Fosdick, *Chronicle of a Generation*, 171; Brandt, *No Magic Bullet*, 104–6.

17. Brandt, *No Magic Bullet*, 98–106; Vandiver, *Black Jack*, 2: 662; Frank W. Weed, *The Medical Department of the United States Army in the World War*, Vol. VI, *Sanitation in the American Expeditionary Forces* (Washington, DC: Government Printing Office, 1926), 906–9.

18. Palmer, *Newton D. Baker*, 1: 298.

19. Nancy K. Bristow, *Making Men Moral: Social Engineering during the Great War* (New York: New York University Press, 1996); Kara Dixon Vuic, *The Girls Next Door: Bringing the Home Front to the Front Lines* (Cambridge, MA: Harvard University Press, 2019), chapter 1.

20. Brandt, *No Magic Bullet*, 115.

21. Joel T. Boone, "The Sexual Aspects of Military Personnel," *Journal of Social Hygiene* 27, no. 3 (March 1941): 114, 116–17.

22. John Boyd Coates, Jr., ed., *Preventive Medicine in World War II*, Volume V, *Communicable Diseases Transmitted Through Contact or by Unknown Means* (Washington, DC: Office of the Surgeon General, Department of the Army, 1960), 140–43, 172–79; Brandt, *No Magic Bullet*, 161–70; Marilyn E. Hegarty, *Victory Girls, Khaki-Wackies, and Patriotutes: The Regulation of Female Sexuality during World War II* (New York: New York University Press, 2008); Aaron Hiltner, *Taking Leave, Taking Liberties: American Troops on the World War II Home Front* (Chicago: University of Chicago Press, 2020); Elizabeth Alice Clement, *Love for Sale: Courting, Treating, and Prostitution in New York City, 1900–1945* (Chapel Hill: University of North Carolina Press, 2006), 240–58.

23. Brandt, *No Magic Bullet*, 161–69; Coates, *Preventive Medicine in World War II*, 143–46, 227–28, 232–34, 240; Jerome H. Greenberg, "Venereal Disease in the Armed Forces," *Medical Aspects of Human Sexuality* (March 1972): 185; Clement, *Love for Sale*, 249–58; Christina S. Jarvis, *The Male Body at War: American Masculinity During World War II* (DeKalb: Northern Illinois University Press, 2010), 72–85.

24. Coates, *Preventive Medicine in World War II*, 284; Mary Louise Roberts, *What Soldiers Do: Sex and the American GI in World War II France* (Chicago: University of Chicago Press, 2013), 174, 182; Hegarty, *Victory Girls*, 46–47, 85, 91–93, 98; Clement, *Love for Sale*, 248; Beth Bailey and David Farber, *The First Strange Place: The Alchemy of Race and Sex in World War II Hawaii* (New York: Free Press, 1992), 99–100; "Annex #1 to Sanitary Report, April 1943, 190th Station Hospital," May 5, 1943, p. 5, HD 730 Neuropsychiatry 1943 Morale and Psychiatry ASF Reports, World War II Administrative Records, ZI, Records of the Office of the Surgeon General (Army), Record Group 112, National Archives and Records Administration, College Park, MD. See also Allan Bérubé, *Coming Out Under Fire: The History of Gay Men and Women in World War Two* (New York: Free Press, 1990), 45–51.

25. Coates, *Preventive Medicine in World War II*, quote on 210, 204–20.

26. Coates, *Preventive Medicine in World War II*, quotes on 271, 273, 272, also 269–76.

27. Kim Munholland, *Rock of Contention: Free French and Americans: At War in New Caledonia, 1940–1945* (New York: Berghahn Books, 2007), quote on 153, also 151–53.

28. Circular No. 49, May 2, 1944, issued by Headquarters, ETOUSA, quoted in Coates, *Preventive Medicine in World War II*, 241.

29. Coates, *Preventive Medicine in World War II*, 243–44.

30. Roberts, *What Soldiers Do*, chapter 6.

31. Coates, *Preventive Medicine in World War II*, 242–50; Roberts, *What Soldiers Do*.

32. Coates, *Preventive Medicine in World War II*, 246.

33. The military gained access to penicillin in 1944. Brandt, *No Magic Bullet*, 161, 170–74.

34. On Germany, see Petra Goedde, *GIs and Germans: Culture, Gender, and Foreign Relations, 1945–1949* (New Haven, CT: Yale University Press, 2003), chapter 3; Maria Höhn, *GIs and Fräuleins: The German-American Encounter in 1950s West Germany* (Chapel Hill: University of North Carolina Press, 2002), chapters 5 and 7. On Cold War sexual containment, see Elaine Tyler May, *Homeward Bound: American Families in the Cold War Era* (New York: Basic Books, 2008). On sexual ideals in the military, see Lt. John G. Morris, "VD Since VE Day," *Army Information Digest* 3, no. 4 (April 1948): 26.

35. He likely also sought to limit the spread of venereal disease, estimated to affect one in four American personnel in country. Robert Kramm, *Sanitized Sex: Regulating Prostitution, Venereal Disease, and Intimacy in Occupied Japan, 1945–1952* (Berkeley: University of California Press, 2017), quote on 30. Social elites in Guantanamo, Cuba, also envisioned sex workers as a buffer between themselves and the American sailors whom they wanted to visit while on leave. Locals desperately wanted the money sailors spent in the local economy but objected to the men's treatment of local women. See Jana K. Lipman, *Guantanamo: A Working-Class History Between Empire and Revolution* (Berkeley: University of California Press, 2008), 115–16.

36. Sarah Kovner, *Occupying Power: Sex Workers and Servicemen in Postwar Japan* (Palo Alto, CA: Stanford University Press, 2012), 74. See also John W. Dower, *Embracing Defeat: Japan in the Wake of World War II* (New York: W. W. Norton, 1999), 123–32; Michiko Takeuchi, "'Pan-Pan Girls' Performing and Resisting Neocolonialism(s) in the Pacific Theater: US Military Prostitution in Occupied Japan, 1945–1952," in *Over There: Living with the US Military Empire from World War Two to the Present*, eds. Maria Höhn and Seungsook Moon (Durham, NC: Duke University Press, 2010), 78–89; Yuki Tanaka, *Japan's Comfort Women: Sexual Slavery and Prostitution during World War II and the US Occupation* (New York: Routledge, 2002); Chris Dixon, *African Americans and the Pacific War* (New York: Cambridge University Press, 2018), 237–38.

37. Seungsook Moon, "Regulating Desire, Managing the Empire: US Military Prostitution in South Korea, 1945–1970," in *Over There*, 39–77, quotes on 54; Susan Zeiger, *Entangling Alliances: Foreign War Brides and American Soldiers in the Twentieth Century* (New York: New York University Press, 2010), 206–14. The growth of private prostitution also contributed to the growth of a black market of military goods and supplies, which sex workers frequently received as payment from American personnel. See Jeong Min Kim, "From Military Supplies to Wartime Commodities: The Black Market for Sex and Goods During the Korean War, 1950–53," *Radical History Review* 133 (January 2019): 11–30.

38. Na Young Lee, "The Construction of Military Prostitution in South Korea During the US Military Rule, 1945–1948," *Feminist Studies* 33, no. 3 (2007): 466.

39. Moon, "Regulating Desire, Managing the Empire," 54. Women continued to migrate to South Korea to work in camptowns on "entertainment" visas for decades to come. See Sealing Cheng, *On the Move for Love: Migrant Entertainers and the US Military in South Korea* (Philadelphia: University of Pennsylvania Press, 2010).

40. Joan Capella, telephone interview by Kara Dixon Vuic, July 12 and 13, 2017; Judy Max, telephone interview by Kara Dixon Vuic, April 13 and May 1, 2017.

41. Kellie Wilson-Buford, *Policing Sex and Marriage in the American Military: The Court-Martial and the Construction of Gender and Sexual Deviance, 1950–2000* (Lincoln: University of Nebraska Press, 2018), 183–88.

42. Greenberg, "Venereal Disease in the Armed Forces," 197–198; Andre J. Ognibene and O'Neill Barrett, Jr., eds., *Internal Medicine in Vietnam*, Volume II, *General Medicine And*

Infectious Diseases (Washington, DC: Office of the Surgeon General and Center of Military History, 1982), 236; R. W. Apple, Jr., "Four G.I.'s Are Accused of Possessing Narcotics—20 Under Inquiry," *New York Times*, January 27, 1966; Lt. Col. Ted A. Cimral, interview by Samuel J. Dennis, Senior Officer Oral History Program, 1985, 5, MHI; Debby Alexander Moore, telephone interview by Kara Dixon Vuic, July 25–28, 2016; Gloria Glover Gates, interview by Anna Snipes, November 17, 2015, recording, The Vietnam Archive, Texas Tech University, Lubbock, TX; Gary E. Skogen, *Not All Heroes: An Unapologetic Memoir of the Vietnam War, 1971–1972* (Washburn, ND: Dakota Institute Press, 2013). For secondary accounts, see Amanda Boczar, "Uneasy Allies: The Americanization of Sexual Policies in South Vietnam," *Journal of American-East Asian Relations* 22 (2015): 187–220; Heather Marie Stur, *Beyond Combat: Women and Gender in the Vietnam War Era* (New York: Cambridge University Press, 2011), 48–61, 171–76; Jeffrey A. Keith, "Producing Miss Saigon: Imaginings, Realities, and the Sensual Geography of Saigon," *Journal of American-East Asian Relations* 22 (2015): 256–67; Sue Sun, "Where the Girls Are: The Management of Venereal Disease by United States Military Forces in Vietnam," *Literature and Medicine* 23, no. 1 (Spring 2004): 66–87; Meredith H. Lair, *Armed with Abundance: Consumerism and Soldiering in the Vietnam War* (Chapel Hill: University of North Carolina Press, 2011), 207.

43. Sydney Gruson, "'R&R Tours on Taiwan," *New York Times*, February 14, 1968; Sun, "*Where the Girls Are*"; Zeiger, *Entangling Alliances*, 220–21; Lair, *Armed with Abundance*, 207–8; Cynthia Enloe, *Maneuvers: The International Politics of Militarizing Women's Lives* (Berkeley: University of California Press, 2000), 69.

44. Kim Willenson, "Some US Bases Open to Viet Prostitutes," *Daily Herald* (Provo, UT), January 24, 1972. Officially, the commanding general of the US army forces in Vietnam explained that the "morale and welfare of the American soldier is of paramount importance" and that some commanders allowed local women onto posts as a means of providing "companionship opportunity" for GIs, not to "encourage or subsidize prostitution or promiscuity." Commanding General US Army Vietnam to Jerry L. Pettis, joint message form draft, 701-07 Congressional Correspondence, Jan-March 1972, Morale and Welfare Branch General Records, Military Personnel Policy Division, DCSPER, Headquarters, USARV, Records of US Forces in Southeast Asia, 1950–1975, Record Group 472, National Archives and Records Administration, College Park, MD.

45. Kevin Sullivan, "3 Servicemen Admit Roles in Rape of Okinawan Girl," *Washington Post*, November 8, 1995; Teresa Watanabe, "Okinawa Rape Suspect's Lawyer Gives Dark Account," *Los Angeles Times*, October 28, 1995; Andrew Pollack, "3 US Servicemen Convicted of Rape of Okinawa Girl," *New York Times*, March 7, 1996.

46. Irvin Molotsky, "Admiral Has to Quit over His Comments on Okinawa Rape," *New York Times*, November 18, 1995; Art Pine, "Admiral Retires After Okinawa Rape Comment," *Los Angeles Times*, November 18, 1995.

47. Paul Eckert, "'Day of Reflection' Held in Okinawa," *Washington Post*, October 5, 1995; Mary Jordan, "In Okinawa's Whisper Alley, GIs Find Prostitutes are Cheap and Plentiful," *Washington Post*, November 23, 1995.

48. Andrew Pollack, "Rape Case in Japan Turns Harsh Light on US Military," *New York Times*, September 20, 1995; Teresa Watanabe, "US, Japan OK Pact on Military Crime Suspects," *Los Angeles Times*, October 26, 1995; Linda Isako Angst, "The Sacrifice of a Schoolgirl: The 1995 Rape Case, Discourses of Power, and Women's Lives in Okinawa," *Critical Asian Studies*, 33, no. 2 (2001): 243–66; Andris Zimelis, "Human Rights, the Sex Industry and Foreign

Troops: Feminist Analysis of Nationalism in Japan, South Korea and the Philippines," *Coopera-tion and Conflict* 44, no. 1 (2009): 51–71.

49. Kathleen Cole, telephone interview by Kara Dixon Vuic, July 12, 2017; Sarah Elizabeth Mendelson, *Barracks and Brothels: Peacekeepers and Human Trafficking in the Balkans* (Wash-ington, DC: CSIS Studies, 2005), 33–34.

50. Zimelis, "Human Rights, the Sex Industry and Foreign Troops," 58–59; Cam Simp-son, "US Stalls on Human Trafficking," *Chicago Tribune*, December 27, 2005; Yuri W. Doolan, "Transpacific Camptowns: Korean Women, US Army Bases, and Military Prostitution in Amer-ica," *Journal of American Ethnic History* 38, no. 4 (2019): 33–54.

51. Jeff Schogol, "Patronizing a Prostitute is Now a Specific Crime for Servicemembers," *Stripes*, January 6, 2006, https://www.stripes.com/news/patronizing-a-prostitute-is-now-a -specific-crime-for-servicemembers-1.43314; Pauline Jelinek, "Anti-Prostitution Rule Drafted for US Forces," *The Washington Post*, September 22, 2004.

52. Rhys Blakely, "US Soldiers Lured into Prostitute Ring," *The* [London] *Times*, Decem-ber 6, 2013; Geoff Ziezulewicz, "Tinder, Sailor, Hooker, Pimp: The US Navy's Sex Traffick-ing Scandal in Bahrain," *Military Times*, June 16, 2020, https://www.militarytimes.com/news /your-military/2020/06/16/tinder-sailor-hooker-pimp-the-us-navys-sex-trafficking-scandal-in -bahrain/.

53. Mark L. Gillem, *America Town: Building the Outposts of Empire* (Minneapolis: Univer-sity of Minnesota Press, 2007), 53–66; David Vine, *Base Nation: How US Military Bases Abroad Harm America and the World* (New York: Metropolitan Books, 2015), chapters 9 and 10; Enloe, *The Morning After*, chapter 5; Cynthia Enloe, *Bananas, Beaches, and Bases: Making Feminist Sense of International Politics* (Berkeley: University of California Press, 1990).

54. See, for example, Gregory A. Daddis, *Pulp Vietnam: War and Gender in Cold War Men's Adventure Magazines* (New York: Cambridge University Press, 2020).

Chapter 6

1. US Senate Committee on Armed Services, *Overseas Construction in the North Atlan-tic and the Mediterranean Areas, Report of the Subcommittee on Military Public Works, Eighty-Second Congress*, 83rd Cong., 1st sess. (Washington, DC: Government Printing Office, 1953).

2. "African Air Bases Defended by Pick," *New York Times*, August 26, 1952; US Senate, Committee on Armed Services, *Investigations of Overseas Air Force Bases: Hearings Before the Subcommittee on Preparedness*, 82nd Cong., 2nd sess. (Washington, DC: Government Printing Office, 1952), 373, 516.

3. In the 1960s the Corps tried to overcome this myopia and better promote its overseas work. "Corps of Engineers Military Construction Mission," information pamphlet, n.d. Military General Files XI-1A, US Army Corps of Engineers Headquarters, Historical Research Office, Alexandria, VA [hereafter ACEHQ].

4. "Corps of Engineers Military Construction Mission," OCE Military General Files, I-1A, ACEHQ. See also Robert P. Grathwol and Donita M. Moorhus, *Bricks, Sand, and Marble: US Army Corps of Engineers Construction in the Mediterranean and Middle East, 1947–1991* (Wash-ington, DC: Center of Military History, US Army, 2010), 10. On Corps construction, Kenneth S. Coates and William R. Morrison, "Soldier-Workers: The US Army Corps of Engineers and the Northwest Defense Projects, 1942–1946," *Pacific Historical Review* 62, no. 3 (1993): 273–304; David P. Billington and Donald C. Jackson, *Big Dams of the New Deal Era: A Confluence of Engi-neering and Politics* (Norman: University of Oklahoma Press, 2006); Lenore Fine and Jesse A.

Remington, *The Corps of Engineers: Construction in the United States* (Washington, DC: Center of Military History, US Army, 2003); Robert P. Grathwol and Donita M. Moorhus, *Building for Peace: US Army Engineers in Europe, 1945–1991* (Washington, DC: Government Printing Office, 2006); Karl C. Dod, *The Corps of Engineers: The War Against Japan* (Washington, DC: Center of Military History, US Army, 2017); *The US Army Corps of Engineers: A History,* 2nd ed. (Alexandria, VA: Office of History, Headquarters, US Army Corps of Engineers, 2008).

5. On US bases, Maria Höhn and Seungsook Moon, eds., *Over There: Living with the US Military Empire from World War Two to the Present* (Durham, NC: Duke University Press, 2010); David Vine, *Base Nation: How US Military Bases Abroad Harm America and the World* (New York: Metropolitan Books, 2015); C. T. Sanders, *America's Overseas Garrisons: A Leasehold Empire* (Oxford, UK: Oxford University Press, 2001); Cynthia Enloe, *Bananas and Beaches: Making Feminist Sense of International Politics,* 2nd ed. (Berkeley: University of California Press, 2014); Catherine Lutz, ed., *The Bases of Empire: The Global Struggle against US Military Posts* (New York: New York University Press, 2009).

6. For engineering construction history after World War II, James M. Carter, *Inventing Vietnam: The United States and State Building, 1954–1968* (New York: Cambridge University Press, 2008); Grathwol and Moorhus, *Building for Peace;* Grathwol and Moorhus, *Bricks, Sand, and Marble;* Kirby Harrison, "Diego Garcia: The Seabees at Work," *US Naval Institute Proceedings* 105, no. 8 (Aug. 1979): 53–61; Daniel L. Haulman, "USAF Combat Airfields in Korea and Vietnam." *Air Power History* 53, no. 4 (2006): 12–19; Frank N. Schubert, *Building Air Bases in the Negev: the US Army Corps of Engineers in Israel, 1979–1982* (Washington, DC: Office of History, Corps of Engineers, and Center of Military History, US Army, 1992); Richard Tregaskis, *Southeast Asia: Building the Bases; The History of Construction in Southeast Asia* (Washington, DC: Government Printing Office, 1975).

7. Adam Moore, *Empire's Labor: The Global Army That Supports US Wars* (Ithaca, NY: Cornell University Press, 2019).

8. "Operation Blue Jay, Phase One, 1 January–12 June, 1951," Military Engineer Files, American Overseas Bases, OPS XII-18, ACEHQ, 18.

9. Lewis A. Pick, "The Story of Blue Jay," *Military Engineer* 45 (July–Aug. 1953): 278–86.

10. "Peace in Strength Seen by Finletter," *New York Times,* June 15, 1950; "Finletter Urges Superiority in Air," *New York Times,* November 4, 1950. Thomas K. Finletter was named secretary of the air force earlier in 1950 and proclaimed his intention to double the number of men in the air force (to nearly 1 million) and to increase the number of air wings from forty-eight to ninety-five.

11. Pick, "The Story of Blue Jay."

12. For the Cold War Arctic, see Ronald E. Doel, Urban Wråkberg, and Suzanne Zeller, "Science, Environment, and the New Arctic," *Journal of Historical Geography* 44 (2014): 2–14; Matthew Farish, "Militarizing a Northern Environment," *Environmental History* 12 (October 2007): 921–50.

13. "Long Range Plan for the Construction of Blue Jay by NAC," June 8, 1951, Military Construction Files, American Overseas Bases, OPS XII-20, ACEHQ. For engineers see "Thule Air Force Base," *Progressive Architecture* 35, no.12 (1953): 107–9.

14. "Note for Colonel Ellis: Blue Jay Project, December 1950 – April 1951," Military Engineer Files, American Overseas Bases, OPS XII-18, ACEHQ, 18; "Big Picture: Operation Blue Jay" (1953), US Army Audiovisual, Office of the Deputy Chief of Staff for Operations, Department of the Army, NARA, https://archive.org/details/gov.archives.arc.2569497.

15. Much of the act was motivated by cost overruns around acquisition of parts and materials. For a great example, see "bearings" and "mis-markings," US Senate Committee on Armed Services, *Armed Services Procurement Act of 1947: Hearings Before the United States Senate Committee on Armed Services*, 80th Cong., 1st sess. (Washington, DC: Government Printing Office, 1947), 12–15.

16. Elliott V. Converse III, "Into the Cold War: An Overview of Acquisition in the Department of Defense, 1945–1958," in *Providing the Means of War, Historical Perspectives on Defense Acquisition, 1945–2000*, ed. Shannon A. Brown (Washington, DC: US Army Center of Military History, 2005), 36–38.

17. Elliott V. Converse III, *Rearming for the Cold War 1945–1960* (Washington, DC: Historical Office, Office of the Secretary of Defense, 2012), 44; Grathwol and Moorhus, *Bricks, Sand, and Marble*, 10–11.

18. Converse, *Rearming for the Cold War*, 48.

19. Numbers are for total contracts, not construction by Corps of Engineers specifically. Converse, *Rearming for the Cold War*, 72, n. 115. Corps of Engineers civil works construction contracts were actually held up as model of competitive bid contracting. Between 1953 and 1955, 83.5 percent of all Corps contracts were competitive, but this data does not include military construction carried out for the other services, such as the air force, so it is difficult to determine precise amounts.

20. US House Committee on Armed Services, *Report to Honorable Carl Vinson, Chairman, House Committee on Armed Services*, 84th Cong., 1st sess. (Washington, DC: Government Printing Office, 1955), 1173, 1177.

21. "Note for Colonel Ellis: Blue Jay Project, December 1950 – April 1951." For meetings and calls see "Big Picture: Operation Blue Jay"; Pick, "The Story of Blue Jay."

22. Corps of Engineers memo to Chief of Engineers, July 2, 1951, Military Engineer Files, American Overseas Bases, OPS XII-20, ACEHQ.

23. "Our History: Military Build-Up," https://www.kiewit.com/about-us/history/military-buildup/ (accessed March 2020), and "Peter Kiewit Sons Inc.," https://www.referenceforbusiness.com/history2/15/Peter-Kiewit-Sons-Inc.html.

24. "Conference, 11 June 1951," Military Engineer Files, American Overseas Bases, OPS, ACEHQ; For decision on CPFF, July 2, 1951, memo "Request for Approval of Award of CPFF Contract for A-E Services on Project Blue Jay," Military Engineer Files, American Overseas Bases, OPS XII-20, ACEHQ.

25. "Flat 3 Expected for African Bases," *New York Times*, July 7, 1953.

26. Grathwol and Moorhus, *Bricks, Sand and Marble*, 53, 40–41.

27. C. W. Carlson, of the Corps of Engineers, to Lyndon B. Johnson, 7 August 1953, ACE XII-29 Moroccan Memos, ACEHQ.

28. Schubert, *Building Air Bases in the Negev*, 47–49.

29. "Additional Statement for the Record," Conference between Corps of Engineers and contractors, June 11, 1951, Military Engineer Files, American Overseas Bases, OPS XII-41; Kiewit said a similar thing: XII-41 Greenland-Okinawa Pdf 8 – 27 Dec 1950 AE contract.

30. For more on this see SIPRE reports through the Corps of Engineers. For US expertise as a force around the world, Michael E. Latham, *Modernization as Ideology: American Social Science and 'Nation Building' in the Kennedy Era* (Chapel Hill: University of North Carolina Press, 2000); for connections between government knowledge and the private sector in Alaska, Andrew Stuhl, *Unfreezing the Arctic: Science, Colonialism, and the Transformation of Inuit Lands*

(Chicago: University of Chicago Press, 2016), chapter 4. B. Alex Beasley writes about how oil companies traded on their expertise around the world in the 1970s and beyond, for example, "The Strange Career of Donald Rumsfeld: Military Logistics and the Routes from Vietnam to Iraq," *Radical History Review* 133 (2019): 56–77. Beasley identifies a relationship of "co-production" that developed in the 1970s and beyond as oil services companies worked with the state to promote and monetize American knowledge. For tight connections between military and civilian sectors, see also Deborah Cowen, *The Deadly Life of Logistics: Mapping Violence in Global Trade* (Minneapolis: University of Minnesota Press, 2014).

31. David Christopher Arnold, "Minnesotans at the Top of the World," *Minnesota History* 65, no. 1 (Spring 2016): 4–13.

32. Arnold, "Minnesotans at the Top of the World."

33. "Transcript of interview with Harold 'Oakie' Priebe, Chief, Heavy Construction Division, Greenland Contractors," September 3, 1959, Military Engineer Files, American Overseas Bases, OPS XII-24, ACEHQ.

34. Construction employment domestically was up 10 percent in 1951 over 1950. Department of Labor statistics for construction do not parse out military construction from public construction, and they specifically leave "secret" military programs off their annual legers. International construction is also absent from these reports (including Alaska), though the number of workers being sent overseas would be relatively small compared to the domestic construction market. See Construction, annual review, 1951, US Bureau of Labor Statistics Bulletin No. 1122, 83rd Cong., 1, Serial Set Vol. No. 11714, Session Vol. No. 35 (1953).

35. "Franco-American Air Base Construction," Corps of Engineers (1955), Military Construction Files XII-29, ACEHQ. On competition, see US Senate, Committee on Armed Services, *Hiring for Work at Overseas Bases: Hearing of the Subcommittee on Preparedness*, 82 Cong., 2nd sess. (Washington, DC: Government Printing Office, 1952), 84.

36. US Senate, *Construction Work for the Army Outside the Continental Limits of the United States: Hearing Before the Committee on Military Affairs*, 76th Cong., 1st sess. (Washington, DC: Government Printing Office, 1939).

37. At the end of 1952, there were 2,204 American employees in Morocco, 1,191 French, and 7,817 local laborers. "Franco-American Air Base Construction," p. 10.

38. Gretchen Heefner, "'A Slice of Their Sovereignty': Negotiating the US Empire of Bases, Wheelus Field, Libya, 1950–1954," *Diplomatic History* 41, no. 1 (January 2017): 50–77.

39. Memo from the Minister of Foreign Affairs to the US Minister, December 1953, Military Files XII-25 Iceland, ACEHQ. "To: Chief, AF Projects Division, Military Construction," November 13, 1953, XII-Iceland, ACEHQ.

40. Grathwol and Moorhus, *Bricks, Sand, and Marble*, 127.

41. *Hiring for Work at Overseas Bases*, 84.

42. "Transcript of Preliminary Negotiations Conference, Kiewit-Groves-Johnson-Cunningham," January 5, 1951, Military Engineer Files, American Overseas Bases, OPS XII-41, 10.

43. For fingerprints, "Overseas Job Cost Put at $718 a Man," *New York Times*, January 12, 1952.

44. "Transcript of interview with Harold 'Oakie' Priebe"; "Exclusive '51er Club," *Northern Kieways Newsletter*, August 1959, Military Engineer Files, American Overseas Bases, OPS XII-Easter Ocean Department, Thule, ACEHQ.

45. *Hiring for Work at Overseas Bases*, 77.

46. Arnold, "Minnesotans at the Top of the World." V. W. Nobles, "They Called It "Blue-Jay,"" *Employment Security Review*, May 1954, 3–7, in Military Engineer Files, American Overseas Bases, OPS XII-Thule, ACEHQ.

47. JFK letter to Pick, September 11, 1951, Military Engineer Files, American Overseas Bases, OPS XII-22, ACEHQ.

48. "Transcript of interview with Harold 'Oakie' Priebe."

49. *Hiring for Work at Overseas Bases*, 1.

50. "Building Men Protest," *New York Times*, November 4, 1951.

51. *Hiring for Work at Overseas Bases*, 90–91.

52. "Moroccan Bases Running Up Bills," *New York Times*, November 1, 1952.

53. *Hiring for Work at Overseas Bases*, 79.

54. On explanation, John R. Hardin to Rep. George Mahon, April 21, 1953, ACE XII-29 Moroccan Memos, ACEHQ; "Moroccan Bases Running Up Bills"; "African Air Bases Defended by Pick," *New York Times*, August 26, 1952.

55. "Pipeline Runs to Nowhere," *Baltimore Evening Sun*, January 9, 1954, in ACE XII-29 Moroccan Memos, ACEHQ.

56. "Air Bases Failed Despite Huge Cost: Long and Morse Fear Stations Overseas Are Vulnerable to Crippling," *New York Times*, February 15, 1953.

57. "Mediterranean Division Report, 1956," Army Corps of Engineers, General Files, Box 2, ACEHQ.

58. For more on economic and local impact, Christopher T. Sandars, *America's Overseas Garrisons: The Leasehold Empire* (New York: Oxford University Press, 2000); Anni P. Baker, *American Soldiers Overseas: The Global Military Presence* (Westport, CT: Praeger 2004); Donna Alvah, *Unofficial Ambassadors: American Military Families Overseas and the Cold War, 1946–1965* (New York: New York University Press 2007).

59. Villard, *Libya*, 6. For details, see Heefner, "A Slice of Their Sovereignty."

60. "Historical Summary Middle East District," Corps of Engineers, 25 June 1950 to 6 September 1951, Box 2, General Files, ACEHQ.

61. Knappen-Tippetts-Abbett Engineering was chosen as the design agent. For Saudi Arabia, Fluor was chosen because it had already been doing work for Aramco.

62. "Request Waiver for Renegotiation Provisions," 7 June 1951, Wheelus Compilation Libya, XII-30, ACEHQ.

63. "Franco-American Air Base Construction," 13.

64. "Mediterranean Division Report," 77.

65. "Historical Summary Middle East District," Corps of Engineers, 25 June 1950 to 6 September 1951, Box 2, General Files, ACEHQ.

66. Grathwol and Moorhus, *Bricks, Sand, and Marble*, 400.

67. Grathwol and Moorhus, *Bricks, Sand, and Marble*, 309.

Chapter 7

I thank Andrew Friedman, Heather Lee, Taryn McKinnon, Seungsook Moon, and Naoko Shibusawa for their advice and support.

1. This chapter adopts the McCune-Reischauer romanization system for Korean words and uses the Korean convention for names (family names before given names) aside from Kang Ki Dong unless common usage dictates otherwise. Citations follow the English-language convention of placing given names before family names. All translations are my own.

2. Ki Dong Kang, *Kanggidonggwa han'guk pandoch'e: kanggidong chasŏjŏn* [Kang Ki Dong and Korea Semiconductor: Autobiography of Kang Ki Dong] (Seoul: Amormundi, 2018), 10–11. Hereafter Kang Autobiography.

3. Kang's task was to produce IC chips that could withstand exposure to Cobalt-60. Kang Autobiography, 20.

4. For the development of the Minuteman II electronics systems, see J. M. Wuerth, "The Evolution of Minuteman Guidance and Control," *Navigation* 23, no. 1 (Spring 1976): 64–75.

5. Kang Autobiography, 246–59. This chapter uses the translation of the company's name (한국반도체). Sources also use the romanization of the company's name, Hankook Semiconductor.

6. While Samsung was not a US military contractor, it did enjoy the support of the US-backed Park Chung Hee military dictatorship. Peter Banseok Kwon, "Building Bombs, Building a Nation: The State, *Chaebol,* and the Militarized Industrialization of South Korea, 1973–1979," *Journal of Asian Studies* 79, no. 1 (February 2020): 17–18.

7. I employ Chandler's definition of "high technology industry" as one that "commercializes—new products based on new scientific advances." Alfred D. Chandler, Jr., *Inventing the Electronic Century* (Cambridge, MA: Harvard University Press, 2009), xi. Like Chandler's work, this chapter focuses on the electronics and computer industries.

8. For example, Walter Isaacson's *Steve Jobs* (New York: Simon & Schuster, 2011) was Amazon's bestselling book in 2011 and then was adapted into a Hollywood film in 2015.

9. Stuart W. Leslie, *The Cold War and American Science: The Military-Industrial-Academic Complex at MIT and Stanford* (New York: Columbia University Press, 1994). See also Thomas Heinrich, "Cold War Armory: Military Contracting in Silicon Valley," *Enterprise & Society* 3, no. 2 (June 2002): 247–84; Christophe Lécuyer, *Making Silicon Valley: Innovation and the Growth of High Tech, 1930–1970* (Cambridge, MA: MIT Press, 2007); Margaret O'Mara, *The Code: Silicon Valley and the Remaking of America* (New York: Penguin, 2019).

10. Daniel Holbrook, Wesley M. Cohen, David A. Hounshell, and Steven Klepper, "The Nature, Sources, and Consequences of Firm Differences in the Early History of the Semiconductor Industry," *Strategic Management Journal* 21, no. 10/11 (October–November 2000): 1017–41; Christophe Lécuyer and David C. Brock, "The Materiality of Microelectronics," *History and Technology* 22, no. 3 (2006): 301–25.

11. Christophe Lécuyer and David C. Brock, *Makers of the Microchip: A Documentary History of Fairchild Semiconductor* (Cambridge, MA: MIT Press, 2010), chapter 1.

12. Hyungsub Choi, "Manufacturing Knowledge in Transit: Technical Practice, Organizational Change, and the Rise of the Semiconductor Industry in the United States and Japan, 1948–1960" (PhD diss., Johns Hopkins University, 2007), 197.

13. John A. Mathews and Dong-Sung Cho, *Tiger Technology: The Creation of a Semiconductor Industry in East Asia* (New York: Cambridge University Press, 2007), especially chapter 3; Sungsoo Song, "Ch'ugyŏgesŏ sŏndoro: samsŏng pandoch'eŭi kisulbalchŏn kwajŏng," ["From Catch-up to Innovation Leader: Technological Development of Semiconductor in Samsung"], *Korean Journal of the History of Science* 30, no. 2 (2008): 517–44; Tony Michell, *Samsung Electronics and the Struggle for Leadership of the Electronics Industry* (Singapore: John Wiley & Sons, 2010); Dong-Won Kim, "Transfer of 'Engineer's Mind': Kim Choong-Ki and the Semiconductor Industry in South Korea," *Engineering Studies* 11, no. 2 (2019), 83–108; Sangwoon Yoo, "Innovation in Practice: The 'Technology Drive Policy' and the 4Mb DRAM R&D Consortium in South Korea in the 1980s and 1990s," *Technology and Culture* 61, no. 2 (April 2020): 385–415.

14. Kang and the US military have been largely overlooked in histories of Samsung and South Korea's high-tech sector. John A. Mathews and Dong-Sung Cho credit Kang for playing "an important role in Samsung's development of semiconductor expertise" in a footnote but provide few details. Mathews and Cho, *Tiger Technology*, 150, footnote 20. Samsung Electronics' official history mentions the acquisition of KSC but not Kang. Chong-man Hong, ed., *Samsŏngjŏnja 20yŏnsa* [*The 20 Year History of Samsung Electronics*] (Seoul: Samsung Electronics, 1989), 166–169. See also the works cited in footnote 12.

15. For a discussion of Taiwanese-American migration and the Taiwanese high-tech industry, see Madeline Y. Hsu, *The Good Immigrants: How the Yellow Peril Became the Model Minority* (Princeton, NJ: Princeton University Press, 2015), 234–35.

16. Kang Autobiography, 26–27.

17. Bruce Cumings, *The Korean War: A History* (New York: Modern Library, 2010), chapter 5.

18. Historian Victoria de Grazia argues that consumer goods were critical to US influence in postwar Europe. De Grazia, *Irresistible Empire: America's Advance Through Twentieth-Century Europe* (Cambridge, MA: Belknap Press of Harvard University Press, 2006). For a discussion of the impact of US goods in South Korea, see Ji-Yeon Yuh, *Beyond the Shadow of Camptown: Korean Military Brides in America* (New York: New York University Press, 2004), chapter 2; Janice C. H. Kim, "Pusan at War: Refuge, Relief, and Resettlement in the Temporary Capital, 1950–1953," *Journal of American-East Asian Relations* 24, no. 2–3 (September 2017): 103–27.

19. Jeong Min Kim, "From Military Supplies to Wartime Commodities: The Black Market for Sex and Goods During the Korean War, 1950–53," *Radical History Review* 133 (January 2019): 11–30.

20. Kang Autobiography, 43.

21. Kim Jang-geun, "*Cheonggyecheon*: Microcosm of Korea's Modernization in the Heart of Seoul," *Koreana* 17, no. 2 (2003): 19–20.

22. Kang Autobiography, 54–57.

23. Kang autobiography, 61–64.

24. Kristen Haring, *Ham Radio's Technical Culture* (Cambridge, MA: MIT Press, 2008), 51.

25. Yuzo Takahashi, "A Network of Tinkerers: The Advent of the Radio and Television Receiver Industry in Japan," *Technology and Culture* 41, no. 3 (July 2000); Lécuyer, *Making Silicon Valley*, 14–22.

26. Haring, *Ham Radio's Technical Culture*, 81.

27. Lécuyer, *Making Silicon Valley*, 48–51.

28. *Sŏultaehakkyo 50yŏnsa, 1946–1996* [Fifty-Year History of the Seoul National University, 1946–1996] (Seoul: Seoul National University Press, 1996), 11–14. Hereafter *Fifty-Year History of the Seoul National University*.

29. For the parallels between Japanese and US deployment of racial tropes during WWII, see Takashi Fujitani, *Race for Empire: Koreans as Japanese and Japanese as Americans During World War II* (Berkeley: University of California Press, 2011).

30. Tae Gyun Park, "The Roles of the United States and Japan in the Development of South Korea's Science and Technology During the Cold War," *Korea Journal* 52, no. 1 (2012): 212–13.

31. While the 1953 armistice ended hostilities, the Korean War is officially ongoing today.

32. UN Command, "Seoul National University Receive New FOA Funds," 13 April 1955, folder 1, box 92, Organizational History Files, Records of the United States Army, Pacific, Record Group 550, US National Archives at College Park, College Park, MD. Hereafter NACP.

33. "USOM Assistance to Education in Korea FY 1954–1967" (November 1966) p. 1, container 15, Entry P 583, Records of the Agency for International Development, Record Group 286 [RG 286], NACP. For context, $30 million in July 1960 would be equivalent to $278 million in August 2021.

34. Kang Ki Dong Oral History, 13 June 1996, IEEE History Center, Hoboken, NJ, http://ethw.org/Oral-History:Ki_Dong_Kang; Jae Kyoon Kim Oral History, 25 August 1996, IEEE History Center, http://ethw.org/Oral-History:Jae_Kyoon_Kim.

35. Kang Autobiography, 68.

36. Kang Autobiography, 84–97.

37. *Fifty-Year History of the Seoul National University*, 92–93.

38. "USOM Assistance to Education in Korea FY 1954–1967," 2.

39. Paul Anderson, "Report of Observations, Activities and Recommendations Concerning College of Engineering Seoul National University," December 1959, US International Cooperation Administration, https://conservancy.umn.edu/handle/11299/150470, 53.

40. Ham radio operators were among the first civilians to hear transmissions from Sputnik. Alan Hall, "The Beep Heard Round the World," *Scientific American*, 1997, https://www.scientificamerican.com/article/the-beep-heard-round-the/.

41. For a discussion of Sputnik on military R&D, see articles by Joseph Manzione, Gregg Herken, and Walter A. McDougall in the January 2000 issue of *Diplomatic History*, on "Technology and US Foreign Relations."

42. O'Mara, *The Code*, 46.

43. Rebecca S. Lowen, *Creating the Cold War University: The Transformation of Stanford* (Berkeley: University of California Press, 1997); Leslie, *The Cold War and American Science*.

44. John Cloud, "Crossing the Olentangy River: The Figure of the Earth and the Military-Industrial-Academic-Complex, 1947–1972," *Studies in History and Philosophy of Science, Part B: Studies in History and Philosophy of Modern Physics* 31B (2000): 374–77.

45. Emerson E. Kimberly, "History of the Department of Electrical Engineering" (Columbus: Ohio State University, 1970), 44–48, https://electroscience.osu.edu/sites/default/files/uploads/Marketing/arv_osu_centennial_histories_electricalengineering.pdf.

46. Kang recalled that his interactions with air force officers inspired an interest in control systems like those found in missile guidance systems during his early years at OSU. Kang Oral History.

47. Kimberly, "History of the Department of Electrical Engineering," 46.

48. Thurston would remain a member of the air force's inactive reserve until 1965.

49. Thurston's work was supported by contract DA-36-039-SC-83874 between the Signal Corps and the OSU Research Foundation. Dawon Kahng, "Phosphorus Diffusion into Silicon Through an Oxide Layer" (PhD diss., Ohio State University, 1959), ii.; Ki Dong Kang, "The Mechanism for Oxidation of Silicon and Diffusion of Donor and Acceptor Impurities into the Oxide for a Silicon-Silicon Dioxide System" (PhD diss., Ohio State University, 1962), ii.

50. The practice was known as "second sourcing." Richard C. Levin, "The Semiconductor Industry," in *Government and Technical Progress: A Cross-Industry Analysis*, ed. Richard R. Nelson (New York: Pergamon Press, 1982), 67–68.

51. Levin, "The Semiconductor Industry," 58–59. John Bardeen and Walter Brattain created the first point-contact transistor at Bell Laboratories in 1947. For a history of semiconductor research, see Bo Lojek, *History of Semiconductor Engineering* (New York: Springer, 2006).

52. Levin, "The Semiconductor Industry," 58. During WWII, the US military funded research on germanium-based transistors at Purdue University. Paul W. Henriksen, "Solid State Physics Research at Purdue," *Osiris* 3, no. 1 (1987): 237–60. Silicon became the standard semiconductor material by the 1960s.

53. Levin, "The Semiconductor Industry," 69.

54. It specifically examined silicon oxidation and boron and phosphorus diffusion. Kang, "Mechanism for Oxidation of Silicon," 1–2.

55. For discussion of Hoerni, Fairchild, and the US military, see Lécuyer and Brock, *Makers of the Microchip*, chapter 1.

56. Kang, "Mechanism for Oxidation of Silicon," 1.

57. Kang Autobiography, 116.

58. Kang Autobiography, 119–24.

59. Kang Autobiography, 127.

60. For an overview of this history, see Margaret O'Mara, "The Uses of the Foreign Student," *Social Science History* 36, no. 4 (Winter 2012): 583–615.

61. Hsu, *The Good Immigrants*, 211–213; O'Mara, "Uses of the Foreign Student," 595.

62. Kahng, "Phosphorous Diffusion into Silicon," 84.

63. Atalla immigrated from Egypt in 1946 to study engineering at Purdue University, where his studies were funded by the air force. Mohamed M. Atalla, "High Speech Compressible Flow in Square Diffusers," (PhD diss., Purdue University, 1949). Hoerni built on Atalla's work. Lojek, *History of Semiconductor Engineering*, 120.

64. Kahng is beyond the scope of this chapter but is deserving of his own study. His career was devoted more to academic research rather than commercial pursuits.

65. John P. DiMoia, "Transnational Scientific Networks and the Research University: The Making of a South Korean Community at the University of Utah, 1948–1980," *East Asian Science, Technology, and Society: An International Journal* 6 (2012): 17–40.

66. Kang Autobiography, 107.

67. J. W. Cohn, "South Korea Emerging as Center of Production to Rival Hong Kong," *Home Furnishings Daily*, May 18, 1967; LGP 3-5 (a) - Promotion Activities (folder), container 3, Entry P 584, RG 286, NACP.

68. Kang Autobiography, 135–37. Arizona became a hub of defense contracting during the Cold War. Jason H. Gart, "The Defense Establishment in Cold War Arizona, 1945–1968," *Journal of Arizona History* 60, no. 3 (Autumn 2019): 319.

69. Motorola Inc., 1965 Annual Report, 2, https://www.motorolasolutions.com/en_us/about/company-overview/history/annual-report-archive.html.

70. C. Lester Hogan, "Daniel Earl Noble 1901–1980," in *Memorial Tributes: National Academy of Engineering* (Washington, DC: National Academies Press, 1984), 2: 225.

71. Kahng urged Kang not to go to Motorola because of its focus on commercial production rather than scientific research. Kang Autobiography, 134.

72. Earl L. Steele Oral History, 2000, IEEE History Center, https://ethw.org/Oral-History:Earl_Steele.

73. Holbrook et al., "The Nature, Sources, and Consequences of Firm Differences in the Early History of the Semiconductor Industry," 1024.

74. Transistors consist of positively (P-type) and negatively (N-type) charged semiconductor wafers. PNP transistors sandwich a negatively charged wafer between two positively

charged ones. Kang's patent proposed a more efficient arrangement of gates (or channels) on the surface of a transistor through which electrical current could travel more efficiently. For a full description, see Ki Dong Kang and David Metz, Semiconductor device with passivated junction, US3302076A, filed September 28, 1966, and issued January 31, 1967. https://patents.google.com/patent/US3302076A/en.

75. Motorola Inc., 1963 Annual Report, 10, https://www.motorolasolutions.com/en_us/about/company-overview/history/annual-report-archive.html.

76. Among the other leading semiconductor firms that worked on the Minuteman project were Signetics Corporation and General Microelectronics. Heinrich, "Cold War Armory," 268.

77. Motorola Inc., 1966 Annual Report, 19, https://www.motorolasolutions.com/en_us/about/company-overview/history/annual-report-archive.html.

78. Kang Autobiography, 176. As well as being ethnically Korean, Kang spoke English, Korean, and Japanese. Therefore, the company often asked Kang to serve as an intermediary with Asian businessmen. Kang Oral History.

79. US firms controlled only six offshore plants in "developing countries" in 1967. US Department of Commerce, *A Report on the US Semiconductor Industry* (Washington, DC: Government Printing Office, 1979), 69.

80. Kang Oral History.

81. Airgram to Department of State, "Biweekly Economic Review No. 2" (28 March 1967), p. 2, box 635, Central Foreign Policy Files, 1967–1969, General Records of the Department of State, RG 59, NACP.

82. William Lazonick, "Globalization of the ICT Labour Force," in *The Oxford Handbook of Information and Communication Technologies*, ed. Chrisanthi Avgerou, Robin Mansell, Danny Quah, and Roget Silverstone (New York: Oxford University Press, 2007), 80.

83. Heinrich, "Cold War Armory," 271–73.

84. Charles E. Sporck Oral History, 2014, Computer History Museum. https://www.computerhistory.org/collections/catalog/102740002, 16. See also Lécuyer, *Making Silicon Valley*, chapter 7.

85. In 1970, the average hourly wage in semiconductor assembly in Asia was less than one-tenth of that in the United States. *A Report on the US Semiconductor Industry*, 75. Cofounder of Fairchild and Intel, Robert Noyce was among the earliest Silicon Valley executives to suggest outsourcing production to Asia. Sporck Oral History, 17.

86. "Biweekly Economic Review No. 2," 2.

87. Airgram to Department of State, "Korean Trade Union Attitude Toward Foreign Investments in Korea," 22 July 1972, enclosure 15, box 916, Subject Numeric File, 1970–73, RG 59, NACP.

88. Levin, "The Semiconductor Industry," 36.

89. As part of an agreement to deploy South Korean troops to Vietnam, the Park government received US funding to establish the Korean Institute of Science and Technology (KIST). Manyong Moon, "Postcolonial Desire and the Tripartite Alliance in East Asia," in *Engineering Asia: Technology, Colonial Development, and the Cold War Order*, eds. Hiromi Mizuno, Aaron S. Moore, and John P. DiMoia (London: Bloomsbury Academic, 2018), 165–88. During subsequent decades, KIST became a focal point of R&D in Korea and produced many of the engineers that would work for its high-tech firms. Kim, "Transfer of 'Engineer's Mind,'" 83–108.

90. *A Report on the US Semiconductor Industry*, 85.

91. One US engineer recalled, "Korea was basically an assembler, with low cost labor but no high tech." Richard Petritz Oral History, 25 August 1996, IEEE History Center, http://ethw.org /Oral-History:Richard_Petritz.

92. In order to avoid the attention of US officials, Kang established KSC as a subsidiary of a US-based firm that he set up in Sunnyvale, California, ICII (Integrated Circuit International, Inc.). Kang Autobiography, 219–22.

93. For Kang's account of KSC, see Kang Autobiography, chapters 6, 7.

94. Kang Autobiography, 246–59.

95. Lécuyer, *Making Silicon Valley*, 278–79.

96. Samsung had previously entered partnerships with the Japanese firms Sanyo and NEC. *The 20-Year History of Samsung Electronics*, 120–30. These agreements did not cover more advanced CMOS large-scale-integration devices like those produced by KSC.

97. Kang Autobiography, 262.

98. Kang Autobiography, 284.

99. For the history of Samsung and the South Korean semiconductor industry during the 1980s and 1990s, see Yoo, "Innovation in Practice."

100. Kang Oral History.

101. Mathews and Cho, *Tiger Technology*, 126.

102. Mathews and Cho, *Tiger Technology*, chapter 3; Yoo, "Innovation in Practice."

103. "Samsung founder's Tokyo Declaration selected as highlight of Korean businesses," December 9, 2019, *The Donga Ilbo*, https://www.donga.com/en/article/all/20191209/1922583/1.

104. "Samsung Topples Intel as Market Leader in 2017," March 29, 2018, *EPS News*, https:// epsnews.com/.

105. Quoted in Walter A. McDougall, "The Cold War Excursion of Science," *Diplomatic History* 24, no. 1 (January 2000): 118.

106. O'Mara, *The Code*, chapter 6.

107. Gabrielle Hecht, ed., *Entangled Geographies: Empire and Technopolitics in the Global Cold War* (Cambridge, MA: MIT Press, 2011), 3.

Chapter 8

1. John W. Finney, "Military Budget Spurs Economy," *New York Times*, February 27, 1974.

2. "Military Spending as a Stimulus to the Economy," *ADA Legislative Newsletter*, March 15, 1974, 2; "Defense Spending—Countup for a Launching," First National City Bank, *Monthly Economic Letter*, April 1974, 13–15.

3. US Senate Committee on Foreign Relations, *Arms Control and the Militarization of Space: Hearing Before a Subcommittee of the Senate Foreign Relations Committee*, 97th Cong., 2nd. sess. (Washington, DC: Government Printing Office, 1982), 63.

4. US Arms Control and Disarmament Agency, *Economic Impacts of Disarmament*, ACDA Publication 2, Economic Series 1 (Washington, DC: Government Printing Office, 1962), 13.

5. Memorandum of Discussion at the 183rd Meeting of the National Security Council, Washington, February 4, 1954. *Foreign Relations of the United States* [hereafter *FRUS*], 1952–1954, China and Japan, Volume XIV, Part 1, eds. David W. Mabon and Harriet D. Schwar (Washington, DC: Government Printing Office, 1985), Document 167, https://history.state.gov /historicaldocuments/frus1952-54v14p1/d167.

6. Harold D. Laswell, "The Garrison State," *American Journal of Sociology* 46, no. 4 (January 1941); Walter J. Oakes, "Toward a Permanent War Economy?" *Politics* (February 1944), https://www.marxists.org/history/etol/writers/vance/1944/02/pwe.htm.

7. A. H. M. Jones, *The Later Roman Empire: A Social Economic and Administrative Survey*, (Oxford: Basil Blackwell, 1964), 2: 66, 834–41; Frederic C. Lane, *Venice: A Maritime Republic* (Baltimore: Johns Hopkins University Press, 1973), 163–65.

8. For creative but ultimately anachronistic extensions of the term "military Keynesianism," see Michael Mann, *The Sources of Social Power: Volume 1, A History of Power from the Beginning to AD 1760* (New York: Cambridge University Press, 1986), 150, 234, 278; Giovanni Arrighi, *The Long Twentieth Century: Money, Power, and the Origins of Our Times* (New York: Verso, 1994), 38.

9. Adam Tooze, "Imagining National Economies: National and International Economics Statistics 1900–1950," in *Imagining Nations*, ed. Geoffrey Cubitt (Manchester, UK: Manchester University Press 1998), 212–28; Timothy Shenk, "Inventing the American Economy," (PhD diss., Columbia University, 2016).

10. Josef Steindl, *Maturity and Stagnation in American Capitalism*, 2nd ed. (New York: Monthly Review Press, 1976); Jamie Martin, "Time and the Economics of the Business Cycle in Modern Capitalism," in *Power and Time: Temporalities in Conflict and the Making of History*, eds. Dan Edelstein, Stefanos Geroulanos, and Natasha Wheatley (Chicago: University of Chicago Press, 2020), 317–34; Alexander Keyssar, *Out of Work: The First Century of Unemployment in Massachusetts* (New York: Cambridge University Press, 1986).

11. Tim Barker, "Macroeconomic Consequences of Peace: American Radical Economists and the Problem of Military Keynesianism, 1938–1975," *Research in the History of Economic Thought and Methodology* 37A (2019): 11–29.

12. John Maynard Keynes, "Will Rearmament Cure Unemployment?" *The Listener*, June 1, 1939; Keynes, "The United States and the Keynes Plan," *New Republic*, July 29, 1940; Henry Morgenthau, *From the Morgenthau Diaries, Vol. 2: Years of Urgency, 1938–1941*, ed. John Morton Blum (Boston: Houghton Mifflin, 1965), 118.

13. Katherine Archibald, *Wartime Shipyard: A Study in Social Disunity* (Berkeley: University of California Press, 1947), 188–189; Nelson Lichtenstein, *Labor's War at Home: The CIO in World War II* (New York: Cambridge University Press, 1987), 203–32.

14. "A WPA for the Brass," *Chicago Daily Tribune*, April 4, 1948.

15. "From Cold War to Cold Peace?" *Business Week*, February 12, 1949.

16. Robert Lekachman, *The Age of Keynes: The Life, Times, Thought and Triumph of the Greatest Economist of Our Age* (New York: Random House, 1966); Robert M. Collins, *The Business Response to Keynes* (New York: Columbia University Press, 1981); Robert M. Collins, *More: The Politics of Growth in Postwar America* (New York: Oxford University Press, 2000); Margaret Weir and Theda Skocpol, "State Structures and the Possibilities for 'Keynesian' Responses to the Great Depression in Sweden, Britain, and the United States," in *Bringing the State Back In*, eds. Peter B. Evans, Dietrich Rueschemeyer, and Theda Skocpol (New York: Cambridge University Press, 1985) 107–163; *The Rise and Fall of the New Deal Order, 1930–1980*, eds. Steve Fraser and Gary Gerstle (New York: Cambridge University Press, 1990); Lizabeth Cohen, *A Consumers' Republic: The Politics of Mass Consumption in Postwar America* (New York: Knopf, 2003).

17. Bruce J. Schulman, *The Seventies: The Great Shift in American, Culture, Society, and Politics* (New York: The Free Press, 2001); Judith Stein, *Pivotal Decade: How the United States Traded Factories for Finance in the Seventies* (New Haven, CT: Yale University Press, 2010); Jefferson Cowie, *Stayin' Alive: The 1970s and the Last Days of the Working Class* (New York: New

Press, 2010); Laura Kalman, *Right Star Rising: A New Politics, 1974–1980* (New York: Norton, 2010); Daniel Rodgers, *Age of Fracture* (Cambridge, MA: Belknap Press of Harvard University Press, 2011).

18. Paul Hammond, "NSC-68: Prologue to Rearmament," in *Strategy, Politics and Defense Budgets*, eds. Warner Schilling, Paul Hammond, and Glenn Snyder (New York: Columbia University Press, 1962) 267–378; Fred Block, "Economic Instability and Military Strength: The Paradoxes of the 1950 Rearmament Decision," *Politics & Society* 10, no. 1 (January 1980): 35–58; John Lewis Gaddis and Paul Nitze, "NSC 68 and the Soviet Threat Reconsidered," *International Security* 4, no. 4 (Spring 1980): 164–76; Lester H. Brune, "Guns and Butter: The Pre-Korean War Dispute over Budget Allocation," *American Journal of Economics and Sociology* 48, no. 3 (July 1989): 357–71; Benjamin Fordham, "Domestic Politics, International Pressure, and Policy Change: The Case of NSC 68," *Journal of Conflict Studies* 17, no. 1 (Spring 1997): 63–88; David M. Hart, *Forged Consensus: Science, Technology, and Economic Policy in the United States, 1921–1953* (Princeton, NJ: Princeton University Press, 1998), 148–52, 193–94; Edmund F. Wehrle, "Guns, Butter, Leon Keyserling, the AFL-CIO and the Fate of Full-Employment Economics," *The Historian*, 66, no. 4 (Winter 2004): 730–48; Curt Cardwell, *NSC 68 and the Political Economy of the Early Cold War* (New York: Cambridge University Press, 2011).

19. Roger Lotchin, *Fortress California, 1910–1961: From Warfare to Welfare* (New York: Oxford University Press, 1992); Bruce J. Schulman, *From Cotton Belt to Sunbelt: Federal Policy, Economic Development, and the Transformation of the South 1938–1980* (Durham, NC: Duke University Press, 1994); Lisa McGirr, *Suburban Warriors: The Origins of the New American Right* (Princeton, NJ: Princeton University Press, 2001); Elizabeth Tandy Shermer, *Sunbelt Capitalism: Phoenix and the Transformation of American Politics* (Philadelphia: University of Pennsylvania Press, 2013).

20. Larry J. Griffin, Joel A. Devine, and Michael Wallace, "Monopoly Capital, Organized Labor, and Military Expenditures in the United States, 1949–1976," *American Journal of Sociology* 88, Supplement: Marxist Inquiries: Studies of Labor, Class, and States (1982): S113–S153; Alex Mintz and Alexander Hicks, "Military Keynesianism in the United States, 1949–1976: Disaggregating Military Expenditures and Their Determination," *American Journal of Sociology* 90, no. 2 (September 1984): 411–17. For an unusual mix of regressions and historical narrative, see Larry W. Isaac and Kevin T. Leicht, "Regimes of Power and the Power of Analytic Regimes: Explaining US Military Procurement Keynesianism as Historical Process," *Historical Methods: A Journal of Quantitative and Interdisciplinary History*, 30, No. 1 (Winter 1997): 28–45.

21. Mannie Kupinsky, "Growth of Aircraft and Parts Industry, 1939 to 1954," *Monthly Labor Review* 77, no. 12 (December 1954); Aerospace Industries Association of America, *Aerospace Facts and Figures* (Washington: 1970).

22. Notable exceptions include *The Rise of the Gunbelt: The Military Remapping of Industrial America*, eds. Ann Markusen, Peter Hall, Scott Campbell, and Sabina Deitrick (New York: Oxford University Press, 1991); Jennifer Mittelstadt, *The Rise of the Military Welfare State* (Cambridge, MA: Harvard University Press, 2015); Michael Brenes, *For Might and Right: Cold War Defense Spending and Remaking of American Democracy* (Amherst: University of Massachusetts Press, 2020).

23. Stein, *Pivotal Decade*; Jefferson Cowie, *The Great Exception: The New Deal and the Limits of American Politics* (Princeton, NJ: Princeton University Press, 2015); Gary Gerstle, "The Rise and Fall (?) of America's Neoliberal Order," *Transactions of the Royal Historical Society*, 28 (December 2018): 241–64.

24. Amy Offner, *Sorting Out the Mixed Economy: The Rise and Fall of Welfare and Developmental States in the Americas* (Princeton, NJ: Princeton University Press, 2019); Gabriel Winant, "Anomalies and Continuities: Positivism and Historicism on Inequality," *Journal of the Gilded Age and Progressive Era* 19, no. 2 (April 2020): 285–95.

25. Theodore J. Lowi, *The End of the Republican Era* (Norman: University of Oklahoma Press, 1996), xxvii.

26. Gerstle, "America's Neoliberal Order," 242, 243, 252.

27. Memorandum of Conversation: December 22, 1973 - Nixon, Schlesinger, Joint Chiefs, box 3, National Security Adviser. Memoranda of Conversations, 1973–1977—Nixon Administration, 1973–74, Gerald R. Ford Presidential Library & Museum, https://www.fordlibrarymuseum.gov/library/document/0314/1552646.pdf.

28. Quinn Slobodian, *Globalists: The End of Empire and the Birth of Neoliberalism* (Cambridge, MA: Harvard University Press, 2018).

29. Offner, *Sorting Out the Mixed Economy*, 17.

30. Michael J. Hogan, *A Cross of Iron: Harry S. Truman and the Origins of the National Security State, 1945–1954* (New York: Cambridge University Press, 1998), 301–04.

31. Bert G. Hickman, *Investment Demand and US Economic Growth* (Washington, DC: Brookings Institution, 1965), 127.

32. Commencement Address at Yale, June 11, 1962. John F. Kennedy Presidential Library, https://www.jfklibrary.org/archives/other-resources/john-f-kennedy-speeches/yale-university-19620611.

33. Howard Norton, "Eisenhower Raps Tax Cut," *Baltimore Sun*, September 9, 1963; Herbert Stein, *The Fiscal Revolution in America* (Chicago: University of Chicago Press, 1969), 441.

34. Arthur Schlesinger, *A Thousand Days: John F. Kennedy in the White House* (New York: Houghton Mifflin, 1965), 630.

35. Richard Nixon, *Six Crises* (New York: Doubleday, 1962), 309–10.

36. Collins, *More*, 107.

37. The Nixon Stand, 1968. Richard G. Lugar Collection, Box 13, GOP Politics/Richard Nixon. University of Indiana Digital Mayoral Archives, https://uindy.historyit.com/item.php?id=312837.

38. Herbert Stein, *Presidential Economics: The Making of Economic Policy from Roosevelt to Reagan and Beyond*, 3rd rev. ed. (Washington, DC: American Enterprise Institute, 1994), 135, 138.

39. On Nixon's economics, see Leonard Silk, *Nixonomics*, 2nd ed. (New York: Praeger, 1973); Stein, *Presidential Economics*, 133–207; Alan Matusow, *Nixon's Economy: Booms, Busts, Dollars, and Votes* (Lawrence: University Press of Kansas, 1998); Nigel Bowles, *Nixon's Business: Authority and Power in Presidential Politics* (College Station: Texas A&M University Press, 2005). On Vietnam costs, see Thomas A. Riddell, "A Political Economy of the American War in Indo-China: Its Costs and Consequences" (PhD diss., American University, 1975).

40. David Rockefeller, an LBJ donor in 1964, backed Nixon in 1968 because he was "willing to accept a somewhat higher level of unemployment in order to achieve a greater rate of price stability." William Hoffman, *David: Report on a Rockefeller* (New York: Dell, 1971), 134.

41. David Stein, "Containing Keynesianism in an Age of Civil Rights: Jim Crow Monetary Policy and the Struggle for Guaranteed Jobs, 1956–1979," in *Beyond the New Deal Order: US Politics from the Great Depression to the Great Recession*, eds. Alice O'Connor, Gary Gerstle, and Nelson Lichtenstein (Philadelphia: University of Pennsylvania Press, 2019), 124–40.

42. Don Irwin, "Nixon Hits 'Pie in Sky' Promises to Negroes," *Los Angeles Times*, April 21, 1968; Whitney M. Young, Jr., "Vietnam-The Peace Dividend," *Chicago Daily Defender*, September 13, 1969.

43. Daniel Patrick Moynihan, *The Politics of a Guaranteed Income: The Nixon Administration and the Family Assistance Plan* (New York: Vintage, 1973), 12.

44. Robert M. Collins, "The Economic Crisis of 1968 and the Waning of the 'American Century,'" *American Historical Review* 101, no. 2 (April 1996): 396–422.

45. Robert P. Bremner, *Chairman of the Fed: William McChesney Martin Jr. and the Creation of the Modern American Financial System* (New Haven, CT: Yale University Press, 2004), 264.

46. Richard A. Hunt, *Melvin Laird and the Foundation of the Post-Vietnam Military, 1969–1973* (Washington, DC: Office of the Secretary of Defense Historical Office, 2015), 282.

47. Arnold Kanter, "Congress and the Defense Budget: 1960–1970," *The American Political Science Review,* 66, no. 1 (March 1972): 129–43; Robert David Johnson, *Congress and the Cold War* (New York: Cambridge University Press, 2005), 105–241; Brenes, *For Might and Right*, 112–56.

48. Robert B. Semple, Jr., "Nixon Links Veto of Education Bill to High Spending, *New York Times*, January 28, 1970.

49. Raford Boddy and James Crotty, "Class Conflict and Macro-Policy: The Political Business Cycle," *Review of Radical Political Economics* 7, no. 1 (April 1975): 15.

50. Marc Linder, *Wars of Attrition: Vietnam, the Business Roundtable, and the Decline of Construction Unions,* 2nd ed. (Iowa City, IA: Fanpihua Press, 2000), 1.

51. Barker, "Macroeconomic Consequences of Peace," 23–24.

52. Stein, *Presidential Economics*, 153.

53. Robert Mayo (Bureau of the Budget) to Nixon, Stimulation of the Economy Through Fiscal Actions, May 24, 1970, US Declassified Documents Online, Gale Document CK2349655973.

54. Letter, Laird to Schultz, 20 October 1970. Reproduced in *Melvin Laird and the Foundation of the Post-Vietnam Military, 1969–1973: Documentary Supplement*, ed. Richard A. Hunt (Washington: Office of the Secretary of Defense Historical Office), 266–71.

55. Minutes of Defense Program Review Committee Meeting, Washington, November 9, 1970, 4:10–5:40 p.m., *FRUS, 1969–1976, Volume XXXIV, National Security Policy, 1969–1972,* ed. M. Todd Bennett (Washington, DC: Government Printing Office, 2011), Document 158, https://history.state.gov/historicaldocuments/frus1969-76v34/d158.

56. Military Budget Battles, November 9, 1970, Kissinger Telephone Conversations, 1969–1977. Digital National Security Archive, https://nsarchive.gwu.edu/digital-national-security-archive [DNSA]. Accession number KA04192, ProQuest document ID1679133717.

57. Matusow, *Nixon's Economy*, 84. Emphasis in original.

58. Memorandum for the Record, Moorer, 27 Nov 1970, *Laird Documentary Supplement*, 285–87.

59. Hunt, *Melvin Laird,* 303.

60. Laird to Schultz, 20 October 1970.

61. Minutes of Defense Program Review Committee Meeting, Washington, November 9, 1970.

62. Laird to Schultz, 20 October 1970; Revisions to Defense Budget, January 13, 1971, Kissinger Telcons, DNSA. Accession number KA04727, ProQuest document ID 1679133908.

63. Lawrence J. Korb, *The Fall and Rise of the Pentagon: American Defense Policies in the 1970s* (Westport, CT: Greenwood Press, 1979), 33, table 5.

64. Defense Budget Cuts. December 30, 1969. Kissinger Telcons, DNSA. Accession number KA01855, ProQuest document ID 1679146899.

65. "Nixon Reportedly Says He Is Now a Keynesian," *New York Times*, January 7, 1971; Richard Nixon, Annual Message to the Congress on the State of the Union, January 22, 1971. Online by Gerhard Peters and John T. Woolley, American Presidency Project [APP], https:// www.presidency.ucsb.edu/node/240562.

66. Matusow, *Nixon's Economy*, 76–77, 106–98.

67. Stephen E. Ambrose, *Nixon: The Triumph of a Politician 1962–1972* (New York: Simon and Schuster, 1989), 587.

68. US Senate, Committee on Banking, Housing, and Urban Affairs, *Emergency Loan Guarantee Legislation, Hearings before the Senate Banking Committee*, 92nd Cong., 1st. sess. (Washington, DC: Government Printing Office, 1971), 126.

69. T. A. Heppenheimer, *The Space Shuttle Decision: NASA's Search for a Reusable Space Vehicle* (Washington, DC: NASA, 1999), 291–330.

70. "The New Poor of Seattle," *Washington Post*, December 2, 1971; Anthony Sampson, *The Arms Bazaar: From Lebanon to Lockheed* (New York: Viking, 1977), 217.

71. Robert A. Wright, "For Some, Life Begins with Lost Job," *New York Times*, July 22, 1971.

72. *Economic Report of the President* (Washington: Government Printing Office, 1971), 45, table II.

73. While standard accounts explain Fed chair Arthur Burns's monetary ease as the result of Nixon's political pressure, concerns about financial instability were also decisive. Compare Edwin Dickens, "The Federal Reserve's Low Interest Rate Policy of 1970–72: Determinants and Constraints," *Review of Radical Political Economics* 28, no. 3 (September 1996), and J. Bradford DeLong, "America's Peacetime Inflation: The 1970s," in *Reducing Inflation: Motivation and Strategy*, eds. Christina D. Romer and David H. Romer (Chicago: University of Chicago Press, 1997), 247–80.

74. For a useful prosopography, embedded in a hyperbolic argument, see Kirkpatrick Sale, *Power Shift: The Rise of the Southern Rim and Its Challenge to the Eastern Establishment* (New York: Vintage), 228–42.

75. Aerospace Industries Association, *Aerospace Facts and Figures* (Washington, DC: 1972/3), 6–7.

76. Federal Open Market Committee, Memorandum of Discussion, March 9, 1971, 64. Historical Materials, Board of Governors of the Federal Reserve System, https://www.federalreserve .gov/monetarypolicy/files/fomcmod19710309.pdf.

77. John Cobbs, "When Companies Get Too Big to Fail," *Business Week*, January 27, 1975, 16.

78. Defense Budget Planning; Includes Follow-up Telephone Conversation at 5:15 p.m, December 11, 1971. Kissinger Telcons, DNSA. Accession number KA07086. ProQuest document ID 1679119354. For Nixon's own doubts about the aircraft in question, see F-111 Aircraft Problems; Strategic Arms Limitation Talks; Includes Follow-up Telephone Conversation at 9:25 a.m., December 23, 1969. Kissinger Telcons, DNSA. Accession number KA01829. ProQuest document ID 1679147372.

79. Heppenheimer, *Shuttle Decision*, 381, 414.

80. Robert Hotz, "The Shuttle Decision," *Aviation Week & Space Technology* (July 31, 1972): 7.

81. Hotz, "Shuttle Decision," 7.

82. Journal I (Green Notebook), 80. Transcript of Arthur F. Burns' Handwritten Journals, January 20, 1969–July 25, 1974, Ford Library. Accession 2006-NLF-057. https://www .fordlibrarymuseum.gov/library/document/0428/Burnstranscript1.pdf.

83. Burns, Journal I, 62.

84. Despite its association with the 1973 oil crisis, the word entered American discourse during the 1970–1971 downturn. See, for example, Lawrence Mayer, "The World Economy: Into a Time of Stagflation," *Fortune*, August 1, 1971, 144.

85. On the shock, see Daniel Sargent, *A Superpower Transformed: The Remaking of American Foreign Relations in the 1970s* (New York: Oxford University Press, 2015), 108–18.

86. Benjamin C. Waterhouse, "Mobilizing for the Market: Organized Business, Wage-Price Controls, and the Politics of Inflation, 1971–1974," *Journal of American History* 100, no. 2 (September 2013).

87. Stein, *Presidential Economics*, 184.

88. Journal II (Blue Notebook), 152–53. Transcript of Burns Journal, Ford Library, https://www.fordlibrarymuseum.gov/library/document/0428/burnstranscript2.pdf.

89. Transcript, Thursday March 23, 1972, 3. Haldeman Diaries, 1972. Richard Nixon Presidential Library and Museum, https://www.nixonlibrary.gov/sites/default/files/virtuallibrary/documents/haldeman-diaries/37-hrhd-audiocassette-ac19b20a-19720323-pa.pdf.

90. Stein, *Presidential Economics*, 184.

91. Memorandum of Conversation, December 22, 1973, Nixon, Schlesinger, Joint Chiefs, Ford Library.

92. Conversation with President Nixon, July 23, 1971. *FRUS*, 1969–1976, Volume XXXIV, Document 188. https://history.state.gov/historicaldocuments/frus1969-76v34/d188.

93. Hunt, *Melvin Laird*, 284; Sargent, *Superpower Transformed*, 155, 158.

94. "Congress Calls It a Sonic Bust," *Newsweek*, April 5, 1971, 19.

95. Stephen MacDonald, "Why an SST: The View from Boeing," *Wall Street Journal*, October 31, 1969.

96. Richard Nixon, Address to the Nation on Domestic Programs, January 22, 1971, APP, https://www.presidency.ucsb.edu/node/239998.

97. Richard Nixon, Special Message to the Congress on the Unemployment Insurance System, July 8, 1969, APP, https://www.presidency.ucsb.edu/node/239562; "Welfare Aid for Strikers Left Up to States in HEW Policy Ruling Backed by Business," *Wall Street Journal*, July 10, 1973.

98. Transcript of a Telephone Conversation Between President Nixon and the President's Assistant for National Security Affairs (Kissinger). *FRUS*, 1969–1976, Volume XIII, Soviet Union, October 1970–October 1971, ed. David C. Geyer (Washington, DC: Government Printing Office, 2011), Document 2, https://history.state.gov/historicaldocuments/frus1969-76v13/d2.

99. "GE Executive Asks Defense Spending Hike," *Los Angeles Times*, June 21, 1972; "Rise in Defense Research Urged by GE Executive," *Los Angeles Times*, June 22, 1972.

100. Sampson, *Arms Bazaar*, 214.

101. Eileen Shanahan, McGovern Calls for Tax Reform, *New York Times*, January 14, 1972; Christopher Lydon, "McGovern Offers a Plan to Cut Defense Outlays," *New York Times*, January 20, 1972.

102. George C. Wilson, "GOP Warns of McGovern Job Losses," *Washington Post*, October 19, 1972.

103. Patrick J. Buchanan and Ken Khachigian, Assault Strategy, June 8, 1972. Reprinted in *From the President: Richard Nixon's Secret Files*, ed. Bruce Oudes (New York: HarperCollins, 1989), 463–74. Emphasis in original.

104. Robert Mason, *Richard Nixon and the Quest for a New Majority* (Chapel Hill: University of North Carolina Press, 2004); Edmund Wehrle, "'Partisan for the Hard Hats': Charles

Colson, George Meany, and the Failed Blue-Collar Strategy," *Labor* 5, no. 3 (Fall 2008): 45–66; Cowie, *Stayin' Alive*, 125–66.

105. Edmund F. Wehrle, "'Aid Where It Is Needed Most': American Labor's Military-Industrial Complex," *Enterprise and Society* 12, no. 1 (March 2011): 96–119.

106. Nicholas von Hoffman, "Bunker for a POW?" *Washington Post,* May 15, 1970.

107. Edmund Wehrle, "Defense Industry," in *Work in America*, eds. Carl E. Van Horn and Herbert A. Schaffner (Santa Barbara: ABC-CLIO, 2003), 1: 125–29, quote at 128.

108. Samuel Lubell, "Jobs Temper Attitudes on Viet War," *Detroit Free Press*, August 15, 1972, 11.

109. Cowie, *Stayin' Alive*, 43–44, 110.

110. Jerry M. Flint, "Auto Union's West Coast Chief Fights to Keep Post," *New York Times*, April 25, 1972.

111. "Activist Loses UAW Job as Western Region Chief," *Wall Street Journal*, April 27, 1972; Sampson, *Arms Bazaar*, 214.

112. Cowie, *Stayin' Alive*, 121–22.

113. The strategy was inspired by Pete Hamill's article "The Revolt of the White Lower Middle Class." Cowie, *Stayin' Alive*, 132.

114. Kevin P. Phillips, *The Emerging Republican Majority* (Princeton, NJ: Princeton University Press, 2015), 521.

115. Bowles, *Nixon's Business*, 76.

116. Lenneal J. Henderson, Jr., "Impact of Military Base Shut-Downs," *The Black Scholar* 5, no. 2 (October 1973): 9–15.

117. Herbert R. Northrup and Richard L. Rowan, *The Negro in Basic Industry: A Study of Racial Policies in Six Industries* (Philadelphia: University of Pennsylvania Press, 1970), 121–26.

118. "In the News: Bayard Rustin," *Bay State Banner*, September 28, 1972.

119. Richard Du Boff, "Full Employment: The History of a Receding Target," *Politics and Society* 7, no. 1 (March 1977): 12; US Bureau of Labor Statistics, Unemployment Rate - White [LNS14000003], retrieved from FRED, Federal Reserve Bank of St. Louis, https://fred.stlouisfed .org/series/LNS14000003.

120. BLS, Unemployment Rate - Black or African American [LNS14000006], FRED, https:// fred.stlouisfed.org/series/LNS14000006.

121. Richard Nixon, Annual Budget Message to the Congress, Fiscal Year 1974, APP, https://www.presidency.ucsb.edu/node/255670.

122. "Defense Spending Boosts Get Mixed Reviews," *Industry Week*, March 18, 1974, 47–53.

123. Memorandum of Conversation, December 19, 1973. *FRUS*, 1969–1976, Volume XXXV, National Security Policy, 1973–1976, ed. M. Todd Bennett (Washington: Government Printing Office, 2014), Document 27.

124. Memorandum of Conversation: December 22, 1973 - Nixon, Schlesinger, Joint Chiefs, Ford Library.

125. Conversation with President Nixon, October 27, 1971. *FRUS*, 1969–1976, Volume XXXIV, Document 199, https://history.state.gov/historicaldocuments/frus1969-76v34/d199.

126. Senator Biden, speaking on S. 3000, Amendment No. 1282, *Congressional Record*, Senate, 93rd Cong., 2nd sess. (June 4, 1974), S 17503.

127. Senator Tower, speaking on S. 3000, Amendment No. 1282, *Congressional Record*, Senate, 93rd Cong., 2nd sess. (June 4, 1974), S 17505.

128. Richard J. Levine, "Major Budget Cuts Unlikely: Congress Smiles on the Pentagon Again," *Los Angeles Times*, March 10, 1974.

129. Richard J. Levine, "Ford to Seek a Defense Spending Increase of $8 Billion, to $93 Billion, for Fiscal '76," *Wall Street Journal*, January 17, 1975.

130. Ernest Volkman, "Congress Buying the Pentagon Line," *Newsday*, April 19, 1976.

131. The Air Combat Fighter—The Largest Aircraft Procurement of the Next 20 Years, December 16, 1974, Defense – general, box 3, Richard B. Cheney Files, Ford Library, https://www.fordlibrarymuseum.gov/library/document/0005/1561364.pdf; Implications of Not Doing Space Flight, enclosed in James C. Fletcher to Mr. Frank G. Zarb. November 6, 1974, Presidential Handwriting, 11/29/1974 (2), box C7, Presidential Handwriting File, Ford Library, https://www.fordlibrarymuseum.gov/library/document/0047/phw19741129-06.pdf.

132. Colin Crouch, "Privatised Keynesianism: An Unacknowledged Policy Regime," *British Journal of Politics & International Relations* 11, no. 3 (August 2009): 382–99; Shenk, "Inventing the American Economy," 312–95.

133. N. Gregory Mankiw, "What Would Keynes Have Done?" *New York Times*, November 28, 2008.

134. "Pentagon Spending is the Economy's Biggest Gun," *Business Week*, October 21, 1985.

135. Letter to Dr. McDowell, c. 1972, reprinted in *Reagan, in His Own Hand*, eds. Kiron Skinner, Annelise Anderson, and Martin Anderson (New York: Free Press, 2001), 453–55.

136. Richard Bergholz, "How GOP Computed M'Govern Job Charge," *Los Angeles Times*, October 1, 1972.

137. Ron Suskind, *The Price of Loyalty: George W. Bush, the White House, and the Education of Paul O'Neill* (New York: Simon and Schuster, 2004), 291.

138. Donald Rumsfeld to Dov Zakheim, Stimulus Package. September 26, 2001. Donald Rumsfeld's Snowflakes, Part I: The Pentagon and US Foreign Policy, 2001–2003, DNSA. Accession number DR00743. ProQuest document ID 2469729556.

139. Martin Feldstein, "Defense Spending Would Be Great Stimulus," *Wall Street Journal*, December 28, 2008.

140. Stephen A. Marglin, *Raising Keynes: A Twenty-First-Century General Theory* (Cambridge, MA: Harvard University Press, 2021).

141. Thus, even a scholar who views the 1964 tax cut as "the defeat of Keynes" refers to the policies in question as "domesticated Keynesianism." Seiichiro Mozumi, "The Kennedy-Johnson Tax Cut of 1964, the Defeat of Keynes, and Comprehensive Tax Reform in the United States," *Journal of Policy History* 30, no. 1 (January 2018): 25–61.

142. Final Grade Sheet, Economics 248B, June 5, 1950, Hansen, Alvin H.: Symposium, box 26, Walter S. Salant Papers, Harry S. Truman Presidential Library and Museum, Independence, MO; James R. Schlesinger, "After Twenty Years: The General Theory," *Quarterly Journal of Economics* 70, no. 4 (November 1956); US House Committee on Appropriations, *Department of Defense Appropriations for 1975: Hearings Before a Subcommittee of the Committee on Appropriations*, 93rd Cong., 2nd. sess. (Washington, DC: Government Printing Office, 1974), 312.

143. Memorandum of Conversation, December 19, 1973, *FRUS*, 1969–1976.

144. Memo, Pursley for Laird, 17 Jul 1972, in *Laird Documentary Supplement*, 529–33.

145. Leonard Silk, "Economic Scene: Military Surge as Spur to Jobs," *New York Times*, September 17, 1982.

146. Adolfo Castilla and Alfredo Coutiño, "Interview to [sic] L.R. Klein," *Estudios de Economía Aplicada* 24, no. 1 (April 2006): 37.

147. Du Boff, "Full Employment."

148. Lisa Adkins, Melinda Cooper, and Martijn Konings, *The Asset Economy: Property Ownership and the New Logic of Inequality* (Medford, MA: Polity Press, 2020).

149. Onur Özgöde, "The Emergence of Systemic Risk: Federal Reserve, Bailouts, and Monetary Government at the Limits," *Socio-Economic Review* (forthcoming), published online February 2021, https://doi.org/10.1093/ser/mwaa053.

150. Gerstle, "America's Neoliberal Order," 243.

151. With PATCO, by contrast, trained military air traffic controllers were ready immediately to replace striking workers. Kim Moody, *An Injury to All: The Decline of American Unionism* (New York: Verso 1992), 87, 304; Philip F. Rubio, *Undelivered: From the Great Postal Strike of 1970 to the Manufactured Crisis of the US Postal Service* (Chapel Hill: University of North Carolina Press, 2020), 102–4.

152. Adam Tooze, "How We Paid for the War on Terror," *Chartbook*, August 21, 2021, https://adamtooze.substack.com/p/chartbook-34-how-we-paid-for-the.

153. George C. Herring, *America's Longest War: The United States and Vietnam, 1950–1975*, 5th ed. (New York: McGraw Hill, 2014), 325.

154. Salman Ahmed et al., "US Foreign Policy for the Middle Class: Perspectives from Ohio," *Carnegie Endowment for International Peace*, December 10, 2018, 87, https://carnegieendowment .org/2018/12/10/u.s.-foreign-policy-for-middle-class-perspectives-from-ohio-pub-77779.

Chapter 9

1. The article, which appeared in the March–April 1972 issue of *Investor: Wisconsin's Business Magazine*, was reproduced in US Senate Committee on Veterans' Affairs, *Educational Benefits Available for Returning Vietnam Era Veterans: Hearings Before the Subcommittee on Readjustment, Education, and Employment*, Part 2, 92nd Cong., 2nd sess. (Washington, DC: Government Printing Office, 1972), 919.

2. "Labor Force Statistics from the Current Population Survey, Unemployment Rate, 1968–1978" (Bureau of Labor Statistics, n.d.), https://beta.bls.gov/dataViewer/view/timeseries /LNS14000000.

3. The data reportedly came from a Louis Harris poll. *Educational Benefits Available for Returning Vietnam Era Veterans*, 992.

4. *Educational Benefits Available for Returning Vietnam Era Veterans*, 919.

5. On whites: "Unemployment Rate-White, 1975–1995," Bureau of Labor Statistics Data Viewer (US Bureau of Labor Statistics, May 2020), https://beta.bls.gov/dataViewer/view/timeseries /LNS14000003. On African Americans: "Unemployment Rate-Black or African American, 1975–1990," Bureau of Labor Statistics Data Viewer (US Bureau of Labor Statistics, May 2020), https:// beta.bls.gov/dataViewer/view/timeseries/LNS14000006. On Hispanics: "Unemployment Rate-Hispanic or Latino, 1975–1990," Bureau of Labor Statistics Data Viewer (US Bureau of Labor Statistics, May 2020), https://beta.bls.gov/dataViewer/view/timeseries/LNS14000009.

6. "Unemployment Rate-Black or African American, 1972–1978," Bureau of Labor Statistics Data Viewer (US Bureau of Labor Statistics, May 2020), https://beta.bls.gov/dataViewer /view/timeseries/LNS14000006.

7. The Urban League numbers were from the first quarter of 1972. *Educational Benefits Available for Returning Vietnam Era Veterans*, 932.

8. Janet M. Wilmoth and Andrew S. London, eds., *Life Course Perspectives on Military Service*, (New York: Routledge, 2012); Alair MacLean and Meredith Kleykamp, "Income Inequality

and the Veteran Experience," *Annals of the American Academy of Political and Social Science* 663 (January 2016): 99–116; Andrew S. London, "Veterans and the Life Course," in *Gerontology: Changes, Challenges, and Solutions* (Santa Barbara, CA: Praeger, 2016). On the concept of "dual entitlement," see Debra Street and Jessica Hoffman, "Military Service, Social Policy, and Later-Life Financial and Health Security" in *Life Course Perspectives on Military Service*, 379–97. Joshua D. Angrist, "Estimating the Labor Market Impact of Voluntary Military Service Using Social Security Data on Military Applicants" *Econometrica* 66, no. 2 (1998): 249–88; Paco Martorell, Trey Miller, Lindsey Daugherty, and Mark Borgschulte, *Effects of Military Service on Earnings and Education, Revisited* (Santa Monica, CA: RAND Corporation, 2014).

9. Richard R. Moser, *The New Winter Soldiers: G.I. And Veteran Dissent During the Vietnam Era* (New Brunswick, NJ: Rutgers University Press, 1996); Andrew E. Hunt, *The Turning: A History of Vietnam Veterans Against the War* (New York: New York University Press, 1999); Gerald Nicosia, *Home to War: A History of the Vietnam Veterans' Movement* (New York: Three Rivers Press, 2001); Wilbur J. Scott, *Vietnam Veterans Since the War: The Politics of PTSD, Agent Orange, and the National Memorial* (Norman: University of Oklahoma Press, 2004); Patrick Hagopian, *The Vietnam War in American Memory: Veterans, Memorials, and the Politics of Healing* (Amherst: University of Massachusetts Press, 2009); Mark Boulton, *Failing Our Veterans: The G.I. Bill and the Vietnam Generation* (New York: New York University Press, 2014); David Kieran, *Forever Vietnam: How a Divisive War Changed American Public Memory* (Amherst: University of Massachusetts Press, 2014).

10. David R Segal, *Recruiting for Uncle Sam: Citizenship and Military Manpower Policy* (Lawrence: University Press of Kansas, 1989); Ronald Schaffer, *America in the Great War: The Rise of the War Welfare State* (New York: Oxford University Press, 1991); Theda Skocpol, *Protecting Soldiers and Mothers: The Political Origins of Social Policy in United States* (Cambridge, MA: Harvard University Press, 1995); Kathleen J. Frydl, *The G.I. Bill* (New York: Cambridge University Press, 2009); Glenn C. Altschuler and Stuart M. Blumin, *The GI Bill : A New Deal for Veterans* (New York: Oxford University Press, 2009); Stephen R. Ortiz, *Beyond the Bonus March and GI Bill : How Veteran Politics Shaped the New Deal Era* (New York University Press, 2010). Jessica L. Adler, *Burdens of War: Creating the United States Veterans Health System* (Baltimore: Johns Hopkins University Press, 2017); Olivier Burtin, "Veterans as a Social Movement: The American Legion, the First Hoover Commission, and the Making of the American Welfare State," *Social Science History* 44, no. 2 (Summer 2020): 329–54.

11. On this concept, Linda Gordon, *Pitied but Not Entitled: Single Mothers and the History of Welfare, 1890–1935* (New York: Free Press, 1994). Other relevant work on the ideology of the US welfare state includes Jill Quadagno, *The Color of Welfare: How Racism Undermined the War on Poverty* (New York: Oxford University Press, 1996); Sanford F. Schram, Joe Soss, and Richard C. Fording, eds., *Race and the Politics of Welfare Reform* (Ann Arbor: University of Michigan Press, 2003); Jennifer Mittelstadt, *From Welfare to Workfare: The Unintended Consequences of Liberal Reform, 1945–1965* (Chapel Hill: University of North Carolina Press, 2005); Michael B. Katz, *The Price of Citizenship: Redefining the American Welfare State* (Philadelphia: University of Pennsylvania Press, 2008); Gunja SenGupta, *From Slavery to Poverty: The Racial Origins of Welfare in New York, 1840–1918* (New York: New York University Press, 2009); Elizabeth Kai Hinton, *From the War on Poverty to the War on Crime: The Making of Mass Incarceration in America* (Cambridge, MA: Harvard University Press, 2017); Richard Rothstein, *The Color of Law: A Forgotten History of How Our Government Segregated America* (New York: Liveright, 2018); Keeanga-Yamahtta Taylor, *Race for Profit: How Banks and the Real Estate Industry Undermined Black Homeownership* (Chapel Hill: University of North Carolina Press, 2019); Julilly

Kohler-Hausmann, *Getting Tough: Welfare and Imprisonment in 1970s America* (Princeton, NJ: Princeton University Press, 2019).

12. On the creation of the AVF, Beth Bailey, *America's Army: Making the All-Volunteer Force* (Cambridge, MA: Harvard University Press, 2009). On the military welfare state, Brian Gifford, "The Camouflaged Safety Net: The US Armed Forces as Welfare State Institution," *Social Politics: International Studies in Gender, State & Society* 13, no. 3 (January 2006): 372–99; Jennifer Mittelstadt, *The Rise of the Military Welfare State* (Cambridge, MA: Harvard University Press, 2015).

13. Christine Scott, "Veterans Affairs: Historical Budget Authority, FY1940-FY2012," Congressional Research Service Report RS22897 (2012), https://sgp.fas.org/crs/misc/RS22897.pdf.

14. This chapter focuses mainly on the experiences of African Americans, but literature on veterans from other marginalized groups shows that martial citizenship is hardly universally defined or experienced, and demonstrates that military service has propelled people into civil rights activism. See, for example, Thomas A. Britten, *American Indians in World War I: At Home and at War* (Albuquerque: University of New Mexico Press, 1997); F. Arturo Rosales and Francisco A. Rosales, *Chicano! The History of the Mexican American Civil Rights Movement* (Houston: Arte Publico Press, 1997); Lea Ybarra, *Vietnam Veteranos: Chicanos Recall the War* (Austin: University of Texas Press, 2004); Hollis D. Stabler, *No One Ever Asked Me: The World War II Memoirs of an Omaha Indian Soldier*, ed. Victoria Smith (Lincoln: University of Nebraska Press, 2008); José A. Ramírez, *To the Line of Fire!: Mexican Texans and World War I* (College Station: Texas A&M University Press, 2009); Cynthia E. Orozco, *No Mexicans, Women, or Dogs Allowed: The Rise of the Mexican American Civil Rights Movement* (Austin: University of Texas Press, 2009); J. Luz Sáenz, *The World War I Diary of José de La Luz Sáenz*, ed. Emilio Zamora, trans. Ben Maya (College Station: Texas A&M University Press, 2014).

15. For example, on unequal access to Civil War disability benefits, Larry M. Logue and Peter Blanck, *Race, Ethnicity, and Disability: Veterans and Benefits in Post-Civil War America* (New York: Cambridge University Press, 2010). On inequity in World War I–era veterans' policy, Jennifer D. Keene, "The Long Journey Home: Federal Veterans' Policy and African-American Veterans of World War I," in *Veterans' Policies, Veterans' Politics: New Perspectives on Veterans in the Modern United States*, ed. Stephen R. Ortiz (Gainesville: University Press of Florida, 2012); Jessica L. Adler, "'The Service I Rendered Was Just as True': African American Soldiers and Veterans as Activist Patients," *American Journal of Public Health* 107, no. 5 (May 2017): 675–83. On World War II and the G.I. Bill, see note 10 and Ira Katznelson and Suzanne Mettler, "On Race and Policy History: A Dialogue about the G.I. Bill," *Perspectives on Politics* 6, no. 3 (September 2008): 519–537; Ira Katznelson, *When Affirmative Action Was White: An Untold History of Racial Inequality* (New York: Norton, 2005); Louis Lee Woods II, "Almost 'No Negro Veteran . . . Could Get a Loan': African-American Veterans, the GI Bill, and the NAACP Campaign against Residential Segregation, 1917–1960," *Journal of African American History* 98, no. 3 (2013), 392–417.

16. Theda Skocpol, Ariane Liazos, and Marshall Ganz, *What a Mighty Power We Can Be: African American Fraternal Groups and the Struggle for Racial Equality* (Princeton, NJ: Princeton University Press, 2006); Donald R. Schaffer, *After the Glory: The Struggles of Black Civil War Veterans* (Lawrence: University Press of Kansas, 2004).

17. On the World War I era, Chad L. Williams, *Torchbearers of Democracy: African American Soldiers in the World War I Era* (Chapel Hill: University of North Carolina Press, 2010); Chad L. Williams, "Vanguards of the New Negro: African American Veterans and Post-World War I Racial Militancy," *Journal of African American History* 92, no. 3 (Summer 2007): 347–70;

Adriane Lentz-Smith, *Freedom Struggles: African Americans and World War I* (Cambridge, MA: Harvard University Press, 2011); Pete Daniel, "Black Power in the 1920s: The Case of Tuskegee Veterans Hospital," *Journal of Southern History* 36, no. 3 (August 1970): 368–88; David A. Davis, "Not Only War Is Hell: World War I and African American Lynching Narratives," *African American Review* 42, no. 3/4 (FallWinter 2008): 477–91; Mark Ellis, *Race, War, and Surveillance: African Americans and the United States* (Bloomington: Indiana University Press, 2001). On the World War II era, see Christopher S. Parker, *Fighting for Democracy: Black Veterans and the Struggle for Democracy in the Postwar South* (Princeton, NJ: Princeton University Press, 2009); Christine Knauer, *Let Us Fight as Free Men: Black Soldiers and Civil Rights* (Philadelphia: University of Pennsylvania Press, 2014); Jennifer E. Brooks, *Defining the Peace: World War II Veterans, Race, and the Remaking of Southern Political Tradition* (Chapel Hill: University of North Carolina Press, 2011); Richard Gergel, *Unexampled Courage: The Blinding of Sgt. Isaac Woodard and the Awakening of President Harry S. Truman and Judge J. Waties Waring* (New York: Sarah Crichton Books; Farrar, Straus and Giroux, 2019). On the post–World War II era, see Jeremy P. Maxwell, *Brotherhood in Combat: How African Americans Found Equality in Korea and Vietnam* (Norman: University of Oklahoma Press, 2018); Bobby White, ed., *Post 8195: Black Soldiers Tell Their Vietnam Stories* (Silver Spring, MD: Beckham Publications Group, 2013); John A. Wood, *Veteran Narratives and the Collective Memory of the Vietnam War* (Athens: Ohio University Press, 2016); James E. Westheider, *Fighting on Two Fronts: African Americans and the Vietnam War* (New York: New York University Press, 1999); James E. Westheider, "African Americans, Civil Rights, and the Armed Forces During the Vietnam War," in *Integrating the US Military: Race, Gender, and Sexual Orientation Since World War II*, ed. Douglas Walter Bristol, Jr., and Heather Marie Stur (Baltimore: Johns Hopkins University Press, 2017); Kimberly Phillips Boehm, *War! What Is It Good For?* (Chapel Hill: University of North Carolina Press, 2013); Gerald F. Goodwin, "Race in the Crucible of War: African American Soldiers and Race Relations in the 'Nam" (PhD diss., Ohio University, 2014); Robert F. Jefferson, ed., *Black Veterans, Politics, and Civil Rights in Twentieth-Century America: Closing Ranks* (Lanham, MD: Lexington Books, 2019).

18. "Democracy in the Foxhole," *Time*, May 26, 1967. According to a note at the front of the issue from the magazine's editor, *Time*'s "entire Saigon staff" and writers based in the United States worked on the article, which painted a generally favorable picture of the integration of the US Armed Forces—an image that would soon be called into question. The quoted sentiments underscore the interconnectedness of military and civilian life and hint at why some army leaders advocated for a "race-conscious approach" to military programs and policies. Beth Bailey, "The US Army and the 'Problem of Race': Afros, Race Consciousness, and Institutional Logic," *Journal of American History*, 106, no. 3 (December 2019): 639–61.

19. John Sibley Butler, "African Americans in the Military," in *The Oxford Companion to American Military History*, ed. John Whiteclay Chambers II (New York: Oxford University Press, 2000), 7–9. Amy Rutenberg notes that when it comes to statistics about inequities in military service, "the picture changes based on whether one looks at the whole [Vietnam] war or simply part of it, the entire military or just draftees," but in the army, "26 percent of black enlisted personnel had combat assignments, a number well out of sync with the percentage of African Americans in the American population at large." Amy J. Rutenberg, *Rough Draft: Cold War Military Manpower Policy and the Origins of Vietnam-Era Draft Resistance* (Ithaca, NY: Cornell University Press, 2019), 165–66.

20. Martin Luther Jr. King, "Beyond Vietnam," April 4, 1967, https://kinginstitute.stanford.edu/king-papers/documents/beyond-vietnam.

21. Rutenberg, *Rough Draft*, 184. In the early 1970s, for example, Vietnam veterans worked in a Black Panther–sponsored clinic in Berkeley, California, and, as one Panther member recalled, "they taught us a lot." Alondra Nelson, *Body and Soul: The Black Panther Party and the Fight Against Medical Discrimination* (Minneapolis: University of Minnesota Press, 2011), 100.

22. Stephen Herbits, quoted in Bailey, *America's Army*, 31.

23. Walter Y. Oi, "The Economic Cost of the Draft," *American Economic Review*, 57, no. 2 (May 1967): 39–62.

24. James C. Miller III and Robert Tollison, "The Implicit Tax on Reluctant Military Recruits," *Social Science Quarterly* 51, no. 4 (March 1971): 924–31.

25. Milton Friedman, "The Case for Abolishing the Draft—and Substituting for It an All-Volunteer Army," *New York Times Magazine*, May 14, 1967. Here, Friedman was likely responding to arguments of sociologists like Morris Janowitz, "The Logic of National Service," in *The Draft: A Handbook of Facts and Alternatives*, ed. Sol Tax (Chicago: University of Chicago Press, 1967), 73–90, cited in Bernard D. Rostker, *I Want You!: The Evolution of the All-Volunteer Force* (Santa Monica, CA: RAND Corporation, 2006).

26. Friedman, "The Case for Abolishing the Draft—and Substituting for It an All-Volunteer Army."

27. Harley L. Browning, Sally C. Lopreato, and Dudley L. Poston, Jr., "Income and Veteran Status: Variations Among Mexican Americans, Blacks and Anglos," *American Sociological Review* 38, no. 1 (February 1973): 74–85.

28. Sally Cook Lopreato and Dudley L. Poston, "Differences in Earnings and Earnings Ability Between Black Veterans and Nonveterans in the United States," *Social Science Quarterly* 57, no. 4 (March 1977): 750–66.

29. James M. Fendrich, "The Returning Black Vietnam-Era Veteran," *Social Service Review* 96, no. 1 (March 1972): 60–75.

30. Phillips Cutright, "The Civilian Earnings of White and Black Draftees and Nonveterans," *American Sociological Review* 39, no. 3 (June 1974): 317–27. While such findings were published simultaneously with conversations about whether the proportion of African Americans being recruited to the new AVF was too high, they do not appear to have shaped them; assessments of veterans' experiences, it seems, did not play a major role in informing conversations about military manpower. Rostker, *I Want You!: The Evolution of the All-Volunteer Force*, 273–275. On the other hand, assessments of AVF recruits' desires and needs—and the priority of increasing the "quality" of recruits—did inform the conceptualization of a new G.I. Bill in the 1980s. See Mittelstadt, *Rise of the Military Welfare State*, 96–108.

31. Quoted in Christina R. Rivers, *The Congressional Black Caucus, Minority Voting Rights, and the US Supreme Court* (Ann Arbor: University of Michigan Press, 2012), 67–68. Also, Kareem U. Crayton, "The Changing Face of the Congressional Black Caucus," SSRN Scholarly Paper (Rochester, NY: Social Science Research Network, 2008), https://doi.org/10.2139/ssrn .1133564; Robert Singh, *The Congressional Black Caucus: Racial Politics in the US Congress* (Thousand Oaks, CA: SAGE Publications, 1997), 55–56; Carol M. Swain, *Black Faces, Black Interests: The Representation of African Americans in Congress* (Cambridge, MA: Harvard University Press, 1993); Carolyn P. DuBose, *The Untold Story of Charles Diggs: The Public Figure, the Private Man* (Arlington, VA: Barton Publishing House, 1998); Matthew Wasniewski, ed., *Black Americans in Congress, 1870–2007*, 3rd ed. (Washington, DC: United States Congress, House Office of History and Preservation, 2008). The seven veteran founding members were Charles Diggs, George Collins, William Lacy Clay, Charles Rangel, Ronald V. Dellums, Ralph Metcalfe, and Parren Mitchell.

32. William L. Clay, *Bill Clay: A Political Voice at the Grass Roots* (Saint Louis: Missouri Historical Society Press, 2004); William L. Clay, *Just Permanent Interests* (New York: Harper Collins, 2000). For a summary of Clay's civil rights activities in the army, https://history.house .gov/People/Detail?id=11058.

33. Congressional Black Caucus's recommendations to President Nixon, March 25, 1971, printed in *Congressional Record*, House, 92nd Cong., 1st sess. (March 30, 1971), 8710–13.

34. "A Report on Racism in the Military," printed in *Congressional Record*, House, 92nd Cong., 1st sess. (November 17, 1971), 41854–58.

35. Marcy L. Karin, "'Other Than Honorable' Discrimination," *Case Western Reserve Law Review* 67, no. 1 (Fall 2016): 135–191; Bradford Adams and Dana Montalto, "With Malice Toward None: Revisiting the Historical and Legal Basis for Excluding Veterans from 'Veteran' Services," *Penn State Law Review* 122 (2017): 69–139.

36. Norman B. Lynch, "The Administrative Discharge: Changes Needed?," *Maine Law Review* 141 (1970): 147–48.

37. On the use of administrative discharges in the early twentieth century: Margot Canaday, *The Straight State: Sexuality and Citizenship in Twentieth-Century America* (Princeton, NJ: Princeton University Press, 2011), chapter 2.

38. Peter Slavin, "The Cruelest Discrimination: Vets with Bad Paper Discharges," *Business and Society Review* 14 (Summer 1975): 25–33.

39. Slavin, "Cruelest Discrimination," 28. That claim, too, seemed borne out by statistics: In 1969, African Americans made up 58 percent of the population at the Long Binh Jail near Saigon. Gerald F. Goodwin, "Black and White in Vietnam," *New York Times*, July 18, 2017. Also see "A Preliminary Statement on Amnesty and Race, Submitted by the American Civil Liberties Union Foundation, Project on Amnesty," in US House, Committee on the Judiciary, *Amnesty: Hearings Before the Subcommittee on Courts, Civil Liberties, and the Administration of Justice*, 93rd Cong., 2nd sess. (Washington, DC: Government Printing Office, 1974), 772–77.

40. US House, Committee on Veterans' Affairs, *Presidential Review Memorandum on Vietnam Era Veterans, released October 10, 1978* (Washington, DC: Government Printing Office, 1979), 12.

41. US Senate, Committee on Veterans' Affairs, *Vietnam Veterans' Readjustment: Hearings before the Committee on Veterans' Affairs*, 96th Cong. 2nd sess. (Washington, DC: Government Printing Office, 1980), 131.

42. Daniel Akaka highlighted the central role of the Committee during a 1992 tribute to Alan Cranston. While heading the group through 1970s and 1980s, Akaka said Cranston had "written or helped to write every major veterans initiative of the last two decades . . . he will be given special credit for drawing attention to the needs of Vietnam veterans, women, minorities, and veterans of . . . recent conflicts." US Senate, *Tributes to the Honorable Alan Cranston of California in the United States Senate upon the Occasion of his Retirement*," S. Pub. 102-26 (Washington, DC: Government Printing Office, 1992).

43. *Educational Benefits Available for Returning Vietnam Era Veterans*, 994–96.

44. *Educational Benefits Available for Returning Vietnam Era Veterans*, 900–905.

45. Faced with a conservative backlash against the visible civil rights advances and upheavals of the 1960s, "ordinary Black people" advocated in the 1970s and 1980s for change via community and national organizations focused on, for example, economic dislocation in rural areas, limited access to credit, restrictive housing policies, police brutality, underfunded schools, and the threat of mass incarceration. In the case of the NABV, leaders deployed their veteran status to

bring attention to a bevy of larger social injustices. The quote is from David Covin, *Black Politics After the Civil Rights Movement: Activity and Beliefs in Sacramento, 1970–2000* (Jefferson, NC: McFarland & Company, 2009), 3. See also Kevin M. Kruse, *White Flight: Atlanta and the Making of Modern Conservatism* (Princeton, NJ: Princeton University Press, 2007); Joseph Crespino, *In Search of Another Country: Mississippi and the Conservative Counterrevolution* (Princeton, NJ: Princeton University Press, 2009); Greta de Jong, *You Can't Eat Freedom: Southerners and Social Justice after the Civil Rights Movement* (Chapel Hill: University of North Carolina Press, 2016); J. Michael Butler, *Beyond Integration: The Black Freedom Struggle in Escambia County, Florida, 1960–1980* (Chapel Hill: University of North Carolina Press, 2016).

46. "Protest Against Police Continues," *Milwaukee Star*, June 1, 1972. At the time of the protest, the group was still known by its original name, used until 1973: the Interested Veterans of the Central City (IVOCC).

47. Richard Morris, "Vet Willie Abney Is No Ordinary Guy," *Milwaukee Star*, April 5, 1973; Ralph Hamilton, "Project Where Recruitment, Counseling, Top Cares," *Milwaukee Star*, August 15, 1974.

48. Deborah Crosby, "Black Vets Conclude First Convention," *Milwaukee Star*, May 9, 1974.

49. *Vietnam Veterans' Readjustment*, 1, 130.

50. "VAV Is Self-Help Group: UWM Program to Aid Veterans," *Milwaukee Star*, February 3, 1973.

51. *Vietnam Veterans' Readjustment*, 130–35.

52. On Project 100,000, see Boehm, *War! What Is It Good For?*, 203–207.

53. *Vietnam Veterans' Readjustment*, 131.

54. *Vietnam Veterans' Readjustment*, 139.

55. *Vietnam Veterans' Readjustment*, 131.

56. Gertrude Schaffner Goldberg, "Employment, Poverty, and Social Welfare," in *New Perspectives on Poverty: Policies, Programs, and Practice*, eds. Elissa D. Giffords and Karen R. Garber (Chicago: Lyceum Books, 2014), 80–132.

57. US Senate Committee on Veterans' Affairs, *Oversight of Veterans Employment Programs: Hearing Before the Subcommittee on Health and Readjustment*, 95th Cong., 1st sess. (Washington, DC: Government Printing Office, 1978), 154–91.

58. Veterans Rehabilitation and Education Amendments of 1980, Pub. L. No. 96-466, 94 Stat. 2171 (1980), 2–5. Also, "Employment and Training" section, F. Ray Marshall, *The Labor Department in the Carter Administration: A Summary Report* (US Department of Labor, 1981). Accessible at https://babel.hathitrust.org/cgi/pt?id=coo.31924078706763&view=1up&seq=1.

59. *Oversight of Veterans Employment Programs*, 176. In 1973, multiple employment programs were consolidated under CETA. Lois Recascino Wise, *Labor Market Policies and Employment Patterns in the United States* (Boulder, CO: Westview Press, 1989). On transitions in labor programs during the administrations of Nixon, Ford, Carter, and Reagan, see Burt S. Barnow, "Thirty Years of Changing Federal, State, and Local Relationships in Employment and Training Programs" *Publius* 23, no. 3 (Summer 1993): 75–94.

60. John David Skrentny, *The Minority Rights Revolution* (Cambridge, MA: Harvard University Press, 2002).

61. R. Candy Tate, Theodore Morocco Coleman's Interview for the Veterans' History Project at Atlanta History Center, December 21, 2017, Atlanta History Center in partnership with the Association for the Study of African American Life and History, Veterans' History Project, https://www.youtube.com/watch?v=47O-6V5eqa8. Also, Morocco Coleman, *Coming Full Circle* (Atlanta: Pen & Press United, 2012).

62. Paul Pierson, *Dismantling the Welfare State?: Reagan, Thatcher and the Politics of Retrenchment* (New York: Cambridge University Press, 1994); Carsten Jensen, Georg Wenzel-burger, and Reimut Zohlnhöfer, "Dismantling the Welfare State? After Twenty-Five Years: What Have We Learned and What Should We Learn?" *Journal of European Social Policy* 29, no. 5 (December 2019): 681–691; Edward D. Berkowitz, *America's Welfare State: From Roosevelt to Reagan* (Baltimore: Johns Hopkins University Press, 1991).

63. The VA's share of the budget was approximately $58.5 million in 1980 and $51.8 million in 1990, in 2011 inflation-adjusted dollars. Scott, "Veterans Affairs: Historical Budget Authority, FY1940-FY2012," 4; Robert J. McMahon, "Rationalizing Defeat: The Vietnam War in American Presidential Discourse, 1975–1995," *Rhetoric & Public Affairs* 2, no. 4 (Winter 1999): 529–49.

64. On efforts to enhance the image of veterans of the war in Vietnam, Patrick Hagopin, *The Vietnam War in American Memory: Veterans, Memorials, and the Politics of Healing* (Amherst: University of Massachusetts Press, 2009), 202.

65. See Sec. 301, Veterans' Compensation, Education, and Employment Amendments of 1982, Pub. L. No. 97-306, 96 Stat. 1429 (1982).

66. US House, Committee on Veterans' Affairs, *Inner-City African American Veterans: Hearing Before the Subcommittee on Oversight and Investigations*, 102nd Cong., 2nd sess. (Washington, DC: Government Printing Office 1993), 62–63. Coleman's points underscore that by the early 1980s, PTSD was entering the popular lexicon as the primary scourge of Vietnam Era veterans. The American Psychiatric Association added the diagnosis of PTSD to its *Diagnostic and Statistical Manual* (*DSM III*) in 1980 at the behest of former service members and their advocates. According to the *DSM*, PTSD was a mental illness that occurred "following a psy-chologically traumatic event," which was accompanied by symptoms including "reexperiencing the traumatic event; numbing of responsiveness to, or reduced involvement with, the external world." *DSM III*, quoted in Wilbur J. Scott, "PTSD in DSM-III: A Case in the Politics of Diagno-sis and Disease," *Social Problems* 37, no. 3 (August 1990): 294–310. Just as studies in the 1970s indicated that Black veterans were more vulnerable to joblessness, studies of the 1980s showed that—due to a variety of factors—they experienced relatively high rates of PTSD.

67. *Permanent Supportive Housing: Evaluating the Evidence for Improving Health Outcomes Among People Experiencing Chronic Homelessness* (Washington, DC: National Academies Press, 2018), Appendix B; Edward D. Berkowitz and Larry DeWitt, *The Other Welfare: Supplemental Security Income and US Social Policy* (Ithaca, NY: Cornell University Press, 2013).

68. US House Committee on Veterans' Affairs, *Homeless and Unemployed Veterans: Hearing Before the Subcommittee on Education, Training and Employment*, 96th Cong., 2nd sess. (Washington, DC: Government Printing Office, 1986), 1, 175. On the history of homelessness, Peter H. Rossi, *Down and Out in America: The Origins of Homelessness* (Chicago: University of Chicago Press, 2013); *Permanent Supportive Housing*, Appendix B.

69. US Senate, Committee on Veterans' Affairs, *Veterans' Administration FY 1988 Budget, the Vet Center Program, and Homeless Veterans Issues: Hearings*, 100th Cong., 1st sess. (Washington, DC: Government Printing Office, 1988), 5–9.

70. The quote is from Drew S. Days III, "Turning Back the Clock: The Reagan Administra-tion and Civil Rights," *Harvard Civil Rights-Civil Liberties Law Review* 19 (1984): 309.

71. "Address by Senator Strom Thurmond (D-SC) at Dedication of Carolina Power and Light Company's Generating Plant, Hartsville, S.C." (June 18, 1960), Clemson Libraries, Strom Thurmond Collection, MS 100, Submissions from 1960, https://tigerprints.clemson.edu/cgi/viewcontent.cgi?article=3058&context=strom.

72. *Veterans' Administration FY 1988 Budget, the Vet Center Program, and Homeless Veterans Issues*, 5–9.

73. *Annual Report of the Secretary of Veterans Affairs, Fiscal Year 1989* (Washington, DC: US Department of Veterans Affairs, 1989), 9.

74. Robert Rosenheck, C. Leda, P. Gallup, B. Astrachan, R. Milstein, P. Leaf, D. Thompson, and P. Errera, "Initial Assessment Data from a 43-Site Program for Homeless Chronic Mentally Ill Veterans," *Psychiatric Services* 40, no. 9 (September 1989): 937–42.

75. Ron E. Armstead, "The Role, Accomplishments, and Challenges of the Congressional Black Caucus Veterans Braintrust," *William Monroe Trotter Institute Publications*, Paper 38 (September 2016), 30.

76. US House, Committee on Veterans' Affairs, *Inner-City African American Veterans: Hearing Before the Subcommittee on Oversight and Investigations*, 102nd Cong., 2nd sess. (Washington, DC: Government Printing Office, 1993); US House Committee on Veterans' Affairs, *African-American Veterans and Community: Post-Traumatic Stress Disorder and Related Issues: Hearings Before the Subcommittee on Oversight and Investigations*, 103rd Cong., 1st sess. (Washington, DC: Government Printing Office, 1994).

77. "Designation of a Chief Minority Affairs Officer in Department of Veterans Affairs," in *Congressional Record*, House, 102nd Cong., 1st sess. (November 25, 1991), 34738–39.

78. Discussion of S. 869, in *Congressional Record*, Senate, 102nd Cong., 1st sess. (November 20, 1991), 17218.

79. "Designation of a Chief Minority Affairs Officer in Department of Veterans Affairs."

80. *Annual Report of the Secretary of Veterans Affairs, Fiscal Year 1995* (Washington, DC: US Department of Veterans Affairs, 1995), 48–49. Maxine Waters, who chaired the 1992 "Inner-City" hearings and sat on both the CBC and the Committee of Veterans Affairs in the early 1990s, wrote the legislation that formed the basis for the Center for Women Veterans, established in November 1994. *H.R. 3013, An Act to Amend Title 38, United States Code, to Establish a Center for Women Veterans in the Department of Veterans Affairs* (Washington, DC: Government Printing Office, 1994); Veterans' Benefits Improvements Act of 1994, Pub. L. No. 103-446, 108 Stat. 4645 (1994).

81. Jesse Bennett, "Veteran Households in US Are Economically Better Off than Those of Non-Veterans" (Pew Research Center, December 9, 2019), https://www.pewresearch.org/fact-tank/2019/12/09/veteran-households-in-u-s-are-economically-better-off-than-those-of-non-veterans/.

82. Lopreato and Poston, "Differences in Earnings and Earnings Ability Between Black Veterans and Nonveterans in the United States."

Conclusion

1. David Vergun, "Pandemic Revealed Supply Chain Vulnerability, Pentagon Official Says," *DOD News* (July 8, 2020), https://www.defense.gov/Explore/News/Article/Article/2267558/pandemic-revealed-supply-chain-vulnerability-pentagon-official-says/ (accessed July 2021). See also Yasmin Tadjdeh, "Pentagon Examining Lessons Learned from Pandemic," *National Defense* 105 (October 2020): 22–23; Jared Serbu, "COVID-19 Successes Set New Expectations for Federal Acquisition Community," *Federal News Network* (April 20, 2021), https://federalnewsnetwork.com/contracting/2021/04/covid-19-successes-set-new-expectations-for-federal-acquisition-community/ (accessed July 2021); Business Executives for National Security (BENS), "Findings and Recommendations of the BENS Commission on the National

Response Enterprise: A Call to Action," February 2021, https://www.bens.org/file/national
-response-enterprise/CNRE-Report-February-2021.pdf (accessed July 2021).

2. Nebaner comments at October 6, 2020, "Resilience" seminar, Center for Government
Contracting, George Mason University, https://business.gmu.edu/govcon/events/conference/.

3. Stew Magnuson, "Bold Action Needed to Solve Rare Earth Problem," *National Defense*,
105 (August 2020): 8.

4. US House, Armed Services Committee, *Subcommittees on Readiness and Military Personnel Joint Hearing, Privatized Military Family Housing: Update on Implementation of Housing
Reforms*, March 10, 2021, https://armedservices.house.gov/2021/3/subcommittees-on-readiness
-and-military-personnel-joint-hearing-privatized-military-family-housing-update-on
-implementation-of-housing-reforms; US Government Accountability Office, *Military Housing:
DOD Needs to Strengthen Oversight and Clarify Its Role in the Management of Privatized Housing*,
GAO-20-281 (Washington, D.C. 2020), https://www.gao.gov/products/gao-20-281.

5. Gina Harkins, "Senators Demand 'Immediate Action' after Explosive Report on Navy Sex
Trafficking Scandal," July 29, 2020, https://www.military.com/daily-news/2020/07/29/senators
-demand-immediate-action-after-explosive-report-navy-sex-trafficking-scandal.html.

CONTRIBUTORS

Jessica L. Adler is associate professor of history at Florida International University in Miami. She is the author of *Burdens of War: Creating the United States Veterans Health System* (2017).

Timothy Barker is a PhD candidate in US history at Harvard University. His essays and reviews have appeared in the *London Review of Books, n+1, Dissent*, and other publications.

Patrick Chung is assistant professor of history at the University of Maryland, College Park. His work has been published in *Diplomatic History, Radical History Review*, and an edited volume titled *Korea and the World: New Frontiers in Korean Studies* (2019).

Gretchen Heefner is associate professor of history at Northeastern University. She is the author of *The Missile Next Door: The Minuteman in the American Heartland* (2012) and is currently writing a book, *From the Red Desert to the Red Planet*, about military engineers in extreme environments.

Jennifer Mittelstadt is professor of history at Rutgers University. She is the author of *From Welfare to Workfare: The Unintended Consequences of Liberal Reform, 1945–1964* (2005) and *The Rise of the Military Welfare State* (2015).

A. Junn Murphy is visiting assistant professor in the Departments of History and Women's, Gender and Sexuality Studies at Brandeis University.

Kara Dixon Vuic is the LCpl. Benjamin W. Schmidt Professor of War, Conflict, and Society in Twentieth-Century America at Texas Christian University. She is the author of *The Girls Next Door: Bringing the Home Front to the*

Front Lines (2019) and *Officer, Nurse, Woman: The Army Nurse Corps in the Vietnam War* (2010).

Sarah Jones Weicksel is the director of research and publications at the American Historical Association and a research associate at the Smithsonian Institution's National Museum of American History. She is the author of several articles on the material culture of war and is currently finishing a book on clothing and violence in the American Civil War era.

Mark R. Wilson is professor of history at the University of North Carolina, Charlotte. He is the author of *The Business of Civil War: Military Mobilization and the State, 1861–1865* (2006) and *Destructive Creation: American Business and the Winning of World War II* (2016).

Daniel Wirls is professor of politics at the University of California, Santa Cruz. His books include *Irrational Security: The Politics of Defense from Reagan to Obama* (2010) and *The Senate: From White Supremacy to Government Gridlock* (2021).

INDEX

ACKNOWLEDGMENTS

This book has a complicated origin story. We met for the first time in September 2015, when we both participated in a Beyond the New Deal conference, hosted by the University of California, Santa Barbara. Placed on the same panel by the conference organizers, we were surprised when we delivered eerily similar papers on the subject of military privatization in the late-twentieth-century United States. After a good laugh, we decided to join forces in our research and writing and began working on a piece that would eventually become the first chapter of this volume. That essay has benefitted from comments provided us in 2018 by participants in a Privatizing the Public Good symposium held at Rutgers University and by participants of Columbia University's 20th Century Politics and Society Workshop.

Also in 2018, Jennifer had the opportunity to teach at the US Army War College, where she created a new course, on the history of the military and the market. Positive encouragement from War College faculty members, including Mark Duckenfield and Jacqueline Whitt, as well as the students in the course, made her realize that it might be fruitful to connect some of the new scholarship dealing with various aspects of military-market relations. At that point, we started to make plans for an edited volume, which became this book.

We are grateful to the many people who accompanied us on the long path to the book's publication. As always, we have been sustained by our families and our home universities (Rutgers University and the University of North Carolina, Charlotte). The most important contributors to this book are the authors of its chapters, who are the ones who deserve any praise this book may garner. It's an exciting time to study the intersection of new military history and new histories of capitalism, and we learned so much from reading the work of the chapter authors, who research at the leading edge of both. Editing this book offered us the chance to think in new ways about advances in military-market histories across subfields and disciplines.

The editorial process with Penn Press strengthened the book at every step. We thank the reviewers of the manuscript, Shane Hamilton and a second anonymous scholar, whose encouragement and critiques guided our work from the first draft of the proposal. Finally, we're grateful to Penn Press editor Bob Lockhart, whose enthusiasm buoyed the book along and whose feedback improved the project immensely.

CPSIA information can be obtained
at www.ICGtesting.com
Printed in the USA
JSHW031059060822
29000JS00003B/3

9 781512 823233